The All Seasons Cookbook

Favorite Recipes Press

Credits

Great American Opportunities, Inc./Favorite Recipes Press

President: Thomas F. McDow III

Editorial Manager: Mary Jane Blount
Editors: Georgia Brazil, Mary Cummings, Jane Hinshaw,
Linda Jones, Mary Wilson
Typography: Pam Newsome, Sara Anglin

Home Economics Advisory Board

Favorite Recipes Press wants to recognize the following persons who graciously serve on our Home Economics Advisory Board:

Carolyn L. Cotton
Home Economics Teacher
Bristow, Oklahoma

Regina M. Haynes
Home Economics Teacher
Waynesville, North Carolina

Brenda D. Long
Home Economics Teacher
Richlands, Virginia

Emily Oates, State Supervisor
Home Economics Education
Little Rock, Arkansas

Alma L. Payne
Home Economics Teacher
Hurst, Texas

Susan Rogers
Home Economics Teacher
Palos Verdes Estates, California

Sue Shackelford
Home Economics Teacher
Hackleburg, Alabama

Sherry Zeigler
Home Economics Teacher
Chillicothe, Ohio

Photography: United Fresh Fruit and Vegetable Association; Mazola Corn Oil; Courtesy of Lewis & Neal; Rice Council; Florida Department of Citrus; Florida Strawberry Growers Association; and Hershey Foods Corporation.

Copyright© 1989 by: Great American Opportunities, Inc.
P.O. Box 305142
Nashville, TN 37230

Library of Congress Catalog Number: 89-1454

ISBN: 0-87197-248-4

Manufactured in the United States of America

First Printing 1989

Contents

Introduction

Welcome to the wonderful world of foods for cooking by the calendar! This book is filled with recipes for all seasons, recipes carefully selected to coincide with the availability of seasonal foodstuffs and to satisfy seasonal appetites.

Home Economics Teachers from across the nation send you their best, and we proudly present these special recipes for your enjoyment.

Great American/Favorite Recipes Press has been associated with Home Economics Teachers for over a quarter century through the publication of Home Economics Teachers Cookbooks, books which have become family favorites in homes the length and breadth of America.

As the Home Economics Teachers cookbooks have evolved over the years to accommodate new lifestyles and changing culinary needs such as greater awareness of the importance of good nutrition, so have there been important and worthwhile changes in the home economics curriculum.

Do you know that home economics is the only subject which specifically prepares our American youth for establishing caring, secure families?

And the home economics curriculum has always responded to the needs of each generation. A generation ago, it was generally "stitching and stirring". Today, home economics is addressing significant and timely issues such as home and resource management, consumer education, individuals and families in crisis, teen pregnancy, and AIDS and other diseases.

America's most precious resource is the family. Help protect it. Please support home economics education in your community!

Tom McDow

Thomas F. McDow III
President

Nutritional Guidelines

The editors have attempted to present these family recipes in a form that allows approximate nutritional values to be computed. Persons with dietary or health problems or whose diets require close monitoring should not rely solely on the nutritional information provided. They should consult their physicians or a registered dietitian for specific information.

Abbreviations for Nutritional Analysis

Cal — Calories
Prot — Protein
Carbo — Carbohydrates

T Fat — Total Fat
Chol — Cholesterol
Calc — Calcium
Potas — Potassium

Sod — Sodium
gr — gram
mg — milligram

Nutritional information for these recipes is computed from information derived from many sources, including materials supplied by the United States Department of Agriculture, computer databanks and journals in which the information is assumed to be in the public domain. However, many specialty items, new products, and processed foods may not be available from these sources or may vary from the average values used in these analyses. More information on new and/or specific products may be obtained by reading the nutrient labels.

Unless otherwise specified, the nutritional analysis of these recipes is based on the following guidelines.
- All measurements are level.
- Alternative ingredients (ie. butter or margarine) are analyzed by the first named.
- Artificial sweeteners vary in use and strength so should be used "to taste," using the recipe ingredients as a guideline.
- Artificial sweeteners using aspertame (NutraSweet and Equal) should not be used in recipes involving prolonged heating which reduces the sweet taste. For details refer to package information.
- Alcoholic ingredients have been analyzed as used, although cooking causes the evaporation of alcohol thus decreasing caloric content.
- Buttermilk, sour cream and yogurt are commercial-type.
- Chicken, cooked for boning and chopping, has been skinned and stewed; this method yields the lowest caloric values.
- Cottage cheese is cream-style with 4.2% creaming mixture. Dry-curd cottage cheese has no creaming mixture.
- Eggs are all large.
- Flour is unsifted all-purpose flour.
- Garnishes, serving suggestions and other optional additions and variations are not included in the analysis.
- Margarine and butter are regular, not whipped or presoftened.
- Milk is whole milk, 3. 5% butterfat. Lowfat milk is 1% butterfat. Evaporated milk is produced by removing 60% of the water from whole milk.
- Oil is any cooking oil. Shortening is hydrogenated vegetable shortening.
- Salt to taste as noted in the method has not been included in the nutritional analysis.

Winter

*O*ne February a few years ago, we had been subjected to endless rain, unremittingly gray skies, and raw cold. Just when even the most devout Winter-lovers were beginning to show the strain something remarkable happened. A huge storm swept down, covering everything with a silvery sheath of ice. By morning, the ordinary world had been transformed into a sparkling Winter dreamland. That night, the skies cleared and the light of the full moon turned icy tree branches into diamonds. So just remember, in the midst of that long and sometimes arduous stretch between Christmas and the first robin, there are times of great beauty and pleasure if we keep our senses open.

Children, however, don't need to be reminded. A busy six-year-old includes in her recital of Winter's pleasures: "apple cider, snowmen, fires in the fireplace, days off from school, getting warm after you've gotten cold, snow angels, Valentine's Day, hot chocolate with marshmallows, and getting the sled out." I would add to my own list our cardinal family at the bird feeder, hot spiced tea, crocuses in the snow, colorful quilts and biscuits and stew for dinner.

Winter is a season in which food becomes synonymous with warmth and comfort and, for most of us, home. This is the season of "beautiful soup," hearty stews, simmering pot roasts, and casseroles that are the fuel for long afternoons of skating.

The trick in Winter cookery is to be a little daring with the ingredients you have available. Take a chance on something new. This cookbook will help you reinvent some classics, celebrate festive days in style and chase away the Winter blues.

A New Year's Day get-together can be as simple or elaborate as you like, from good caviar, pâté, and champagne to a soup-and-salad buffet supper.

Winter claims the most romantic day of the year, as well as the greenest day. A fireside brunch or candlelight dinner on February 14th makes the day special just for two. Then on March 17, well-timed to put us in a good mood before we confront the tax man or spring cleaning, the entire population of the United States seems to have Irish ancestry.

And if, despite all the merriment, good food, and good times Winter brings, you should still catch a passing case of Winter doldrums, keep in mind that one of Winter's main pleasures is the anticipation of glorious Spring.

PHOTOGRAPHS FOR THESE RECIPES ON COVER AND PAGE 1.

FRESH FRUIT BETTY

1 1/3 cups graham
   cracker crumbs
1/4 cup melted
   butter
1/4 cup sugar
1/2 teaspoon
   cinnamon
1/4 teaspoon nutmeg
1 large apple,
   peeled, sliced

1 banana, sliced
1 large pear, peeled,
   sliced
2/3 cup chopped
   pecans
1 1/4 cups orange
   juice
2 tablespoons lemon
   juice

□ Preheat oven to 350 degrees.
□ Mix crumbs, butter, sugar, and spices in bowl. Mix fruit and pecans in bowl.
□ Layer fruit and crumb mixtures 1/2 at a time in 2-quart casserole. Pour juices over top.
□ Bake for 1 hour. Serve warm.
□ Yield: 8 servings.

WINTER POT ROAST VEGETABLES

6 cups sliced onions
2 tablespoons oil
4 carrots, peeled,
   sliced

4 turnips, peeled,
   cubed
1 cup sliced celery
1 cup beef broth

□ Sauté onions in oil in saucepan.
□ Add vegetables and broth. Simmer, covered, for 30 minutes or until tender.
□ Serve with favorite pot roast.
□ Yield: 8 servings.

BRIGHTON BEACH BORSCH

2 pounds beef cubes
2 tablespoons oil
6 cups beef broth
2 cups water
2 cups sliced carrots
1 (16-ounce) can
   tomatoes
4 medium potatoes,
   peeled, chopped

2 cups shredded
   cabbage
2 cups sliced celery
1/2 teaspoon nutmeg
Salt and pepper to
   taste
4 cups julienne beets
3 cups orange juice
Sour cream

□ Brown beef in oil in large saucepan.
□ Add broth and water; deglaze saucepan. Cook, covered, over low heat for 1 hour, stirring occasionally.
□ Add carrots, tomatoes, potatoes, cabbage, celery and seasonings.
□ Simmer for 20 minutes. Add beets and orange juice.
□ Simmer for 20 minutes. Serve with sour cream.
□ Yield: 4 servings.

SAVORY PUMPKIN SOUP

1 small onion, finely
   chopped
1 tablespoon butter
2 cups orange juice
1 (16-ounce) can
   pumpkin
1 cup milk

3/4 cup chicken broth
1 teaspoon grated
   orange rind
1 teaspoon ginger
Salt and pepper to
   taste

□ Sauté onion in butter in saucepan. Add remaining ingredients.
□ Simmer, covered, for 10 minutes.
□ Ladle into bowls.
□ Garnish with toasted pumpkin seed and orange slices.
□ Yield: 4 servings.

SOPA DE TORTILLA CON NARANJA

8 small tortillas
1/4 cup oil
1/2 cup chopped
   onion
1 clove of garlic,
   minced
2 1/2 cups chicken
   broth
1 (4-ounce) can
   chopped green
   chilies

1 1/2 cups orange
   juice
1 (8-ounce) can
   tomato sauce
1 tablespoon
   chopped
   coriander
1 pound chicken
   breast filets
1 cup shredded
   Cheddar cheese

□ Cut tortillas into 1/4-inch strips. Fry in oil in skillet until crisp; drain on paper towels.
□ Sauté onion and garlic in remaining oil until tender. Add broth, green chilies, orange juice, tomato sauce and coriander.
□ Simmer, covered, for 5 minutes.
□ Cut chicken into 1/2-inch strips. Add to soup.
□ Simmer, uncovered, for 8 minutes or until chicken is cooked, stirring occasionally.
□ Place tortilla strips in soup bowls; ladle soup over top. Sprinkle with cheese.
□ Yield: 4 servings.

Winter Foods

January	February	March	
	ARTICHOKES		**Vegetables**
	BROCCOLI		
		BRUSSELS SPROUTS	
CARROTS			
	ENDIVE		
COLLARD GREENS			
		KALE	
	LEEKS		
		PARSNIPS	
	NEW POTATOES		
	RADISHES		
		RUTABAGAS	
	SPINACH		
	WINTER SQUASH		
	TURNIPS		

January	February	March	
CRANBERRIES			**Fruits**
	GRAPEFRUIT		
	KUMQUATS		
		ORANGES	
		WINTER PEARS	
PERSIMMONS		PINEAPPLE	
RHUBARB			
TANGELOS			
		TANGERINES	

January	February	March	
CHICKEN	(ROASTERS AND STEWERS)	LAMB	**Meats**
	OYSTERS		
PORK			
TURKEY	VEAL		

January

Bean Pot Soup

Alice White, Texas

2	**cups dried pinto beans**
1	**pound ham, chopped**
1	**(18-ounce) can tomatoes, drained**
3	**medium onions, chopped**
3	**cloves of garlic, minced**
4	**cups chicken stock**
4	**cups water**
¼	**cup chopped green pepper**
3	**tablespoons chopped parsley**
¼	**cup packed light brown sugar**
1	**tablespoon chili powder**
1	**teaspoon salt**
1	**teaspoon crushed bay leaves**
1	**teaspoon oregano**
½	**teaspoon cumin**
½	**teaspoon rosemary**
½	**teaspoon celery seed**
½	**teaspoon thyme**
½	**teaspoon marjoram**
½	**teaspoon basil**
¼	**cup pearl barley**
½	**cup chopped green onions**

Combine beans with water to cover generously in 6-quart saucepan. Let stand overnight; drain. Add ham, tomatoes, onions, garlic, chicken stock, 4 cups water, green pepper, parsley, light brown sugar, chili powder, salt, bay leaves, oregano, cumin, rosemary, celery seed, thyme, marjoram, basil and barley. Bring to a boil; reduce heat. Simmer, covered, for 2 hours or until beans are tender. Ladle into soup bowls. Garnish with green onions.

Yield: 8 servings. Approx Per Serving: Cal 279;
Prot 16.6 gr; Carbo 27.0 gr; T Fat 11.9 gr;
Chol 27.5 mg; Calc 72.5 mg;
Potas 745.0 mg; Sod 1539.0 mg.

Note: Give a soup basket as a gift. Pack a basket containing one 16-ounce package beans, a 1-pound canned ham, an 18-ounce can tomatoes, 3 whole onions and 3 whole cloves of garlic, three 13-ounce cans chicken broth, 1 small green pepper and a bag containing a mixture of brown sugar, spices and barley. Add a recipe card for soup, packets of corn bread mix and soup bowls if desired.

Avocado Dip Picante

Lea Jenkins, Texas

Peel avocados; discard seed. Mash in bowl. Add mayonnaise, Worcestershire sauce and picante sauce; mix well. Chill for 2 hours or longer. Serve with tortilla chips.

Yield: 8 servings. Approx Per Serving: Cal 167; Prot 1.7 gr; Carbo 8.8 gr; T Fat 15.3 gr; Chol 2.9 mg; Calc 11.5 mg; Potas 468.0 mg; Sod 122.0 mg.

3   **large ripe avocados**
6   **tablespoons mayonnaise**
1   **teaspoon Worcestershire sauce**
3   **tablespoons picante sauce**
    Tortilla chips

Baked Mushroom Squares

Donna M. Prange, Wisconsin

Preheat oven to 350 degrees. Sauté mushrooms and onion in butter in skillet. Add lemon juice, Worcestershire sauce and garlic salt. Cook until liquid is absorbed, stirring frequently. Chill in refrigerator if desired. Press roll dough into greased 9 x 13-inch baking dish. Spread cream cheese over dough. Sprinkle with Parmesan cheese. Spoon mushroom mixture over top. Bake for 20 minutes or until crust is brown. Cut into squares. Serve hot.

Yield: 24 servings. Approx Per Serving: Cal 84; Prot 1.9 gr; Carbo 5.0 gr; T Fat 6.4 gr; Chol 13.6 mg; Calc 22.3 mg; Potas 61.0 mg; Sod 255.0 mg.

1   **(16-ounce) can mushrooms, drained**
2   **tablespoons minced onion**
2   **tablespoons butter or margarine**
1   **teaspoon lemon juice**
1   **teaspoon Worcestershire sauce**
½   **teaspoon garlic salt**
1   **(8-count) can refrigerator crescent rolls**
8   **ounces cream cheese, softened**
¼   **cup Parmesan cheese**

Piquant Sausage Balls

Lisa Stanley, Kentucky

Preheat oven to 325 degrees. Shape sausage into 1-inch balls. Arrange on rack in broiler pan. Bake for 25 minutes, turning once. Mix catsup and remaining ingredients in large bowl. Add sausage balls. Refrigerate overnight. Simmer sausage balls in sauce in saucepan until heated through. Serve hot.

Yield: 2 servings. Approx Per Serving: Cal 618; Prot 14.1 gr; Carbo 38.4 gr; T Fat 45.9 gr; Chol 77.6 mg; Calc 53.3 mg; Potas 487.0 mg; Sod 1381.0 mg.

½   **pound mild sausage**
¼   **cup catsup**
¼   **cup red wine vinegar**
¼   **cup packed light brown sugar**
1½   **teaspoons soy sauce**
⅛   **teaspoon ground ginger**

New England Chowder

2½   **pounds haddock**
2   **cups water**
1¾   **cups thinly sliced onions**
5   **tablespoons butter**
    or margarine
2   **tablespoons all-purpose flour**
2½   **cups chopped potatoes**
2   **cups chopped celery**
1   **bay leaf**
1   **teaspoon salt**
¼   **teaspoon pepper**
4   **cups milk**
1   **cup half and half**
1   **cup sour cream**
3   **tablespoons butter**

Simmer haddock in water in saucepan for 5 minutes. Remove haddock. Boil fish broth for 10 minutes or until reduced to 1⅔ cups. Sauté onions in 5 tablespoons butter in stockpot for 5 minutes. Add flour; mix well. Stir in broth gradually. Add vegetables, seasonings and ⅔ of the haddock. Simmer for 20 minutes or until potatoes are tender. Bring milk just to the boiling point in saucepan; remove from heat. Whisk in half and half and sour cream. Reheat over low heat; do not boil. Stir into potato mixture. Add remaining haddock. Cook over low heat for 5 minutes. Remove bay leaf. Top with 3 tablespoons butter. Cool. Chill for 1 to 2 days. Reheat over low heat. Ladle into soup bowls.

Yield: 12 servings. Approx Per Serving: Cal 295; Prot 24.5 gr; Carbo 15.1 gr; T Fat 15.0 gr; Chol 69.4 mg; Calc 171.0 mg; Potas 796.0 mg; Sod 364.0 mg.

Marinated Avocados and Mushrooms

Marian Castro, California

½   **cup oil**
3   **tablespoons tarragon vinegar**
2   **tablespoons lemon juice**
2   **tablespoons water**
1   **tablespoon minced parsley**
1   **clove of garlic, minced**
¾   **teaspoon salt**
    Dash of pepper
2   **large avocados**
8   **ounces fresh mushrooms**

Combine first 8 ingredients in jar; shake to mix. Peel and slice avocados. Cut mushrooms into halves. Combine with avocados in shallow dish. Pour dressing over avocados and mushrooms. Chill for several hours, basting occasionally. Drain; place in serving dish.

Yield: 8 servings. Approx Per Serving: Cal 251; Prot 2.14 gr; Carbo 7.71 gr; T Fat 25.3 gr; Chol 0.0 mg; Calc 12.3 mg; Potas 572.0 mg; Sod 209.0 mg.

Shropshire Sandwiches

Carolyn Myers, Louisiana

Preheat oven to 375 degrees. Blend butter and flour in saucepan over medium heat. Add salt, mustard and cayenne pepper. Stir in milk gradually. Cook until thickened, stirring constantly. Remove from heat. Add Cheddar cheese; stir until melted. Arrange toast slices in lightly buttered 9 x 13-inch baking dish. Top each slice with turkey. Spoon cheese sauce over top. Sprinkle with Parmesan cheese and paprika. Bake for 15 minutes or until light brown. Top each sandwich with bacon.

Yield: 6 servings. Approx Per Serving: Cal 564; Prot 35.5 gr; Carbo 21.0 gr; T Fat 37.2 gr; Chol 128.0 mg;Calc 484.0 mg; Potas 383.0 mg; Sod 999.0 mg.

3	**tablespoons melted butter or margarine**
3	**tablespoons all-purpose flour**
½	**teaspoon salt**
¼	**teaspoon dry mustard**
	Cayenne pepper to taste
2	**cups milk**
2	**cups shredded Cheddar cheese**
6	**slices bread, toasted**
12	**ounces thinly sliced turkey**
6	**tablespoons Parmesan cheese**
	Paprika to taste
12	**slices crisp-fried bacon**

Beef Goulash

Melt ¼ cup butter in heavy saucepan. Cook until golden brown, stirring constantly. Blend in flour. Cook over low heat until golden brown, stirring constantly. Stir in broth gradually. Add Tabasco sauce. Cook until thickened, stirring constantly; set aside. Sauté onions and garlic in ¼ cup butter in large saucepan. Add beef cubes. Cook until brown on all sides. Stir in reserved sauce, tomatoes and seasonings. Simmer, covered, for 1½ to 2 hours or until beef is tender. Remove bay leaf. Serve over Spaetzle.

Yield: 6 servings. Approx Per Serving: Cal 1087; Prot 71.3 gr; Carbo 57.6 gr; T Fat 61.6 gr; Chol 414.0 mg; Calc 94.9 mg; Potas 1234.0 mg; Sod 996.0 mg.

¼	**cup butter or margarine**
¼	**cup all-purpose flour**
2	**cups beef broth**
½	**teaspoon Tabasco sauce**
4	**cups sliced onions**
2	**cloves of garlic, minced**
¼	**cup butter or margarine**
3	**pounds boneless round or chuck, cut into 1-inch cubes**
1	**(8-ounce) can tomatoes, drained, chopped**
4	**teaspoons paprika**
1	**bay leaf**
½	**teaspoon marjoram**
½	**teaspoon salt**

Spaetzle

Combine flour, salt and spices in bowl. Add eggs and water; beat until smooth. Drop by ⅛ teaspoonfuls into boiling salted water in saucepan. Cook for 1 minute or just until dumplings rise to surface. Remove to serving dish with slotted spoon. Drizzle with melted butter. Serve with Beef Goulash.

3	**cups all-purpose flour**
1	**teaspoon salt**
	Dash of nutmeg
	Dash of paprika
4	**eggs**
¾	**cup water**
	Melted butter or margarine

Boliche

1	**3-pound boneless round steak**
1	**tablespoon vinegar**
1	**teaspoon olive oil**
1	**teaspoon pepper**
1	**teaspoon garlic salt**
1	**teaspoon salt**
1	**large onion, chopped**
½	**cup chopped green pepper**
4	**slices bacon, chopped**
¼	**cup chopped cooked ham**
¼	**cup chopped pepperoni**
6	**stuffed green olives, sliced**
2	**tablespoons tomato sauce**
1	**cup water**
½	**cup red wine**
2	**tablespoons all-purpose flour**
¼	**cup water**

Pound round steak to ½-inch thickness with meat mallet. Place in shallow dish. Pour mixture of vinegar, oil and seasonings over steak. Marinate in refrigerator for several hours. Preheat oven to 300 degrees. Sauté onion, green pepper and bacon in skillet until green pepper is tender. Add ham, pepperoni and olives. Cook for 5 minutes. Drain steak. Spoon vegetable mixture onto steak; roll up. Secure with butcher's string. Place in roasting pan. Pour mixture of tomato sauce, 1 cup water and wine over roast. Cover tightly. Bake for 1½ hours or until steak is tender. Place on heated serving plate; remove string. Thicken pan juices with mixture of flour and ¼ cup water. Serve with steak.

Yield: 6 servings. Approx Per Serving: Cal 749; Prot 63.2 gr; Carbo 5.45 gr; T Fat 49.6 gr; Chol 199.0 mg; Calc 32.5 mg; Potas 1009.0 mg; Sod 940.0 mg.

Ground Beef and Broccoli Wellington

Rachelle Young, Washington

1	**pound fresh broccoli**
1	**pound ground beef**
1	**cup shredded mozzarella cheese**
½	**cup chopped onion**
½	**cup sour cream**
¼	**teaspoon salt**
¼	**teaspoon pepper**
2	**(8-count) cans refrigerator crescent dinner rolls**
1	**egg, beaten**
1	**tablespoon poppy seed**

Trim broccoli; cut into small pieces. Cook in a small amount of water in saucepan until tender; drain. Preheat oven to 375 degrees. Brown ground beef in skillet, stirring until crumbly; drain. Stir in broccoli, cheese, onion, sour cream, salt and pepper; mix well. Separate crescent roll dough into 4 rectangles. Place 2 rectangles on baking sheet, overlapping long sides; press edges to seal. Spoon half the ground beef mixture onto center. Fold long edges to enclose filling; seal edges. Repeat with remaining roll dough and ground beef mixture. Brush with egg; sprinkle with poppy seed. Bake for 18 to 22 minutes or until golden brown.

Yield: 8 servings. Approx Per Serving: Cal 463; Prot 22.1 gr; Carbo 26.7 gr; T Fat 29.7 gr; Chol 102.0 mg; Calc 130.0 mg; Potas 529.0 mg; Sod 658.0 mg.

Sesame Chicken

Betty Stevenson, Oregon

Preheat oven to 375 degrees. Combine flour, salt and pepper in plastic bag. Add chicken pieces; shake to coat well. Shake off excess flour. Roll chicken in oil. Arrange in single layer in shallow baking pan. Bake for 30 minutes. Turn chicken pieces over. Sprinkle with lemon juice, sesame seed and onion. Drizzle wine around chicken pieces. Bake for 20 minutes longer or until tender, basting occasionally.

Yield: 4 servings. Approx Per Serving: Cal 541; Prot 21.6 gr; Carbo 24.0 gr; T Fat 38.2 gr; Chol 46.9 mg; Calc 33.5 mg; Potas 239.0 mg; Sod 51.9 mg.

1	**cup all-purpose flour**
	Salt and pepper to taste
1	**3-pound chicken, cut up**
½	**cup oil**
2	**teaspoons lemon juice**
½	**cup sesame seed**
3	**tablespoons minced onion**
½	**cup white wine**

Stuffed Pork Chops

Sylvia Malone, Oregon

Preheat oven to 350 degrees. Cut pocket in each pork chop from outside edge to bone. Cook rice according to package directions. Sauté celery and 3 tablespoons onion in margarine in skillet. Stir in rice, 2 tablespoons parsley, poultry seasoning, salt and pepper. Stuff rice mixture into pockets in chops. Secure chops with skewers. Arrange in buttered baking dish. Chill in refrigerator if desired. Bake, covered, for 1 hour. Bake, uncovered, for 30 minutes longer. Combine sour cream and remaining ingredients in small saucepan. Heat mixture to serving temperature, stirring constantly; do not boil. Serve over pork chops.

Yield: 4 servings. Approx Per Serving: Cal 708; Prot 34.1 gr; Carbo 25.6 gr; T Fat 51.4 gr; Chol 139.0 mg; Calc 75.7 mg; Potas 524.0 mg; Sod 284.0 mg.

4	**1¼-inch thick pork chops**
½	**cup rice**
⅓	**cup chopped celery**
3	**tablespoons chopped onion**
2	**tablespoons margarine**
2	**tablespoons chopped parsley**
⅛	**teaspoon poultry seasoning**
	Salt and pepper to taste
¾	**cup sour cream**
¼	**cup salad dressing**
1	**tablespoon chopped onion**
1	**tablespoon chopped parsley**
½	**teaspoon Worcestershire sauce**
½	**teaspoon sugar**

Louisiana Corn and Rice Pudding

Betty Sue Stuart, Missouri

2 **eggs**
2 **cups cooked long grain rice**
1 **(10-ounce) package frozen cream-style corn, thawed**
½ **cup minced onion**
½ **cup chopped green pepper**
1 **cup shredded Cheddar cheese**

Preheat oven to 350 degrees. Beat eggs in bowl until foamy. Add remaining ingredients; mix well. Spoon into greased 1½-quart baking dish. Bake for 45 minutes or until set and edges are brown. Let stand for 10 minutes before serving.

Yield: 6 servings. Approx Per Serving: Cal 223; Prot 9.8 gr; Carbo 27.1 gr; T Fat 8.4 gr; Chol 111.0 mg; Calc 150.0 mg; Potas 143.0 mg; Sod 629.0 mg.

Hoppin' Juan

Janet McCamant, Colorado

1 **cup brown rice**
1 **(10-ounce) package frozen black-eyed peas**
2 **cloves of garlic, minced**
¾ **cup chopped onion**
1 **(4-ounce) can chopped green chilies, drained**
2 **tablespoons milk**
¾ **cup ricotta cheese**
3 **cups shredded Monterey Jack cheese**

Preheat oven to 350 degrees. Cook brown rice and black-eyed peas separately according to package directions. Combine with garlic, onion, green chilies and salt in bowl; mix well. Mix milk, ricotta cheese and 2 cups Monterey Jack cheese in bowl. Alternate layers of rice mixture and cheese mixture in greased baking dish until all ingredients are used, ending with rice mixture. Bake for 25 minutes or until bubbly. Sprinkle with remaining Monterey Jack cheese. Bake for 5 minutes longer.

Yield: 8 servings. Approx Per Serving: Cal 499; Prot 28.5 gr; Carbo 30.4 gr; T Fat 29.3 gr; Chol 89.1 mg; Calc 706.0 mg; Potas 344.0 mg; Sod 481.0 mg.

Parsnips with Maple Syrup

Helen B. Davis, Vermont

12 **medium parsnips**
1 **tablespoon salt**
⅓ **cup maple syrup**
⅓ **cup orange juice**
1 **tablespoon grated orange rind**
½ **cup butter or margarine**

Preheat oven to 350 degrees. Parboil parsnips; drain. Slice lengthwise. Place in 9x12-inch baking dish. Sprinkle with salt. Combine syrup, orange juice and rind in bowl; mix well. Pour over parsnips. Dot with butter. Bake until parsnips are tender and glazed.

Yield: 6 servings. Approx Per Serving: Cal 311; Prot 2.3 gr; Carbo 43.1 gr; T Fat 16.7 gr; Chol 41.4 mg; Calc 95.1 mg; Potas 627.0 mg; Sod 503.0 mg.

Super Spinach Casserole

Berndena McCleskey, Indiana

Wash spinach; discard stems. Combine with boiling water in saucepan. Cook, covered, for 5 minutes; drain. Add onion flakes, bread, cheeses, eggs and garlic salt; mix well. Melt butter in 1-quart baking dish. Add spinach mixture. Microwave on Medium-High for 10 minutes. Top with French-fried onions. Microwave for 2 minutes longer.

Yield: 6 servings. Approx Per Serving: Cal 213; Prot 11.2 gr; Carbo 13.6 gr; T Fat 13.2 gr; Chol 163.0 mg; Calc 191.0 mg; Potas 496.0 mg; Sod 395.0 mg.

1	*pound fresh spinach*
¼	*cup boiling water*
1	*teaspoon dried onion flakes*
2	*slices dark rye bread, cubed*
½	*cup shredded Cheddar cheese*
½	*cup cottage cheese*
3	*eggs, slightly beaten*
	Dash of garlic salt
1½	*tablespoons butter or margarine*
1	*(3½-ounce) can French-fried onions*

Glazed Acorn Squash

Preheat oven to 350 degrees. Cut squash into quarters; discard seed. Place in shallow baking dish. Combine remaining ingredients in bowl; mix well. Pour over squash. Bake, covered, for 30 minutes, basting with pan juices. Bake, uncovered, for 10 minutes or until tender, basting frequently.

Yield: 6 servings. Approx Per Serving: Cal 323; Prot 3.1 gr; Carbo 49.2 gr; T Fat 15.5 gr; Chol 0.0 mg; Calc 116.0 mg; Potas 1116.0 mg; Sod 190.0 mg.

3	*medium acorn squash*
½	*cup melted margarine*
6	*tablespoons orange juice*
¼	*cup honey*
¼	*teaspoon cinnamon*
¼	*teaspoon ginger*

Winter Vegetable Melange

Combine turnips, rutabagas and carrots in large saucepan. Add 2 inches salted water. Bring to a boil; reduce heat. Simmer, covered, for 15 to 20 minutes or until vegetables are tender; drain. Place in serving dish. Mix butter and remaining ingredients in small bowl. Pour over vegetables; mix gently.

Yield: 6 servings. Approx Per Serving: Cal 106; Prot 1.2 gr; Carbo 8.7 gr; T Fat 7.8 gr; Chol 20.7 mg; Calc 38.4 mg; Potas 303.0 mg; Sod 106.0 mg.

1½	*cups julienne white turnip strips*
1½	*cups julienne rutabaga strips*
2	*cups julienne carrot strips*
¼	*cup melted butter or margarine*
1	*tablespoon chopped fresh parsley*
2	*teaspoons lemon juice*

Carrot Corn Bread

Delores H. Clocker, Washington

1 cup all-purpose flour
1 cup cornmeal
¼ cup sugar
1 tablespoon baking powder
¼ cup butter or margarine
1 egg
1 cup buttermilk
2 medium carrots, shredded

Preheat oven to 425 degrees. Sift dry ingredients into bowl. Cut in butter until crumbly. Beat egg in bowl. Add buttermilk and carrots; mix well. Stir into dry ingredients. Pour into greased 9x9-inch baking pan. Bake for 25 minutes or until brown. Cut into squares.

Yield: 8 servings. Approx Per Serving: Cal 212; Prot 4.9 gr; Carbo 31.7 gr; T Fat 7.5 gr; Chol 50.9 mg; Calc 71.7 mg; Potas 160.0 mg; Sod 218.0 mg.

Wholesome Wheat Bread

2 cups whole wheat flour
2 packages (2 tablespoons) dry yeast
1 teaspoon salt
1 teaspoon cinnamon
1 cup dark corn syrup
½ cup Hellmann's mayonnaise
1 cup water
2 eggs
3½ to 4 cups whole wheat flour
1 tablespoon melted butter or margarine

Mix first 4 ingredients in mixer bowl. Heat corn syrup, mayonnaise and water to 120 degrees in saucepan. Add to flour mixture. Beat at medium speed for 2 minutes. Beat in eggs and 2 cups flour. Beat at medium speed for 2 minutes. Stir in enough remaining flour to make medium dough. Knead on floured surface for 10 minutes or until smooth and elastic. Place in greased bowl, turning to grease surface. Let rise, covered, for 1 hour. Divide into 2 portions. Let rest for 10 minutes. Shape each into 4x8-inch oval; cut slashes in top. Place on greased and floured baking sheet. Let rise for 1½ hours. Preheat oven to 350 degrees. Bake for 30 minutes or until loaves test done. Brush with butter. Cool on wire rack.

Yield: 24 servings. Approx Per Serving: Cal 171; Prot 4.8 gr; Carbo 33.0 gr; T Fat 3.2 gr; Chol 25.4 mg; Calc 22.6 mg; Potas 129.0 mg; Sod 144.0 mg.

Apple Pie Squares

Preheat oven to 350 degrees. Cream 1 cup butter and 2 cups sugar in mixer bowl until light and fluffy. Add eggs 1 at a time, beating well after each addition. Add vanilla and mixture of baking powder and 2 cups flour; mix well. Stir in remaining 3½ cups flour. Divide into 2 portions. Pat 1 portion over bottom of greased 10 x 15-inch baking pan. Combine apples and next 5 ingredients in bowl; mix well. Spoon into prepared pan. Dot with sliced butter. Divide remaining dough into 15 portions; shape into balls and flatten. Arrange over apples. Mix ½ cup flour, ½ cup sugar and cinnamon in small bowl. Cut in ¼ cup butter until crumbly. Sprinkle over top. Bake for 45 minutes. Remove from oven; cut into squares. Bake for 15 minutes longer or until golden brown. Serve warm or cold.

Yield: 15 servings. Approx Per Serving: Cal 702; Prot 7.1 gr; Carbo 99.6 gr; T Fat 32.1 gr; Chol 129.0 mg; Calc 32.3 mg; Potas 230.0 mg; Sod 261.0 mg.

1 **cup butter or margarine, softened**
2 **cups sugar**
3 **eggs**
1 **teaspoon vanilla extract**
½ **teaspoon baking powder**
5½ **cups all-purpose flour**
9 **cups sliced peeled Jonathan apples**
1 **cup sugar**
1 **teaspoon nutmeg**
1 **teaspoon vanilla extract**
1 **cup raisins**
½ **cup chopped pecans**
1 **stick butter or margarine, sliced**
½ **cup all-purpose flour**
½ **cup sugar**
1½ **teaspoons cinnamon**
¼ **cup butter or margarine**

Pears au Chocolat

Drain pears well. Mix cocoa and sugar in bowl. Blend in cream, salt and flavorings. Soften gelatin in cold water in double boiler pan. Place over hot water. Heat until gelatin is dissolved. Stir into cocoa mixture. Beat for several minutes or until of spreading consistency. Spoon into individual dessert dishes. Place pears cut side down on mousse. Chill for 1 hour or longer. Spoon fudge sauce over pears. Garnish with shaved chocolate. Chill until serving time.

Yield: 6 servings. Approx Per Serving: Cal 441; Prot 7.7 gr; Carbo 53.5 gr; T Fat 24.3 gr; Chol 67.9 mg; Calc 79.9 mg; Potas 309.0 mg; Sod 58.5 mg.

12 **canned pear halves**
5 **tablespoons cocoa**
7 **tablespoons sugar**
1¼ **cups heavy cream**
Dash of salt
¾ **teaspoon vanilla extract**
¼ **teaspoon mint extract**
1½ **teaspoons unflavored gelatin**
1½ **tablespoons cold water**
½ **cup fudge sauce**
½ **(1-ounce) square semisweet chocolate, shaved**

February

Crab Salad in Orange Cups

4	**large navel oranges**
¼	**cup chopped fresh pineapple**
8	**ounces cooked crab meat**
2	**small green onions, chopped**
½	**cup finely chopped celery**
¼	**cup mayonnaise**
1	**teaspoon fresh lemon juice**
¼	**cup chopped almonds**
4	**lemon slices**
4	**parsley sprigs**

Slice top off each orange. Scoop out and reserve orange pulp. Cut top edges of orange shells into zigzag pattern. Cut small slice from bottom of each so orange shells will stand upright. Set aside. Chop enough reserved orange pulp to measure ⅓ cup. Combine with pineapple, crab meat, green onions and celery in bowl. Add mayonnaise and lemon juice; mix well. Spoon into orange shells. Sprinkle with almonds. Garnish tops with twisted lemon slices and parsley sprigs.

Yield: 4 servings. Approx Per Serving: Cal 239; Prot 15.0 gr; Carbo 24.1 gr; T Fat 10.4 gr; Chol 60.4 mg; Calc 151.0 mg; Potas 575.0 mg; Sod 278.0 mg.

Chilled Cherry Soup

Susanne Jones, Maryland

Combine pie filling, chicken broth, wine, nutmeg and cloves in saucepan. Simmer for several minutes, stirring frequently. Cool. Stir in sour cream. Chill in refrigerator. Ladle into soup bowls. Garnish each serving with 1 orange slice and 1 parsley sprig.

Yield: 4 servings. Approx Per Serving: Cal 389; Prot 4.8 gr; Carbo 57.9 gr; T Fat 12.5 gr; Chol 6.6 mg; Calc 68.5 mg; Potas 297.0 mg; Sod 548.0 mg.

1	**(21-ounce) can cherry pie filling**
1	**cup chicken broth**
1	**cup dry white wine**
	Pinch of nutmeg
	Pinch of cloves
½	**cup sour cream**
4	**orange slices**
4	**parsley sprigs**

Cream of Squash Soup

Laura Hill, Tennessee

Peel, seed and chop squash and apples. Sauté squash, apples and onion in butter in skillet just until tender. Sprinkle with flour. Cook for several minutes, stirring gently. Bring chicken broth and seasonings to a boil in saucepan. Add squash mixture. Simmer for 20 minutes. Cool to lukewarm. Process a small amount at a time in food processor or blender until smooth. Return to saucepan. Bring to a simmer. Mix egg yolks and half and half in bowl. Stir a small amount of hot mixture into egg mixture; stir egg mixture into hot mixture. Heat just to serving temperature, stirring gently; do not boil.

Yield: 6 servings. Approx Per Serving: Cal 175; Prot 6.0 gr; Carbo 18.6 gr; T Fat 9.2 gr; Chol 109.0 mg; Calc 78.8 mg; Potas 478.0 mg; Sod 919.0 mg.

1	**pound butternut squash**
2	**medium Granny Smith apples**
1	**medium onion, chopped**
2	**tablespoons butter or margarine**
1	**tablespoon all-purpose flour**
4	**cups chicken broth**
¼	**teaspoon rosemary**
¼	**teaspoon marjoram**
1	**teaspoon salt**
½	**teaspoon white pepper**
2	**egg yolks, slightly beaten**
½	**cup half and half**

Everybody's Favorite Slaw

Shred cabbage. Soak in ice water to cover in large bowl until crisp; drain. Combine mayonnaise and remaining ingredients in small bowl; mix well. Pour over cabbage; toss to mix. Chill for 1 hour or longer.

Yield: 8 servings. Approx Per Serving: Cal 113; Prot 1.6 gr; Carbo 11.7 gr; T Fat 7.6 gr; Chol 5.6 mg; Calc 55.9 mg; Potas 282.0 mg; Sod 309.0 mg.

1	**(2-pound) head cabbage**
¾	**cup mayonnaise**
1½	**tablespoons fresh lemon juice**
½	**teaspoon salt**
¼	**teaspoon white pepper**
¼	**teaspoon dry mustard**
½	**teaspoon sugar**

Seven Bean Salad

Maxine Adams, Louisiana

1 *(16-ounce) can green beans*
1 *(16-ounce) can wax beans*
1 *(16-ounce) can red kidney beans*
1 *(16-ounce) can lima beans*
1 *(16-ounce) can navy beans*
1 *(16-ounce) can garbanzo beans*
1 *(16-ounce) can black beans*
1 *cup chopped onion*
½ *cup chopped green pepper*
1¼ *cups sugar*
1 *cup vinegar*
1 *cup oil*
½ *teaspoon celery seed*
Salt and pepper to taste

Drain beans. Combine with onion, green pepper, sugar, vinegar, oil, celery seed, salt and pepper in bowl; mix well. Chill, covered, for 24 hours, stirring occasionally. Store unused portion in refrigerator for several days.

Yield: 16 servings. Approx Per Serving: Cal 334; Prot 9.0 gr; Carbo 44.5 gr; T Fat 14.7 gr; Chol 0.0 mg; Calc 59.3 mg; Potas 423.0 mg; Sod 249.0 mg.

Beefy Broccoli Strudel

Sally Luman, Illinois

1 *pound lean ground beef*
1 *medium onion, minced*
1 *pound fresh broccoli*
1½ *cups shredded mozzarella cheese*
½ *cup sour cream*
¼ *cup bread crumbs*
1¼ *teaspoons salt*
¼ *teaspoon pepper*
8 *ounces phyllo dough*
½ *cup melted butter or margarine*

Preheat oven to 350 degrees. Brown ground beef with onion in skillet, stirring until crumbly; drain. Trim broccoli; cut into small pieces. Cook in a small amount of water in saucepan until tender; drain. Combine ground beef, broccoli, cheese, sour cream, bread crumbs and seasonings in bowl; mix well. Open phyllo on waxed paper-lined surface. Brush each layer with butter. Spoon ground beef mixture onto half the dough. Roll as for jelly roll from ground beef end. Place seam side down on baking sheet. Bake for 45 minutes or until brown. Cut into slices.

Yield: 6 servings. Nutritional information not available.

Oven Barbecued Pork Roast

Mary-Margaret Norman, West Virginia

Preheat oven to 325 degrees. Cut eight 1-inch slits in roast. Place 1 whole clove of garlic in each slit. Place roast in roasting pan. Bake for 2 hours. Combine preserves and remaining ingredients in saucepan. Bring to a boil; reduce heat. Simmer for 10 minutes. Brush roast with apricot mixture. Bake for 1 hour longer or to 185 degrees on meat thermometer, basting several times. Place roast on serving plate. Remove whole garlic cloves. Serve with remaining apricot sauce.

Yield: 12 servings. Approx Per Serving: Cal 467; Prot 48.8 gr; Carbo 23.6 gr; T Fat 18.8 gr; Chol 160.0 mg; Calc 25.5 mg; Potas 692.0 mg; Sod 565.0 mg.

1	**6-pound lean pork roast**
8	**cloves of garlic**
1	**(12-ounce) jar apricot preserves**
⅓	**cup soy sauce**
2	**tablespoons dark brown sugar**
2	**cloves of garlic, crushed**
¼	**teaspoon crushed red pepper**
⅛	**teaspoon pepper**
½	**teaspoon grated fresh gingerroot**

Veal Stew

Preheat oven to 325 degrees. Sauté onion in oil in Dutch oven. Add veal, bay leaf, salt and pepper. Brown veal on all sides, stirring frequently. Bake, covered, for 45 minutes. Add tomatoes, potatoes and wine. Bake for 20 minutes longer. Add green beans. Bake for 20 to 30 minutes or until veal and beans are tender. Remove bay leaf. Serve with homemade bread and sweet butter.

Yield: 6 servings. Approx Per Serving: Cal 589; Prot 78.5 gr; Carbo 24.9 gr; T Fat 17.5 gr; Chol 311.0 mg; Calc 90.6 mg; Potas 1729.0 mg; Sod 954.0 mg.

1	**large onion, chopped**
3	**tablespoons oil**
3	**pounds veal cubes**
1	**small bay leaf**
1½	**teaspoons salt**
½	**teaspoon white pepper**
1	**(29-ounce) can plum tomatoes**
3	**medium potatoes, peeled, cut into quarters**
⅓	**cup dry white wine**
2	**cups cut fresh green beans**

Buttermilk Chicken

Laura Hill, Tennessee

Preheat oven to 400 degrees. Marinate chicken in buttermilk in bowl for 15 minutes. Combine flour, salt and pepper in bowl. Remove chicken from buttermilk; reserve buttermilk. Roll chicken in flour mixture, coating well. Melt butter in shallow baking dish in oven. Heat until butter is bubbly. Arrange chicken, skin side down, in prepared baking dish. Bake for 30 minutes. Turn chicken pieces over. Bake for 15 minutes. Mix soup with reserved buttermilk. Pour mixture over chicken. Bake for 15 minutes longer.

Yield: 4 servings. Approx Per Serving: Cal 645; Prot 58.3 gr; Carbo 33.0 gr; T Fat 29.7 gr; Chol 193.0 mg; Calc 195.0 mg; Potas 679.0 mg; Sod 929.0 mg.

1	**medium chicken, cut up**
2	**cups buttermilk**
1	**cup all-purpose flour**
	Salt and pepper to taste
¼	**cup butter or margarine**
1	**(10-ounce) can cream of chicken soup**

Chili Chicken Pie

Ann Hetrick, Pennsylvania

1	**cup sliced mushrooms**
2	**tablespoons margarine**
2	**cups chopped cooked chicken**
1	**cup chili sauce**
¼	**cup water**
2	**tablespoons brown sugar**
1	**tablespoon mustard**
1	**(10-count) can refrigerator flaky biscuits**
¼	**cup shredded Cheddar cheese**

Preheat oven to 375 degrees. Sauté mushrooms in margarine in saucepan. Add chicken, chili sauce, water, brown sugar and mustard; mix well. Cook until bubbly. Spoon into 8 x 12-inch baking dish. Arrange biscuits over chicken mixture. Sprinkle with cheese. Bake for 20 to 25 minutes or until brown.

Yield: 5 servings. Approx Per Serving: Cal 453; Prot 22.5 gr; Carbo 41.8 gr; T Fat 21.9 gr; Chol 55.9 mg; Calc 69.8 mg; Potas 546.0 mg; Sod 1369.0 mg.

Cornish Hens with Apple Stuffing

6	**medium green onions, sliced**
½	**cup sliced mushrooms**
¼	**cup butter or margarine**
1	**small apple, chopped**
½	**cup chopped pecans**
6	**slices bread, torn into pieces**
	Salt and pepper to taste
¼	**cup (about) dry white wine**
4	**Cornish game hens**
2	**tablespoons oil**
8	**slices lean bacon**

Preheat oven to 350 degrees. Sauté green onions and mushrooms in butter in skillet. Mix with apple, pecans, bread, salt and pepper in bowl. Add enough wine to bind mixture. Wash game hens and pat dry inside and out. Stuff with apple mixture. Close cavities with skewers. Brush hens with oil. Place breast side up on rack in roasting pan. Roast for 30 minutes. Arrange bacon slices on hens. Roast for 30 minutes longer or until tender.

Yield: 4 servings. Approx Per Serving: Cal 916; Prot 74.9 gr; Carbo 30.5 gr; T Fat 53.3 gr; Chol 244.0 mg; Calc 116.0 mg; Potas 867.0 mg; Sod 712.0 mg.

Scallops Thermidor

Laurie Burdo, Michigan

1	**pound scallops**
8	**ounces mushrooms, sliced**
4	**medium green onions, chopped**
¼	**cup melted butter or margarine**
¼	**cup all-purpose flour**
1	**cup milk**
⅓	**cup dry white wine**
1	**tablespoon lemon juice**
1	**tablespoon chopped parsley**
½	**teaspoon dry mustard**
	Dash of cayenne pepper
1	**cup shredded Swiss cheese**

Preheat oven to 400 degrees. Sauté scallops, mushrooms and green onions in butter in skillet. Remove with slotted spoon. Blend flour into butter in skillet. Stir in milk gradually. Cook until thickened, stirring constantly. Add sautéed scallop mixture, wine, lemon juice, parsley, dry mustard and cayenne pepper; mix well. Simmer until heated through. Spoon into individual greased baking shells or ramekins. Sprinkle with cheese and paprika. Bake for 10 to 15 minutes or until brown.

Yield: 4 servings. Approx Per Serving: Cal 432; Prot 38.2 gr; Carbo 16.5 gr; T Fat 13.7 gr; Chol 115.0 mg; Calc 387.0 mg; Potas 828.0 mg; Sod 423.0 mg.

Shrimpaghetti

Peel and devein shrimp; cut into bite-sized pieces. Sauté onion and garlic in margarine and olive oil in heavy saucepan. Stir in soup, water, chopped parsley and salt. Simmer until slightly thickened. Add shrimp. Simmer for 5 minutes. Cook spaghetti according to package directions just until tender; drain. Place on serving platter. Top with shrimp sauce. Sprinkle with cheese. Garnish with parsley sprigs.

Yield: 4 servings. Approx Per Serving: Cal 609; Prot 34.4 gr; Carbo 54.0 gr; T Fat 28.1 gr; Chol 225.0 mg; Calc 145.0 mg; Potas 522.0 mg; Sod 1442.0 mg.

1   *pound medium shrimp*
1   *medium onion, chopped*
1   *clove of garlic, crushed*
2   *tablespoons margarine*
⅓   *cup olive oil*
1   *(10-ounce) can tomato soup*
½   *cup water*
1   *tablespoon chopped parsley*
1   *teaspoon salt*
1   *(8-ounce) package spaghetti*
¼   *cup Parmesan cheese*
    Parsley sprigs

Seafood and Wild Rice Casserole

Charlene Butler, Iowa

Preheat oven to 350 degrees. Combine wild rice, long grain rice, celery, onion, green pepper, water chestnuts and pimento in bowl. Add soup; mix well. Fold in crab meat and shrimp. Spoon into greased baking dish. Chill in refrigerator for several hours if desired. Bake for 1½ hours.

Yield: 8 servings. Approx Per Serving: Cal 180; Prot 13.1 gr; Carbo 23.8 gr; T Fat 3.4 gr; Chol 70.7 mg; Calc 52.4 mg; Potas 287.0 mg; Sod 563.0 mg.

2   *cups cooked wild rice*
1   *cup cooked long grain rice*
1½   *cups chopped celery*
1   *medium onion, chopped*
½   *cup chopped green pepper*
1   *(7-ounce) can sliced water chestnuts, drained*
1   *(2-ounce) can chopped pimento, drained*
1½   *(10-ounce) cans cream of mushroom soup*
1   *cup crab meat*
1   *cup peeled shrimp*

Velvety Baked Eggs

3 **ounces cream cheese,**
  softened
⅓ **cup milk**
2 **eggs, beaten**
¼ **teaspoon salt**
¼ **teaspoon dry mustard**

Preheat oven to 375 degrees. Melt cream cheese in double boiler pan over hot water or in glass bowl in microwave. Remove from heat. Blend in milk gradually. Add eggs and seasonings; mix well. Pour into 2 greased individual ramekins or custard cups. Place in pan of hot water. Bake for 20 minutes.

Yield: 2 servings. Approx Per Serving: Cal 252; Prot 10.5 gr; Carbo 3.6 gr; T Fat 21.7 gr; Chol 326.0 mg; Calc 107.0 mg; Potas 170.0 mg; Sod 478.0 mg.

Sweet and Sour Cabbage

Frances Dodge, Maine

2 **medium onions, sliced**
2 **tablespoons oil**
1 **medium Granny Smith apple**
4 **cups shredded cabbage**
2 **tablespoons light brown sugar**
½ **cup cider vinegar**
1 **cup water**

Sauté onions in oil in skillet. Chop apple. Add to skillet with remaining ingredients; mix well. Cook, covered, for 20 minutes or until tender-crisp. Spoon into serving bowl.

Yield: 8 servings. Approx Per Serving: Cal 70; Prot 0.7 gr; Carbo 10.2 gr; T Fat 3.6 gr; Chol 0.0 mg; Calc 26.0 mg; Potas 164.0 mg; Sod 8.2 mg.

Chuck Wagon Beans

Debra Meadows, Wyoming

1 **(16-ounce) can green beans**
1 **medium green pepper**
2 **cups cooked pinto beans**
2 **cups cooked kidney beans**
1 **(16-ounce) can pork and beans**
1 **medium onion, chopped**
1 **(8-ounce) bottle of chili sauce**
⅔ **cup packed brown sugar**

Preheat oven to 325 degrees. Drain green beans. Chop green pepper. Combine with green beans and remaining ingredients in bowl. Spoon into 2-quart baking dish. Bake for 3 hours.

Yield: 20 servings. Approx Per Serving: Cal 113; Prot 4.7 gr; Carbo 24.1 gr; T Fat 0.5 gr; Chol 1.5 mg; Calc 41.1 mg; Potas 325.0 mg; Sod 339.0 mg.

Winter Corn Casserole

Lucretia Pippen, Louisiana

Preheat oven to 300 degrees. Sauté onion and green pepper in butter in saucepan. Add corn, uncooked rice, jalapeño pepper, sugar and seasonings; mix well. Spoon into greased 9 x 13-inch baking dish. Chill in refrigerator if desired. Bake for 30 minutes or until bubbly. Sprinkle with cheese. Bake for 10 minutes longer.

Yield: 12 servings. Approx Per Serving: Cal 265; Prot 7.4 gr; Carbo 28.8 gr; T Fat 14.3 gr; Chol 40.5 mg; Calc 144.0 mg; Potas 171.0 mg; Sod 418.0 mg.

1	**medium onion, chopped**
1	**medium green pepper, chopped**
½	**cup butter or margarine**
2	**(16-ounce) cans cream-style corn**
2	**cups minute rice**
1	**jalapeño pepper, chopped**
1	**tablespoon sugar**
	Salt and pepper to taste
2	**cups shredded Cheddar cheese**

Potato and Broccoli Casserole

Julia Novy, Ohio

Preheat oven to 350 degrees. Cook potatoes in boiling water to cover in saucepan until tender; drain. Add cream cheese, milk, butter and egg. Beat until smooth. Fold in half the French-fried onions. Spread over bottom and sides of buttered 8 x 12-inch baking dish. Bake for 30 minutes. Cook broccoli in a small amount of water in saucepan until tender; drain. Place in potato shell. Sprinkle with cheese and remaining onions. Bake for 5 minutes or until cheese is melted.

Yield: 8 servings. Approx Per Serving: Cal 270; Prot 9.1 gr; Carbo 27.6 gr; T Fat 14.5 gr; Chol 73.3 mg; Calc 159.0 mg; Potas 575.0 mg; Sod 189.0 mg.

6	**medium potatoes, peeled, chopped**
3	**ounces cream cheese, softened**
¼	**cup milk**
2	**tablespoons butter or margarine**
1	**egg**
1	**(3-ounce) can French-fried onions**
2	**bunches fresh broccoli**
1	**cup shredded Cheddar cheese**

Macaroni Mousse

Nancy Whisinnand, Nebraska

Preheat oven to 350 degrees. Cook macaroni according to package directions; drain. Pour hot milk over bread crumbs in bowl. Stir in butter and cheese until melted. Add salt, pepper and eggs; mix well. Place macaroni in greased baking dish. Pour cheese sauce over top. Bake for 1 hour.

Yield: 8 servings. Approx Per Serving: Cal 366; Prot 14.9 gr; Carbo 37.4 gr; T Fat 17.1 gr; Chol 147.0 mg; Calc 230.0 mg; Potas 208.0 mg; Sod 321.0 mg.

1½	**cups elbow macaroni**
1½	**cups milk, scalded**
1	**cup soft bread crumbs**
¼	**cup butter or margarine**
1½	**cups shredded Cheddar cheese**
¼	**teaspoon salt**
⅛	**teaspoon pepper**
3	**eggs, well beaten**

Cottage Cheese Biscuits

Tricia Leonard, Maryland

<table>
<tr><td>2</td><td>packages (2 tablespoons) dry yeast</td></tr>
<tr><td>½</td><td>cup warm (115-degree) water</td></tr>
<tr><td>2</td><td>cups cottage cheese</td></tr>
<tr><td>¼</td><td>cup sugar</td></tr>
<tr><td>1</td><td>teaspoon salt</td></tr>
<tr><td>½</td><td>teaspoon soda</td></tr>
<tr><td>2</td><td>eggs, beaten</td></tr>
<tr><td>5</td><td>cups all-purpose flour</td></tr>
</table>

Dissolve yeast in warm water in bowl. Heat cottage cheese in saucepan over low heat until warm. Combine cottage cheese, sugar, salt, soda, eggs, yeast and 1 cup flour in mixer bowl; mix well. Beat for 2 minutes. Add remaining flour; mix well. Place in greased bowl, turning to grease surface. Let rise, covered, for 1½ hours or until doubled in bulk. Shape into 24 balls on floured surface. Arrange in 3 greased 9-inch baking pans. Let rise, covered, for 30 minutes or until doubled in bulk. Preheat oven to 350 degrees. Bake for 20 minutes or until brown. Serve hot.

Yield: 24 servings. Approx Per Serving: Cal 121; Prot 5.4 gr; Carbo 21.0 gr; T Fat 1.5 gr; Chol 25.4 mg; Calc 17.6 mg; Potas 54.6 mg; Sod 183.0 mg.

Raspberry Coffee Cake

<table>
<tr><td>3</td><td>ounces cream cheese, softened</td></tr>
<tr><td>¼</td><td>cup butter or margarine, softened</td></tr>
<tr><td>2</td><td>cups buttermilk baking mix</td></tr>
<tr><td>⅓</td><td>cup milk</td></tr>
<tr><td>½</td><td>cup seedless raspberry preserves</td></tr>
<tr><td>1</td><td>cup confectioners' sugar</td></tr>
<tr><td>1</td><td>to 2 tablespoons milk</td></tr>
</table>

Preheat oven to 425 degrees. Blend cream cheese and butter in bowl. Add baking mix; mix until crumbly. Add ⅓ cup milk; mix well. Knead 8 to 10 times in bowl. Roll into 8 x 12-inch rectangle on greased baking sheet. Spread preserves in 3-inch wide strip down center of rectangle. Cut ½-inch wide strips from edge to preserves. Fold alternately over preserves. Bake for 15 minutes or until golden brown. Blend confectioners' sugar with enough milk to make glaze of desired consistency. Drizzle over coffee cake. Serve warm.

Yield: 4 servings. Approx Per Serving: Cal 941; Prot 11.9 gr; Carbo 139.0 gr; T Fat 38.0 gr; Chol 58.0 mg; Calc 203.0 mg; Potas 285.0 mg; Sod 1763.0 mg.

Streusel Pie

Barbara Blum, Vermont

Preheat oven to 350 degrees. Mix peanut butter and confectioners' sugar in bowl until crumbly. Sprinkle ⅔ of the mixture into pie shell. Mix flour, ½ cup sugar and salt in double boiler pan. Stir in milk gradually. Cook over boiling water until thickened, stirring constantly. Stir a small amount of hot mixture into beaten egg yolks; stir egg yolks into hot mixture. Cook for several minutes longer, stirring frequently. Remove from heat; stir in butter and vanilla. Pour into pie shell. Beat egg whites with cream of tartar in mixer bowl until stiff peaks form. Add ½ cup sugar gradually, beating until very stiff. Spread over filling, sealing to edge; sprinkle with remaining peanut butter mixture. Bake for 15 to 20 minutes or until light brown. Cool. Chill until serving time.

⅓	**cup peanut butter**
¾	**cup confectioners' sugar**
1	**baked 9-inch pie shell**
⅓	**cup all-purpose flour**
½	**cup sugar**
⅛	**teaspoon salt**
2	**cups milk, scalded**
3	**egg yolks, beaten**
2	**tablespoons butter or margarine**
½	**teaspoon vanilla extract**
3	**egg whites**
¼	**teaspoon cream of tartar**
½	**teaspoon sugar**

Yield: 8 servings. Approx Per Serving: Cal 371;
Prot 9.3 gr; Carbo 40.2 gr; T Fat 20.0 gr;
Chol 118.0 mg; Calc 84.7 mg;
Potas 198.0 mg; Sod 299.0 mg.

Cappucino Mix

Eileen Winkler, California

Combine creamer, sugar, coffee powder and hard candies in blender container. Process at high speed until well mixed. Store in airtight container. Dissolve 1 tablespoon mix in ¾ cup boiling water in cup. Top with whipped cream.

⅓	**cup powdered nondairy creamer**
⅓	**cup sugar**
¼	**cup instant coffee powder**
4	**orange-flavored hard candies Whipped cream**

Yield: 15 servings. Approx Per Serving: Cal 36;
Prot 0.1 gr; Carbo 7.4 gr; T Fat 0.7 gr;
Chol 0.0 mg; Calc 1.1 mg;
Potas 18.5 mg; Sod 4.9 mg.

March

Fresh Parsnip Slaw

½ **cup sour cream**
1 **tablespoon freshly squeezed lemon juice**
2 **tablespoons finely chopped onion**
2 **tablespoons finely chopped parsley**
1 **teaspoon sugar**
½ **teaspoon salt**
⅛ **teaspoon pepper**
6 **medium parsnips**
2 **medium apples**

Combine sour cream, lemon juice, onion, parsley, sugar, salt and pepper in bowl; mix well. Peel parsnips; shred coarsely. Add to dressing; mix well. Chill, covered, for several hours. Chop unpeeled apples. Add to salad; mix well.

Yield: 6 servings. Approx Per Serving: Cal 106; Prot 1.3 gr; Carbo 17.1 gr; T Fat 4.3 gr; Chol 8.5 mg; Calc 45.4 mg; Potas 263.0 mg; Sod 193.0 mg.

Sopa con Queso

Karen Strubbe, California

Combine tomato, green chilies, water, garlic salt and pepper in saucepan. Bring to a boil; reduce heat. Simmer, covered, for 5 minutes. Blend in evaporated milk and soups. Cook until heated through. Place ¼ cup cheese cubes in each soup bowl. Ladle hot soup over cheese.

Yield: 8 servings. Approx Per Serving: Cal 206; Prot 11.8 gr; Carbo 10.5 gr; T Fat 13.4 gr; Chol 42.6 mg; Calc 366.0 mg; Potas 300.0 mg; Sod 645.0 mg.

1 **medium tomato, peeled, chopped**
1 **(4-ounce) can chopped green chilies, drained**
2½ **cups water**
½ **teaspoon garlic salt**
¼ **teaspoon pepper**
1 **(13-ounce) can evaporated milk**
1 **(10-ounce) can cream of potato soup**
1 **(10-ounce) can onion soup**
2 **cups cubed Monterey Jack cheese**

Greek Salad

Anita Rukus, Connecticut

Remove outer leaves from lettuce; arrange on serving plate. Shred remaining lettuce finely. Spoon potato salad into center of prepared plate; sprinkle with shredded lettuce. Slice tomatoes into wedges and cucumbers into spears. Alternate tomato and cucumber slices around edge. Top with cheese, green pepper, shrimp, olives and scallions. Drizzle mixture of vinegar, olive oil, oregano and salt and pepper over top.

Yield: 8 servings. Approx Per Serving: Cal 318; Prot 9.8 gr; Carbo 17.8 gr; T Fat 22.7 gr; Chol 104.0 mg; Calc 165.0 mg; Potas 596.0 mg; Sod 803.0 mg.

1 **large head lettuce**
3 **cups favorite potato salad**
2 **large tomatoes**
2 **large cucumbers**
6 **ounces feta cheese, crumbled**
8 **green pepper rings**
8 **cooked peeled shrimp**
8 **black olives**
8 **medium scallions**
¼ **cup white vinegar**
⅓ **cup olive oil**
¼ **teaspoon oregano**
Salt and pepper to taste

Burritos Ensaladas

Carol McLennan, Oklahoma

8	**flour tortillas**
¾	**cup chopped broccoli**
¾	**cup shredded carrots**
¾	**cup chopped onion**
¾	**cup shredded cabbage**
¾	**cup alfalfa sprouts**
¾	**cup sliced avocado**
1½	**tablespoons chopped dill pickle**
¼	**cup salad dressing**

Preheat oven to 250 degrees. Wrap tortillas in damp cloth. Warm in oven for 15 minutes. Combine broccoli, carrots, onion and cabbage in glass bowl. Microwave, loosely covered, on High for 10 minutes or until tender-crisp; drain well. Add alfalfa sprouts, avocado and pickle; mix gently. Spread tortillas with salad dressing. Spoon vegetable mixture onto tortillas; roll tightly to enclose filling. Place on serving plate.

Yield: 8 servings. Approx Per Serving: Cal 183; Prot 3.9 gr; Carbo 25.8 gr; T Fat 8.6 gr; Chol 1.9 mg; Calc 41.0 mg; Potas 281.0 mg; Sod 277.0 mg.

Continental Steak Rolls

Joyce Emerson, Missouri

1	**pound tenderized round steak**
¼	**cup all-purpose flour**
¼	**teaspoon salt**
⅛	**teaspoon pepper**
2	**tablespoons shortening**
3	**tablespoons minced onion**
3	**tablespoons minced mushrooms**
1	**(8-count) can refrigerator crescent rolls**
1	**tablespoon melted butter or margarine**
1	**cup sour cream**
½	**teaspoon minced parsley**
¼	**teaspoon salt**

Preheat oven to 375 degrees. Cut steak into 4 rectangular pieces. Coat with mixture of flour, ¼ teaspoon salt and pepper. Brown on both sides in shortening in skillet; drain on paper towel. Sauté onion and mushrooms in pan drippings in skillet. Place about 1½ tablespoons on each steak piece; fold over to enclose filling. Unroll roll dough. Leave 2 triangles together to form rectangle; press perforations to seal. Place steak roll in center of each rectangle; fold over dough to enclose steak roll, sealing edges. Place seam side down on baking sheet. Bake for 12 to 15 minutes or until golden. Blend butter and sour cream in saucepan over low heat. Add parsley and ¼ teaspoon salt. Heat to serving temperature; do not boil. Serve over steak rolls.

Yield: 4 servings. Approx Per Serving: Cal 746; Prot 34.7 gr; Carbo 30.6 gr; T Fat 53.1 gr; Chol 128.0 mg; Calc 79.9 mg; Potas 654.0 mg; Sod 717.0 mg.

Recipes for this photograph on page 84.

Hawaiian Meatballs

Combine first 4 ingredients in bowl; mix well. Shape into small balls. Coat with flour. Brown in shortening in skillet; drain. Chill in refrigerator if desired. Combine brown sugar and next 4 ingredients in skillet. Stir in vinegar, catsup, soy sauce, water and pineapple. Bring to a boil, stirring constantly. Add meatballs. Simmer, covered, for 10 minutes or until heated through. Serve over rice as main dish or from chafing dish for buffet.

Yield: 8 servings. Approx Per Serving: Cal 371; Prot 23.4 gr; Carbo 23.3 gr; T Fat 20.7 gr; Chol 143.0 mg; Calc 38.6 mg; Potas 417.0 mg; Sod 745.0 mg.

2   *pounds lean ground beef*
2   *eggs*
½   *cup chopped green onions*
½   *teaspoon garlic salt*
2   *tablespoons all-purpose flour*
2   *tablespoons shortening*
6   *tablespoons light brown sugar*
¼   *teaspoon dry mustard*
½   *teaspoon garlic salt*
½   *teaspoon onion powder*
2   *tablespoons cornstarch*
¼   *cup vinegar*
6   *tablespoons catsup*
2   *tablespoons soy sauce*
1   *cup water*
1   *(8-ounce) can crushed pineapple*

Ham and Broccoli Pie

Kathy Rinas, Missouri

Preheat oven to 375 degrees. Place dried potatoes in bowl; reserve sauce mix packet. Pour boiling water over potatoes. Let stand for 15 minutes; drain. Add 1 tablespoon margarine and 1 egg; toss until coated. Press into greased 9-inch pie plate. Bake for 10 minutes. Mix ham, broccoli, ½ cup cheese, 2 eggs and onion in bowl. Blend 2 tablespoons margarine, reserved sauce mix packet and dry mustard in saucepan. Stir in milk. Bring to a boil, stirring constantly. Mix into ham mixture. Pour into potato shell. Top with ½ cup cheese. Bake for 30 minutes. Let stand for several minutes before serving.

Yield: 6 servings. Approx Per Serving: Cal 361; Prot 21.0 gr; Carbo 9.7 gr; T Fat 27.0 gr; Chol 191.0 mg; Calc 280.0 mg; Potas 424.0 mg; Sod 1049.0 mg.

1   *(6-ounce) package scalloped potatoes*
4   *cups boiling water*
1   *tablespoon melted margarine*
1   *egg*
1½ *cups chopped ham*
1   *(10-ounce) package frozen chopped broccoli, thawed*
½   *cup shredded Swiss cheese*
2   *eggs*
¼   *cup chopped onion*
2   *tablespoons melted margarine*
¼   *teaspoon dry mustard*
1   *cup milk*
½   *cup shredded Swiss cheese*

Recipes for this photograph on page 120.

Creole Pork Chops

Sandra Jones, North Carolina

6	center cut pork chops
3	tablespoons peanut oil
2	medium onions, sliced
2	cloves of garlic, minced
¼	cup chopped green pepper
½	cup dry white wine
1	(16-ounce) can tomatoes
3	tablespoons lemon juice
1½	tablespoons Worcestershire sauce
1	teaspoon salt
¼	teaspoon pepper
1	bay leaf
	Tabasco sauce to taste
3	cups hot cooked rice

Brown pork chops on both sides in 1½ tablespoons hot oil in skillet; drain chops and discard drippings. Add 1½ tablespoons oil. Sauté onions and garlic in skillet for 3 minutes. Add green pepper. Sauté for 1 minute. Add wine. Bring to a boil, stirring to deglaze skillet. Return chops to skillet; spoon sauce over chops. Add tomatoes, lemon juice, seasonings and enough water to cover chops if necessary. Simmer, lightly covered, for 1 hour or until chops are tender, turning occasionally. Remove chops to warm serving platter. Remove bay leaf. Cook sauce over high heat until thickened to desired consistency. Spoon over chops. Serve over rice.

Yield: 6 servings. Approx Per Serving: Cal 642; Prot 48.0 gr; Carbo 7.2 gr; T Fat 44.6 gr; Chol 164.0 mg; Calc 44.9 mg; Potas 882.0 mg; Sod 636.0 mg.

Parmesan Chicken Bake

Beverly Moulton, California

8	chicken breasts
½	cup melted butter or margarine
1	cup fine whole wheat bread crumbs
¾	cup Parmesan cheese
1	clove of garlic, minced
¼	cup chopped parsley
½	teaspoon seasoned salt

Preheat oven to 350 degrees. Rinse chicken breasts; pat dry. Dip into melted butter; coat with mixture of remaining ingredients. Arrange skin side up in shallow baking pan. Sprinkle with any remaining butter and crumb mixture. Bake for 50 minutes or until tender.

Yield: 8 servings. Approx Per Serving: Cal 457; Prot 36.4 gr; Carbo 13.4 gr; T Fat 28.4 gr; Chol 129.0 mg; Calc 148.0 mg; Potas 393.0 mg; Sod 643.0 mg.

Asparagus Brunch Casserole

Laura Hill, Tennessee

Melt butter in saucepan over low heat. Blend in flour. Cook for 1 to 2 minutes, stirring constantly. Stir in milk, Sherry and seasonings gradually. Cook until thickened, stirring constantly. Stir in cheese until melted. Pour half the sauce into shallow baking dish. Cut asparagus into 1-inch pieces. Sprinkle in prepared dish. Break eggs carefully over asparagus. Cover with remaining cheese sauce. Chill, tightly covered, overnight if desired. Preheat oven to 325 degrees. Bake for 50 minutes.

Yield: 6 servings. Approx Per Serving: Cal 350; Prot 18.8 gr;Carbo 7.9 gr; T Fat 26.0 gr; Chol 337.0 mg; Calc 375.0 mg; Potas 284.0 mg; Sod 556.0 mg.

3   **tablespoons butter or margarine**
3   **tablespoons all-purpose flour**
1½   **cups milk**
¼   **cup Sherry**
½   **teaspoon salt**
¼   **teaspoon pepper**
2   **cups shredded Cheddar cheese**
12   **large cooked asparagus spears**
6   **eggs**

Delmonico Potatoes

Cook potatoes in boiling salted water in saucepan until tender; drain. Cool. Peel and slice potatoes. Place in buttered baking dish. Combine milk and remaining ingredients in saucepan. Cook over low heat until cheese melts and sauce is smooth, stirring constantly. Pour over potatoes. Refrigerate, covered, overnight. Preheat oven to 325 degrees. Bake for 1 hour or until browned.

Yield: 10 servings. Approx Per Serving: Cal 240; Prot 8.5 gr; Carbo 23.4 gr; T Fat 12.8 gr; Chol 43.4 mg; Calc 206.0 mg; Potas 418.0 mg; Sod 374.0 mg.

8   **red potatoes**
1   **cup milk**
½   **cup whipping cream**
2   **cups shredded sharp Cheddar cheese**
1   **teaspoon dry mustard Dash of nutmeg**
1   **teaspoon salt Dash of pepper**

Curried Spinach

Wilma Paul, Pennsylvania

1	**pound spinach**
1	**tablespoon oil**
2	**tablespoons all-purpose flour**
½	**teaspoon curry powder**
¼	**teaspoon salt**
⅛	**teaspoon pepper**
1	**cup milk**
3	**hard-boiled eggs, sliced**

Cook spinach in a small amount of water in saucepan for 10 minutes or until tender; drain. Keep warm. Blend oil, flour, curry powder, salt and pepper in saucepan. Stir in milk gradually. Cook over low heat until thickened, stirring constantly. Place spinach in serving dish; add egg slices. Pour sauce over top of spinach.

Yield: 4 servings. Approx Per Serving: Cal 166; Prot 10.3 gr; Carbo 10.3 gr; T Fat 10.0 gr; Chol 214.0 mg; Calc 241.0 mg; Potas 662.0 mg; Sod 287.0 mg.

Green Noodles

Kelly Schrader, Kansas

4	**ounces noodles**
2	**pounds fresh spinach**
3	**tablespoons melted butter or margarine**
2	**tablespoons all-purpose flour**
½	**teaspoon salt**
⅛	**teaspoon pepper**
½	**teaspoon paprika**
1	**cup sour cream**
8	**ounces Cheddar cheese, shredded**

Preheat oven to 400 degrees or use microwave oven. Cook noodles using package directions; drain. Wash spinach; remove stems. Cook spinach in a small amount of water in saucepan over low heat or microwave on High in glass dish just until tender; drain and chop. Combine butter, flour, salt, pepper and paprika in saucepan; mix well. Stir in sour cream. Cook over low heat until thickened, stirring constantly. Remove from heat. Fold in spinach. Layer half the noodles, half the cheese and all the spinach mixture in greased 8 x 12-inch glass baking dish. Layer remaining noodles and cheese on top. Bake for 15 minutes or microwave on High for 5 minutes.

Yield: 6 servings. Approx Per Serving: Cal 397; Prot 17.6 gr; Carbo 23.5 gr; T Fat 27.1 gr; Chol 72.3 mg; Calc 474.0 mg; Potas 980.0 mg; Sod 600.0 mg.

Rice and Carrot Ring

Nelle Motschenbacher, Oregon

Preheat oven to 375 degrees. Combine carrots, rice, cheese, seasonings and egg yolks in bowl; mix well. Beat egg whites until stiff peaks form. Fold gently into carrot mixture. Spoon into greased ring mold. Place ring in larger pan of hot water. Bake for 45 minutes. Unmold onto serving plate. Serve with creamed turkey or seafood.

Yield: 6 servings. Approx Per Serving: Cal 213; Prot 9.7 gr; Carbo 22.5 gr; T Fat 9.2 gr; Chol 157.0 mg; Calc 173.0 mg; Potas 188.0 mg; Sod 186.0 mg.

2 **cups mashed cooked carrots**
2 **cups cooked rice**
1 **cup shredded Cheddar cheese**
  Salt, pepper and garlic salt
  to taste
3 **eggs, separated**

Quick Pretzels

Charlene Travis, Washington

Preheat oven to 375 degrees. Separate roll dough into rectangles; seal perforations. Cut each rectangle into 4 strips; shape each strip into 15-inch rope. Shape each into pretzel on ungreased baking sheet. Brush with beaten egg; sprinkle with salt. Bake for 8 to 12 minutes or until golden brown. Serve hot with mustard.

Yield: 16 servings. Approx Per Serving: Cal 55; Prot 1.1 gr; Carbo 5.5 gr; T Fat 3.1 gr; Chol 17.1 mg; Calc 1.8 mg; Potas 35.3 mg; Sod 119.0 mg.

1 **(8-count) can refrigerator**
  crescent rolls
1 **egg, beaten**
  Coarse salt
  Prepared mustard

Whole Wheat Soda Gems

Mary Lockwood, Nebraska

Preheat oven to 400 degrees. Combine dry ingredients in bowl. Add buttermilk; stir just until moistened. Spoon into greased muffin cups. Bake for 20 minutes.

Yield: 12 servings. Approx Per Serving: Cal 90; Prot 2.7 gr; Carbo 19.9 gr; T Fat 0.5 gr; Chol 0.8 mg; Calc 30.6 mg; Potas 86.7 mg; Sod 179.0 mg.

1½ **cups whole wheat flour**
1 **teaspoon soda**
½ **cup (scant) sugar**
½ **teaspoon salt**
1 **cup buttermilk**

Philadelphia Butter Cake

1	*package (2 tablespoons) dry yeast*
½	*cup warm (110-degree) milk*
¼	*cup sugar*
¼	*teaspoon salt*
½	*cup shortening*
1	*egg*
2¼	*cups all-purpose flour*
1	*tablespoon vanilla extract*
2½	*cups sugar*
1	*cup butter or margarine, softened*
	Pinch of salt
1	*egg*
¼	*cup light corn syrup*
1	*cup all-purpose flour*
¼	*cup water*
1	*tablespoon vanilla extract*
¼	*cup confectioners' sugar*

Dissolve yeast in warm milk in bowl. Cream ¼ cup sugar, ¼ teaspoon salt and shortening in mixer bowl until light and fluffy. Add 1 egg. Beat for 1 minute. Add 2¼ cups flour, yeast mixture and 1 tablespoon vanilla. Beat with dough hook or by hand for 3 minutes. Knead on floured surface for 1 minute. Place in greased bowl, turning to grease surface. Let rise, covered, for 1 hour or until doubled in bulk. Cream 2½ cups sugar, butter and pinch of salt in bowl until light and fluffy. Add 1 egg and corn syrup; mix well. Stir in 1 cup flour, water and 1 tablespoon vanilla. Set aside. Preheat oven to 375 degrees. Press dough over bottom and sides of 10 x 15-inch cake pan. Prick with fork. Spoon in filling. Let stand for 20 minutes. Sift confectioners' sugar over filling. Bake for 15 to 20 minutes. or until set. Do not overbake; topping will be gooey.

Yield: 20 servings. Approx Per Serving: Cal 329; Prot 3.0 gr; Carbo 46.4 gr; T Fat 15.3 gr; Chol 53.1 mg; Calc 17.7 mg; Potas 44.0 mg; Sod 135.0 mg.

Butter Crunch Delight

Judy Anderson, Iowa

20	*Oreo cookies, finely crushed*
5	*(2-ounce) Butterfinger candy bars, crushed*
½	*cup melted butter or margarine*
½	*gallon mint chocolate chip ice cream, softened*

Mix cookie and candy crumbs in bowl. Reserve ½ cup for topping. Mix butter with remaining crumbs. Press into 9 x 13-inch pan. Spread ice cream over crumb mixture. Sprinkle reserved crumbs over top. Freeze until firm.

Yield: 12 servings. Approx Per Serving: Cal 562; Prot 5.4 gr; Carbo 49.5 gr; T Fat 39.7 gr; Chol 60.0 mg; Calc 129.0 mg; Potas 288.0 mg; Sod 289.0 mg.

Steamed Carrot Pudding

Fae Allen, California

Grease and flour three or four 16-ounce cans. Cream shortening and brown sugar in mixer bowl until light and fluffy. Add carrots, potatoes, raisins and nuts; mix well. Stir in mixture of hot water and soda. Sift dry ingredients together. Add to vegetable mixture; mix well. Fill prepared cans ⅔ full. Cover with waxed paper; secure with rubber band. Place on rack in saucepan. Add water to half the depth of cans. Steam, covered, for 3 hours. Serve hot with Hard Sauce.

Yield: 16 servings. Approx Per Serving: Cal 233;
      Prot 1.8 gr; Carbo 31.6 gr; T Fat 12.0 gr;
      Chol 10.0 mg; Calc 21.7 mg;
      Potas 180.0 mg; Sod 145.0 mg.

6   *tablespoons shortening*
¾   *cup packed light brown sugar*
¾   *cup grated carrots*
¾   *cup grated potatoes*
¾   *cup raisins*
¾   *cup chopped nuts*
2   *teaspoons hot water*
1   *teaspoon soda*
1   *cup all-purpose flour*
½   *teaspoon salt*
½   *teaspoon cinnamon*
¼   *teaspoon cloves*
¼   *teaspoon nutmeg*

Hard Sauce

Beat butter in mixer bowl until fluffy. Sift in confectioners' sugar gradually, beating until fluffy. Add lemon juice. Beat until smooth. Add enough cream gradually to make of desired consistency. Chill until serving time.

3   *tablespoons butter*
   or margarine, softened
1   *cup confectioners' sugar*
1   *tablespoon lemon juice*
4   *tablespoons cream*

Shortbread Cookies

Barbara Shoemaker, Maryland

Preheat oven to 300 degrees. Cream butter and confectioners' sugar in mixer bowl for 3 minutes. Add flour gradually. Beat well after each addition. Beat at high speed for 10 minutes. Drop by spoonfuls onto ungreased cookie sheet. Bake for 25 minutes or until light brown. Remove to wire rack to cool.

Yield: 18 servings. Approx Per Serving: Cal 141;
      Prot 1.1 gr; Carbo 11.4 gr; T Fat 10.3 gr;
      Chol 27.6 mg; Calc 4.5 mg;
      Potas 12.5 mg; Sod 86.3 mg.

1   *cup butter or margarine,*
   softened
¾   *cup confectioners' sugar*
1½   *cups all-purpose flour*

Micro Brittle

1 cup unroasted pecans,
  almonds, cashews or peanuts
1 cup sugar
½ cup light corn syrup
⅛ teaspoon salt
1 tablespoon margarine
1 teaspoon soda
1 teaspoon vanilla extract

Combine nuts, sugar, corn syrup and salt in 1½-quart glass casserole. Microwave on High (600 to 700 watts) for 7 minutes, stirring once. Blend in margarine. Microwave on High for 2 to 3 minutes longer or until nuts are golden brown. Stir in soda and vanilla. Pour onto greased baking sheet. Let stand until cool. Break into pieces. Store in airtight container.

Yield: 8 servings. Approx Per Serving: Cal 265; Prot 1.2 gr; Carbo 43.0 gr; T Fat 11.5 gr; Chol 0.0 mg; Calc 15.7 mg; Potas 63.3 mg; Sod 176.0 mg.

Mocha Fudge Pies

½ cup butter or margarine,
  softened
1½ cups packed dark brown sugar
6 eggs
24 ounces semisweet chocolate
4 teaspoons instant coffee
  powder
2 teaspoons almond extract
½ cup all-purpose flour
1 to 1½ cups chopped walnuts
2 unbaked 9-inch pie shells
2 cups whipping cream
2 tablespoons sugar
¼ cup chopped maraschino
  cherries
2 teaspoons chocolate sprinkles

Preheat oven to 375 degrees. Cream butter and brown sugar in mixer bowl until light and fluffy. Blend in eggs 1 at a time. Melt chocolate in double boiler pan over hot water. Add to creamed mixture gradually, stirring constantly. Add coffee powder, flavoring, flour and walnuts; mix well. Spoon into pie shells. Bake for 25 minutes. Cool on wire racks. Whip cream in bowl until soft peaks form. Add sugar gradually, beating constantly until stiff peaks form. Fold in cherries. Spread over pies. Garnish with chocolate sprinkles. Chill.

Yield: 12 servings. Approx Per Serving: Cal 909; Prot 12.4 gr; Carbo 82.4 gr; T Fat 64.4 gr; Chol 212.0 mg; Calc 97.5 mg; Potas 481.0 mg; Sod 318.0 mg.

A Trifle Irish

Janet Crawford, Connecticut

Prepare gelatin according to package directions. Pour into shallow pan. Chill until firm. Slice jelly rolls 1-inch thick. Layer in glass serving bowl, sprinkling each layer with orange juice. Mix egg yolks, sugar and salt in bowl. Scald milk in heavy saucepan. Stir in Irish Mist. Stir a small amount of hot mixture into egg mixture; stir egg mixture into hot mixture. Cook over low heat until thickened, stirring constantly. Stir in vanilla and butter. Pour over jelly roll layers. Chill for several hours. Beat egg whites until stiff peaks form. Whip cream with confectioners' sugar in bowl until stiff peaks form. Fold in egg whites. Sprinkle almonds over trifle. Spoon whipped cream mixture over top. Cut gelatin into shamrocks with cookie cutter. Place on top of trifle.

Yield: 8 servings. Nutritional information not available.

1	*(3-ounce) package lime gelatin*
2	*(16-ounce) packages bakery jelly rolls*
1	*cup orange juice*
3	*egg yolks*
¼	*cup sugar*
¼	*teaspoon salt*
1½	*cups milk*
½	*cup Irish Mist liqueur*
1	*teaspoon vanilla extract*
1	*tablespoon butter or margarine*
3	*egg whites*
1	*cup whipping cream*
2	*tablespoons confectioners' sugar*
½	*cup slivered almonds*

Vermont Cooler

Combine softened ice cream, milk and maple syrup in mixer bowl. Beat until smooth. Scoop remaining ice cream into tall glasses. Pour mixture over ice cream. Garnish with mixture of pecans and butter brickle chips.

Yield: 6 servings. Nutritional information not available.

1	*pint vanilla ice cream, softened*
4	*cups cold milk*
½	*cup maple syrup*
1	*pint vanilla ice cream*
¼	*cup chopped pecans*
¼	*cup butter brickle chips*

Café Viennese

Place 1 tablespoon hot chocolate mix in each cup. Add coffee gradually, stirring until mix dissolves. Add 1 cinnamon stick and dollop of whipped cream to each cup. Top with chocolate shavings.

Yield: 2 servings. Approx Per Serving: Cal 129; Prot 1.1 gr; Carbo 17.3 gr; T Fat 7.9 gr; Chol 20.4 mg; Calc 20.5 mg; Potas 244.0 mg; Sod 41.3 mg.

2	*tablespoons instant hot chocolate mix*
2	*cups hot brewed coffee*
2	*cinnamon sticks*
¼	*cup whipped cream*
1	*tablespoon chocolate shavings*

Spring

*I*n its earliest awakenings Spring is the elusive season. After months of Winter's monotonous color scheme, we're impatient for color as well as for warmth. Then one morning the light has changed slightly. The air seems lighter. The grass is a shade greener. Spring has announced her imminent arrival.

For the cook—and the lucky ones for whom she cooks — this season offers splendid gifts of fresh foods at the height of their goodness. After winter weeks spent cruising the supermarket aisles in search of inspiration, it's positively exhilarating to find those first fresh fruits and vegetables.

Where I live there's a short wonderful time in which you'll find local strawberries side by side with elegant little baskets of fresh raspberries, blueberries, and blackberries. In our house this is the cue to polish up our pie-baking techniques and churn up a batch of vanilla ice cream.

In the Spring spectacular side by side with strawberries is asparagus. For most of my youth, asparagus was spoken of reverently as a luxurious commodity that was hard to find and even harder to afford. Now, it's available a large part of the year in most supermarkets. Simply steamed and served with lemon juice and butter, it's easy to see why this vegetable was one of the mainstays of the Roman nobleman.

The list of Spring foods goes on, each with its own mini-season: lettuce in dozens of varieties, peaches, cucumbers, squash, nectarines, cherries, melons, fresh turnip greens, and another favorite, first in the South and now prized all over the country, Vidalia onions from Georgia. Lamb appears in the butcher's case, and pork and hams are appealing. Seasonal fish become available again, and tender pink veal is at its best.

Spring is the season in which some of our happiest celebrations take place and for which some of our most elegant, fanciful food is served. This is a time for intimate celebrations such as a Father's Day brunch or a Mother's Day supper. Easter Dinner offers a wonderful opportunity to serve the whole clan, while nostalgic bridal showers and graduation luncheons call for gala desserts, extra special entrées, and creative hors d'oeuvres and finger foods. Whether your major social event this Spring is an Easter egg hunt for the younger set or a wedding reception, here you'll find recipes that will help your party shine.

PHOTOGRAPHS FOR THESE RECIPES ON COVER AND PAGE 2.

FRENCH HERBED SALAD DRESSING

1 cup corn oil	1 teaspoon mixed
1/3 cup lemon juice	dried tarragon,
1 tablespoon sugar	chives and parsley
1/2 teaspoon paprika	1 clove of garlic,
1/4 teaspoon dry	crushed
mustard	1 teaspoon salt

□ Combine all ingredients in 1-pint jar; shake well.
□ Chill in refrigerator.
□ Discard garlic. Shake well.
□ Serve on assorted salad greens.
□ Yield: 1 1/3 cups.

SOUTH OF THE BORDER DRESSING

1 cup corn oil	2 teaspoons sugar
1/3 cup white vinegar	1 1/2 teaspoons salt
1/4 cup orange juice	1 teaspoon cumin
1 tablespoon minced	1 teaspoon oregano
onion	1/4 teaspoon crushed
1 small clove of	red pepper
garlic, crushed	flakes

□ Combine all ingredients in 1-pint jar; shake well.
□ Chill in refrigerator.
□ Discard garlic. Shake well.
□ Serve on assorted salad greens.
□ Yield: 1 1/2 cups.

SPRING SALAD DRESSING

1 cup corn oil	2 teaspoons dillweed
1/2 cup lime juice	1/2 teaspoon celery
1 1/2 teaspoons salt	seed
1 teaspoon sugar	1 small clove of
1 teaspoon minced	garlic, crushed
onion	

□ Combine all ingredients in 1-pint jar; shake well.
□ Chill in refrigerator.
□ Discard garlic. Shake well.
□ Serve on assorted salad greens.
□ Yield: 1 1/2 cups.

STRAWBERRY TOP-HAT SOUFFLÉ

1 quart strawberries	1 tablespoon vanilla
3/4 cup sugar	extract
1 envelope	1 cup whipping
unflavored gelatin	cream, whipped
2 egg yolks, beaten	

□ Reserve 4 strawberries for garnish.
□ Process remaining strawberries in blender to yield 2 1/2 cups purée.
□ Mix sugar and dry gelatin in double boiler. Blend in purée.
□ Cook over simmering water until sugar dissolves, stirring constantly.
□ Whisk 1/2 cup hot mixture into beaten egg yolks; whisk egg yolk mixture into hot mixture.
□ Cook for 2 minutes or until slightly thickened, stirring constantly.
□ Blend with vanilla in large bowl.
□ Chill until mixture mounds when dropped from spoon.
□ Fold in whipped cream. Spoon into 1-quart soufflé dish with 2-inch waxed paper collar.
□ Chill until firm. Remove collar.
□ Garnish with reserved strawberries.
□ Serve with Custard Sauce.
□ Yield: 8 servings.

CUSTARD SAUCE

2 cups milk, scalded	4 egg yolks, beaten
1/4 cup sugar	1 1/2 teaspoons
Pinch of salt	vanilla extract

□ Heat milk, sugar and salt in double boiler over simmering water until sugar dissolves, stirring constantly.
□ Whisk 1/4 cup hot mixture into beaten egg yolks; whisk egg yolks into hot mixture.
□ Cook custard over simmering water for 2 minutes or until thickened, stirring constantly.
□ Remove from heat; stir in vanilla.
□ Place in pan of ice water; stir constantly until cool.
□ Yield: 2 cups.

Spring Foods

April	May	June	
	███ ARTICHOKES		**Vegetables**
ASPARAGUS ███████████████			
	███ BROCCOLI	BEETS ████	
	██ LEEKS	GREEN BEANS ██	
CABBAGE ████████			
	██ CARROTS ████████		
CUCUMBERS ████████			
	███ ENDIVE		
	KOHLRABI ███████████		
LETTUCE ██			
	OKRA ███████████████		
GREEN ONIONS ██			
PEAS ██			
		NEW POTATOES ████	
██████████████████████	██ RADISHES		
		██ SPINACH	
		APRICOTS ████	**Fruits**
		BLACKBERRIES ███	
		BLUEBERRIES ███	
	██ RHUBARB	RASPBERRIES ███	
STRAWBERRIES ██			
	SWEET CHERRIES ███		
	██ GRAPEFRUIT	SOUR CHERRIES ████	
		FIGS ██	
		KIWIFRUIT ████	
		LEMONS/LIMES ███	
MANGOS ██			
		MELONS ███	
		NECTARINES ███	
		██ PINEAPPLE	
	PEACHES ███		
	CLINGSTONE PLUMS ███		
	CHICKEN (BROILER-FRYERS) ████		**Meats**
	████ LAMB		
██ OYSTERS			
██ VEAL			

April

Devonshire Strawberries

Grace Welch, Illinois

1	**envelope unflavored gelatin**
¾	**cup cold water**
1	**cup sour cream**
1	**cup whipping cream**
½	**cup sugar**
1	**teaspoon vanilla extract**
4	**cups sliced fresh strawberries**

Soften gelatin in cold water in small saucepan. Heat over low heat until gelatin dissolves. Stir into sour cream in bowl; set aside. Whip cream in mixer bowl until thickened. Add sugar gradually, beating until soft peaks form. Fold in vanilla and sour cream gently. Rinse 1-quart mold with cold water. Spoon sour cream mixture into mold. Chill until firm. Unmold onto serving plate. Arrange strawberries around mold.

Yield: 8 servings. Approx Per Serving: Cal 238; Prot 2.7 gr; Carbo 19.7 gr; T Fat 17.3 gr; Chol 53.5 mg; Calc 63.6 mg; Potas 188.0 mg; Sod 28.6 mg.

Spring Garden Salad

Sally Taft, Ohio

Tear iceburg lettuce, Bibb lettuce, endive and spinach into bite-sized pieces. Combine greens with radishes and mushrooms in large salad bowl. Drizzle dressing over salad; toss gently. Top with croutons. Serve immediately.

Yield: 6 servings. Approx Per Serving: Cal 180; Prot 2.9 gr; Carbo 7.3 gr; T Fat 16.6 gr; Chol 0.0 mg; Calc 59.8 mg; Potas 472.0 mg; Sod 88.3 mg.

½ medium head iceburg lettuce
1 large head Bibb lettuce
1 bunch endive
1 (8-ounce) package fresh spinach
1 bunch radishes, sliced
8 ounces fresh mushrooms, sliced
¾ cup oil and vinegar dressing
¾ cup herb-seasoned croutons

Fresh Spinach Salad Bowl

Blend flour and 1 tablespoon oil in small saucepan. Stir in water. Cook until thickened, stirring constantly. Stir a small amount of hot mixture into egg yolk; stir egg yolk into hot mixture. Add ¼ cup oil, lemon juice, dry mustard and ½ teaspoon salt; beat until smooth. Chill until serving time. Wash spinach; pat dry. Tear into bite-sized pieces; discard stems. Combine with onion, celery, radishes, eggs, ½ teaspoon salt and pepper in bowl. Chill until serving time. Drizzle dressing over salad; toss lightly.

Yield: 8 servings. Approx Per Serving: Cal 143; Prot 5.8 gr; Carbo 5.5 gr; T Fat 11.7 gr; Chol 137.0 mg; Calc 106.0 mg; Potas 555.0 mg; Sod 375.0 mg.

1 tablespoon all-purpose flour
1 tablespoon oil
½ cup water
1 egg yolk, beaten
¼ cup oil
3 tablespoons lemon juice
½ teaspoon dry mustard
½ teaspoon salt
1½ pounds fresh spinach
1 small onion, thinly sliced
½ cup thinly sliced celery
½ cup thinly sliced radishes
3 hard-boiled eggs, sliced
½ teaspoon salt
¼ teaspoon pepper

French Vegetable Salad

1	*pound asparagus*
½	*cup Ocean Spray jellied cranberry sauce*
½	*cup yogurt*
1	*clove of garlic, crushed*
2	*tablespoons chopped parsley*
⅓	*cup chopped celery*
1	*tablespoon catsup*
4	*medium tomatoes, cut into wedges*
½	*medium avocado, cut into wedges*
1	*(8-ounce) can artichoke hearts*
½	*medium head romaine*

Steam asparagus in a small amount of water in covered saucepan for 10 minutes or until tender; drain. Chill in refrigerator. Beat cranberry sauce in bowl until smooth. Stir in yogurt, garlic, parsley, celery and catsup. Chill, covered, in refrigerator. Arrange asparagus spears, tomato wedges, avocado wedges and artichoke hearts on romaine-lined serving plate. Drizzle with cranberry dressing.

Yield: 6 servings. Approx Per Serving: Cal 139; Prot 5.6 gr; Carbo 24.4 gr; T Fat 3.8 gr; Chol 2.5 mg; Calc 89.0 mg; Potas 835.0 mg; Sod 91.1 mg.

Zesty Pasta Salad

Louise Watt, New York

8	*ounces pasta shells*
½	*cup shelled fresh peas*
¼	*cup chopped pimento*
½	*cup sliced ripe olives*
¼	*cup chopped green onions*
¼	*cup chopped fresh parsley*
1	*clove of garlic, minced*
1	*(7-ounce) jar marinated artichoke hearts*
1	*cup Italian salad dressing*
½	*cup Parmesan cheese*

Cook pasta shells according to package directions; drain. Rinse with cold water; drain. Blanch peas in a small amount of water in saucepan; drain. Combine pasta, peas, pimento, olives, green onions, parsley and garlic in bowl. Add artichoke hearts with marinade and desired amount of salad dressing; mix lightly. Chill, covered, in refrigerator for 12 to 24 hours. Serve at room temperature. Sprinkle with Parmesan cheese just before serving.

Yield: 4 servings. Approx Per Serving: Cal 633; Prot 14.5 gr; Carbo 58.1 gr; T Fat 47.0 gr; Chol 7.9 mg; Calc 204.0 mg; Potas 369.0 mg; Sod 875.0 mg.

Baked Tenderloin Flambé

Preheat oven to 400 degrees. Place tenderloin in baking dish. Spread with butter. Bake for 20 minutes. Mix Sherry, mustard, soy sauce and scallions in saucepan. Cook until reduced by ⅓. Pour over tenderloin. Bake for 10 minutes longer or to desired degree of doneness. Place tenderloin on flame-proof serving platter. Spoon pan drippings over tenderloin. Pour Cognac over top; ignite. Serve immediately.

Yield: 8 servings. Approx Per Serving: Cal 787; Prot 65.8 gr; Carbo 15.1 gr; T Fat 38.6 gr; Chol 237.0 mg; Calc 39.5 mg; Potas 1063.0 mg; Sod 1141.0 mg.

1   *(4-pound) beef tenderloin*
¾   *cup butter or margarine, softened*
2   *cups Sherry*
3   *tablespoons mustard*
6   *tablespoons soy sauce*
¾   *cup chopped scallions*
¾   *cup warmed Cognac*

Beef and Mushroom Stir-Fry

Dian Callahan, South Dakota

Cut steak diagonally into thin strips; place in bowl. Slice onions lengthwise; add to steak. Add mixture of soy sauce, vinegar, water, sugar, garlic and ginger. Chill, covered, for 2 hours or longer, stirring occasionally. Stir-fry mushrooms in hot oil in wok for 2 minutes. Add steak with marinade. Stir-fry for 5 minutes. Add cabbage, bean sprouts and water chestnuts. Stir-fry for 5 minutes longer. Serve over rice.

Yield: 8 servings. Approx Per Serving: Cal 615; Prot 35.9 gr; Carbo 53.8 gr; T Fat 28.1 gr; Chol 94.7 mg; Calc 53.8 mg; Potas 883.0 mg; Sod 1107.0 mg.

2   *pounds flank steak*
2   *medium onions*
½   *cup soy sauce*
1   *tablespoon vinegar*
¼   *cup water*
2   *tablespoons sugar*
1   *teaspoon minced garlic*
¾   *teaspoon ginger*
1   *pound fresh mushrooms, sliced*
¼   *cup oil*
2   *cups finely shredded cabbage*
2   *cups fresh bean sprouts*
1   *(8-ounce) can sliced water chestnuts, drained*
6   *cups hot cooked rice*

Saucy Rice Balls

Cheryl Colwell Hansen, New York

1	*pound ground beef*
½	*cup chopped onion*
2	*cloves of garlic, chopped*
1	*(15-ounce) can tomato sauce*
2	*teaspoons sugar*
1	*teaspoon basil*
½	*teaspoon salt*
½	*teaspoon pepper*
2	*cups long grain rice*
4	*cups chicken broth*
3	*tablespoons butter*
	or margarine
1½	*cups Parmesan cheese*
	Garlic powder to taste
	Italian seasoning to taste
5	*egg yolks*
8	*ounces mozzarella cheese,*
	cut into 16 cubes
5	*egg whites*
2	*cups seasoned bread crumbs*
1	*cup oil*

Brown ground beef in saucepan, stirring until crumbly. Drain, reserving 2 tablespoons pan drippings. Sauté onion and garlic in reserved drippings until tender. Stir in tomato sauce, sugar, basil, salt and pepper. Simmer for 1 hour, stirring occasionally. Bring rice, chicken broth and butter to a boil in saucepan; reduce heat. Simmer, covered, until rice is tender. Cool. Add Parmesan cheese, garlic powder, Italian seasoning and egg yolks; mix well. Shape by ⅓ cupfuls into balls. Make indentation in each rice ball. Insert 1 cube mozzarella cheese. Shape to enclose cheese completely. Roll in lightly beaten egg whites; coat with bread crumbs. Chill ground beef sauce and rice balls for 2 to 24 hours. Preheat oven to 400 degrees. Heat oil in large heavy skillet. Brown rice balls several at a time in oil in skillet over medium heat; drain. Place in baking dish. Bake for 10 minutes. Reheat ground beef sauce to serving temperature. Place rice balls in serving bowl. Spoon sauce over top.

Yield: 6 servings. Approx Per Serving: Cal 827; Prot 47.1 gr; Carbo 68.0 gr; T Fat 38.8 gr; Chol 332.0 mg; Calc 570.0 mg; Potas 747.0 mg; Sod 2738.0 mg.

Ham Cups with Peas

Marjorie Yandell, Kentucky

1	*egg, beaten*
2	*tablespoons milk*
3	*tablespoons minced onion*
¾	*cup soft bread crumbs*
½	*teaspoon dry mustard*
8	*ounces cooked ham, ground*
1	*tablespoon butter*
	or margarine
½	*teaspoon curry powder*
1	*tablespoon all-purpose flour*
⅛	*teaspoon salt*
	Dash of pepper
⅔	*cup milk*
1	*cup fresh peas, cooked*

Combine egg, 2 tablespoons milk, onion, bread crumbs and dry mustard in bowl. Add ham; mix well. Divide into 2 portions. Press over bottom and sides of two 6-ounce ramekins, forming shells. Microwave on High for 3 minutes or until set. Remove ham cups carefully to warm serving plate. Microwave butter and curry powder in 2-cup glass measure for 20 seconds or until butter is melted. Blend in flour, salt and pepper. Stir in ⅔ cup milk. Microwave for 2 minutes or until thickened, stirring every 30 seconds. Stir in peas. Spoon into ham cups carefully.

Yield: 2 servings. Approx Per Serving: Cal 549; Prot 30.7 gr; Carbo 29.7 gr; T Fat 34.0 gr; Chol 219.0 mg; Calc 172.0 mg; Potas 749.0 mg; Sod 1948.0 mg.

Crab Florentine

Linda Clapper, Florida

Preheat oven to 350 degrees. Cook spinach in a small amount of water in saucepan for 10 minutes; drain. Layer spinach, rice, 1 cup cheese and crab meat in 1½-quart casserole. Sprinkle with lemon juice. Blend sour cream, salt and oregano in bowl. Spread over crab meat. Top with tomato sauce. Bake for 20 minutes. Sprinkle with ½ cup cheese. Bake for 5 minutes longer.

Yield: 6 servings. Approx Per Serving: Cal 263; Prot 19.3 gr; Carbo 19.9 gr; T Fat 11.9 gr; Chol 73.2 mg; Calc 336.0 mg; Potas 733.0 mg; Sod 728.0 mg.

1 **pound spinach, chopped**
1½ **cups cooked rice**
1 **cup shredded mozzarella cheese**
2 **cups crab meat**
1 **tablespoon lemon juice**
⅔ **cup sour cream**
½ **teaspoon salt**
½ **teaspoon oregano**
1 **(8-ounce) can tomato sauce**
½ **cup shredded mozzarella cheese**

Vegetable Vermicelli

Bonnie Borelles, New Jersey

Fry bacon in skillet until crisp; remove with slotted spoon. Drain, reserving 3 tablespoons pan drippings. Sauté mushrooms, carrots, cauliflower, peas, zucchini, pepper, green onions and garlic in reserved drippings for 5 minutes or just until tender. Cook vermicelli al dente in boiling water in saucepan; drain. Add butter; toss until butter is melted. Add mixture of eggs and cream; mix well. Add sautéed vegetables, crisp bacon and cheese; toss lightly. Serve immediately.

Yield: 6 servings. Approx Per Serving: Cal 568; Prot 23.3 gr; Carbo 63.1 gr; T Fat 24.3 gr; Chol 235.0 mg; Calc 243.0 mg; Potas 421.0 mg; Sod 513.0 mg.

8 **slices bacon, chopped**
½ **cup sliced mushrooms**
½ **cup sliced carrots**
½ **cup sliced cauliflower**
½ **cup fresh green peas**
½ **cup sliced zucchini**
½ **sweet red pepper, cut into strips**
¼ **cup sliced green onions**
1 **clove of garlic, sliced**
1 **(16-ounce) package vermicelli**
¼ **cup butter or margarine, sliced**
4 **eggs, beaten**
¼ **cup heavy cream**
1 **cup Parmesan cheese**

Green Beans and Walnuts

Joe Lucente, Maryland

2	**pounds fresh green beans**
½	**cup fresh mint leaves**
¾	**cup oil**
¼	**cup tarragon vinegar**
½	**teaspoon minced garlic**
¾	**teaspoon salt**
¼	**teaspoon white pepper**
1	**cup crumbled feta cheese**
1	**cup chopped red onion**
1	**cup chopped toasted walnuts**

Trim green beans; break into 2-inch pieces. Cook in a small amount of boiling salted water in saucepan for 4 minutes. Rinse in cold water; drain and pat dry. Combine mint, oil, vinegar, garlic, salt and pepper in food processor or blender container. Process until smooth. Combine with feta cheese in salad bowl. Add green beans and onion; toss lightly. Sprinkle with walnuts. Chill for several minutes to overnight.

Yield: 8 servings. Approx Per Serving: Cal 363; Prot 6.8 gr; Carbo 14.5 gr; T Fat 33.2 gr; Chol 12.5 mg; Calc 145.0 mg; Potas 465.0 mg; Sod 363.0 mg.

Spring Onion Pie

Sharon Wells, Texas

2	**cups chopped green onions**
2	**tablespoons butter** **or margarine**
1	**unbaked 9-inch pie shell**
8	**ounces cream cheese, softened**
2	**eggs**
½	**cup milk**
	Dash of Tabasco sauce
¼	**teaspoon salt**
	Paprika

Preheat oven to 350 degrees. Sauté green onions lightly in butter in skillet. Spread in pie shell. Beat cream cheese in mixer bowl until light. Add eggs, milk, Tabasco sauce and salt; beat until smooth. Pour into prepared pie shell. Sprinkle with paprika. Bake for 35 to 45 minutes or until knife inserted in center comes out clean.

Yield: 8 servings. Approx Per Serving: Cal 272; Prot 6.2 gr; Carbo 13.1 gr; T Fat 22.2 gr; Chol 109.0 mg; Calc 65.6 mg; Potas 153.0 mg; Sod 380.0 mg.

Lemony New Potatoes

Patricia Peralez, Texas

2½	**pounds small new potatoes**
2	**tablespoons chopped scallions**
½	**cup butter or margarine**
1½	**tablespoons lemon juice**
½	**teaspoon nutmeg**
½	**teaspoon pepper**
2	**teaspoons grated lemon rind**

Combine potatoes with water to cover in saucepan. Cook, covered, for 30 minutes or just until tender; drain and rinse. Remove skins carefully. Sauté scallions in butter in skillet. Stir in lemon juice, nutmeg and pepper. Add potatoes. Heat to serving temperature. Spoon into serving dish. Sprinkle with lemon rind.

Yield: 8 servings. Approx Per Serving: Cal 257; Prot 3.4 gr; Carbo 36.1 gr; T Fat 11.7 gr; Chol 31.1 mg; Calc 18.6 mg; Potas 604.0 mg; Sod 108.0 mg.

Rice Primavera

Penny Richardson, Oklahoma

Preheat oven to 350 degrees. Alternate layers of rice, cheese, pimento, mushrooms and peas in greased 2-quart casserole until all ingredients are used. Beat eggs, milk and salt in bowl until smooth. Pour over layers. Toss bread cubes with melted butter in bowl. Sprinkle over casserole. Chill in refrigerator if desired. Bake for 45 minutes or until set and brown.

Yield:　8 servings. Approx Per Serving: Cal 271; Prot 11.4 gr; Carbo 29.7 gr; T Fat 11.8 gr; Chol 100.0 mg; Calc 202.0 mg; Potas 252.0 mg; Sod 454.0 mg.

3	*cups cooked rice*
1¼	*cups shredded Cheddar cheese*
1	*(2-ounce) jar pimento, drained*
1	*cup sliced fresh mushrooms*
2	*cups tiny fresh green peas*
2	*eggs*
1¼	*cups milk*
1	*teaspoon salt*
1	*cup bread cubes*
2	*tablespoons melted butter or margarine*

Peppy Batter Bread

Dissolve yeast in ¼ cup lukewarm water. Combine shortening, sugar, potato flakes, cream cheese, salt and 1 cup boiling water in bowl; beat until well blended. Add evaporated milk and eggs; mix well. Stir in yeast mixture. Add 2 cups flour. Beat at medium speed for 2 minutes. Mix in remaining flour by hand to make stiff batter. Let rise, covered, in warm place for 45 minutes or until doubled in bulk. Stir vigorously for 35 to 40 strokes. Spoon into greased 2-quart casserole. Let rise, covered, for 30 minutes or until doubled in bulk. Preheat oven to 350 degrees. Bake bread for 40 to 45 minutes or until golden. Remove immediately to wire rack. Brush with margarine; sprinkle with lemon pepper. Serve warm or cold.

Yield:　12 servings. Approx Per Serving: Cal 281; Prot 7.9 gr; Carbo 41.8 gr; T Fat 14.3 gr; Chol 67.8 mg; Calc 47.7 mg; Potas 205.0 mg; Sod 319.0 mg.

1	*package (1 tablespoon) dry yeast*
¼	*cup warm (115-degree) water*
2	*tablespoons shortening*
1	*tablespoon sugar*
1	*cup dry potato flakes*
3	*ounces cream cheese*
1	*teaspoon salt*
1	*cup boiling water*
¼	*cup evaporated milk*
2	*eggs*
3½	*cups all-purpose flour*
¼	*cup melted margarine*
	Lemon pepper

Creamy Coconut Mold

Margaret Damm, Montana

2	envelopes unflavored gelatin
1½	cups cold water
24	ounces cottage cheese
1	(14-ounce) can sweetened condensed milk
3	ounces cream cheese, softened
1	cup flaked coconut
1	cup chopped nuts
½	teaspoon almond extract
3	cups fresh strawberries

Sprinkle gelatin over cold water in saucepan; let stand until softened. Heat until gelatin is dissolved, stirring constantly. Combine cottage cheese, sweetened condensed milk, cream cheese, coconut, nuts and flavoring in bowl; mix well. Stir in gelatin. Chill until partially set; mix well. Spoon into lightly oiled 1½-quart ring mold. Chill for 3 hours or until set. Unmold onto serving plate. Place strawberries in center and around ring.

Yield: 6 servings. Approx Per Serving: Cal 588; Prot 24.9 gr; Carbo 50.2 gr; T Fat 33.7 gr; Chol 54.7 mg; Calc 287.0 mg; Potas 607.0 mg; Sod 591.0 mg.

Fondant Easter Eggs

½	cup butter or margarine, softened
1	teaspoon vanilla extract
1	teaspoon salt
⅔	cup sweetened condensed milk
6	cups sifted confectioners' sugar
¾	cup flaked coconut
1	(8-ounce) can almond paste
8	(1-ounce) squares semisweet chocolate
2	tablespoons melted paraffin

Cream butter, vanilla and salt in mixer bowl until light. Blend in sweetened condensed milk. Add 5 cups confectioners' sugar gradually, mixing well after each addition. Knead in remaining confectioners' sugar until fondant is smooth and easily handled. Divide into 2 portions. Knead coconut into 1 portion and almond paste into remaining portion. Shape into eggs; place on waxed paper. Chill for several hours to overnight. Let eggs stand at room temperature for 15 minutes. Melt chocolate with paraffin in double boiler pan over hot water; blend well. Dip eggs into chocolate. Place on waxed paper. Let stand until dry. Pipe Butter Cream Frosting through decorating tube onto eggs.

Yield: 24 servings. Approx Per Serving: Cal 331; Prot 2.5 gr; Carbo 51.6 gr; T Fat 14.4 gr; Chol 21.7 mg; Calc 52.2 mg; Potas 140.0 mg; Sod 159.0 mg.

Butter Cream Frosting

⅓	cup butter or margarine, softened
1	teaspoon vanilla extract
3	cups sifted confectioners' sugar
1	tablespoon egg white Food coloring
1	to 2 tablespoons heavy cream

Cream butter in mixer bowl until light. Add vanilla and confectioners' sugar gradually, mixing well after each addition. Blend in egg white. Tint with food coloring as desired. Add enough cream to make of desired consistency.

Nutritional information not available.

Strawberry Cream Pie

Chill bowl and beaters of electric mixer. Reserve 3 strawberries. Process remaining strawberries in blender until smooth; set aside. Mix ¾ cup orange juice and sugar in saucepan. Sprinkle gelatin over top. Let stand for 1 minute or until softened. Heat until gelatin is dissolved, stirring constantly. Cool to room temperature. Combine ½ cup orange juice and dry milk powder in chilled mixer bowl. Beat at high speed until soft peaks form. Add gelatin and orange rind gradually, beating constantly. Beat for 2 minutes or until smooth. Beat in safflower oil gradually. Fold in puréed strawberries. Chill until mixture mounds when dropped from spoon. Spoon into Whole Wheat Pie Shell. Chill until firm. Cut reserved strawberries into halves. Garnish pie with strawberry halves and mint leaves.

Yield: 6 servings. Approx Per Serving: Cal 347; Prot 7.3 gr; Carbo 49.8 gr; T Fat 14.4 gr; Chol 1.0 mg; Calc 107.2 mg; Potas 672.2 mg; Sod 97.6 mg.

1	*pint fresh strawberries*
¾	*cup orange juice*
2	*tablespoons sugar*
1	*envelope unflavored gelatin*
½	*cup chilled orange juice*
½	*cup nonfat dry milk powder*
2	*teaspoons grated orange rind*
3	*tablespoons safflower oil*
1	*baked Whole Wheat Pie Shell*
	Mint leaves

Whole Wheat Pie Shell

Combine whole wheat flour, all-purpose flour and salt in bowl; make well in center. Mix safflower oil, lemon juice and water in bowl. Pour into well. Stir just until moistened. Shape into ball. Roll into circle between 2 sheets waxed paper. Peel off top sheet. Invert into pie plate; peel off remaining paper. Trim and flute edges; prick with fork. Chill for 1 hour. Preheat oven to 400 degrees. Cover pastry with aluminum foil weighted with dried beans or pastry weights. Bake for 10 minutes. Remove foil and weights. Bake for 5 minutes or until firm. Cool.

Yield: 1 pie shell. Approx Per Pie Shell: Cal 774; Prot 14.1 gr; Carbo 87.6 gr; T Fat 42.7 gr; Chol 0.0 mg; Calc 37.2 mg; Potas 295.2 mg; Sod 376.2 mg.

½	*cup whole wheat flour*
½	*cup all-purpose flour*
⅛	*teaspoon salt*
3	*tablespoons safflower oil*
1	*tablespoon lemon juice*
3½	*tablespoons (or more) warm water*

May

Shrimp Vinaigrette in Snow Peas

 3 **pounds large shrimp, peeled**
 1 **bay leaf**
 ½ **cup olive oil**
 2 **tablespoons wine vinegar**
 3 **tablespoons Dijon-style mustard**
 1 **tablespoon minced shallot**
 1 **teaspoon minced fresh gingerroot**
 1 **clove of garlic, minced**
 1 **tablespoon minced fresh dill**
   Pinch of sugar
   Salt and pepper to taste
 24 **snow peas**

Bring a generous amount of water to a boil in saucepan. Add shrimp and bay leaf. Cook for 2 minutes or just until shrimp turn pink;drain. Place in ice water immediately; drain and pat dry. Place in glass bowl. Mix olive oil, vinegar, mustard, shallot, ginger, garlic, dill and sugar in bowl. Add salt and pepper. Pour over shrimp; toss to mix. Chill, covered, for 24 to 48 hours, tossing every 12 hours. Blanch pea pods in boiling water in saucepan for 10 seconds. Place in ice water immediately. Split pods apart; drain and pat dry. Drain shrimp; wrap pea pod half around each shrimp, securing with toothpick. Arrange on serving plate or attach with toothpick to half cabbage head on serving plate.

Yield: 48 servings. Approx Per Serving: Cal 54; Prot 6.0 gr; Carbo 0.9 gr; T Fat 2.8 gr; Chol 43.1 mg; Calc 18.4 mg; Potas 67.4 mg; Sod 54.5 mg.

The Springiest Green Salad

Chop summer sausage. Cut artichoke hearts into quarters. Combine sausage, artichoke hearts, mushrooms, onion rings and salad dressing in bowl; toss lightly. Chill, covered, for several hours. Mix greens in salad bowl. Drain sausage mixture, reserving marinade. Pour marinade over greens; toss to mix well. Add sausage mixture; toss lightly. Sprinkle with Parmesan cheese.

Yield: 4 servings. Approx Per Serving: Cal 703; Prot 22.8 gr; Carbo 22.8 gr; T Fat 67.2 gr; Chol 55.2 mg; Calc 393.0 mg; Potas 851.0 mg; Sod 2077.0 mg.

8 **ounces summer sausage**
1 **(15-ounce) can artichoke hearts, drained**
4 **ounces mushrooms, sliced**
1 **small red onion, sliced**
1 **cup Italian salad dressing**
2 **cups torn Bibb lettuce**
2 **cups torn Boston lettuce**
1 **cup torn curly endive**
1 **cup torn escarole**
1 **cup torn watercress**
1 **cup torn dandelion greens**
Parmesan cheese

German Potato Salad

Cook potatoes in water to cover in saucepan until tender; drain. Peel and slice potatoes. Split knockwurst lengthwise; slice as desired. Sauté knockwurst in 2 tablespoons margarine in skillet. Add onion. Cook until onion is tender, stirring frequently. Remove knockwurst and onion with slotted spoon. Blend 3 tablespoons margarine and flour in skillet; remove from heat. Add vinegar, apple juice, sugar and pepper. Simmer until thickened, stirring constantly. Add knockwurst and onion; mix well. Let stand, covered, for several minutes. Add potatoes; mix gently. Heat to serving temperature. Spoon into serving dish.

Yield: 6 servings. Approx Per Serving: Cal 666; Prot 20.8 gr; Carbo 38.4 gr; T Fat 47.9 gr; Chol 86.7 mg; Calc 29.0 mg; Potas 890.0 mg; Sod 1602.0 mg.

6 **medium potatoes**
2 **pounds knockwurst**
2 **tablespoons margarine**
1 **medium onion, sliced**
3 **tablespoons margarine**
2 **tablespoons all-purpose flour**
¾ **cup red wine vinegar**
¾ **cup apple juice**
1½ **teaspoons sugar**
¼ **teaspoon pepper**

Pot Roast Pacifica

Karen Strubbe, California

1	**(4-pound) sirloin tip roast**
2	**tablespoons lemon juice**
6	**slices bacon, chopped**
1	**medium onion, chopped**
1	**clove of garlic, minced**
1½	**cups orange juice**
1	**cup chopped peeled tomato**
1	**tablespoon sugar**
1	**tablespoon salt**
1	**teaspoon thyme**
1	**bay leaf**
1	**teaspoon nutmeg**
¼	**teaspoon pepper**
	Pinch of basil
	Pinch of rosemary
3	**tablespoons cornstarch**
¼	**cup cold water**

Brush roast with lemon juice. Let stand for 5 minutes. Sauté bacon, onion and garlic in large skillet until bacon is crisp. Remove bacon, onion and garlic. Brown roast in pan drippings. Add mixture of onion, bacon, orange juice, tomato and seasonings. Simmer for 3 hours or until roast is tender. Remove roast to heated serving platter. Skim pan juices. Remove bay leaf. Add enough water to pan juices to measure 3 cups. Stir in mixture of cornstarch and ¼ cup cold water. Cook until thickened, stirring constantly. Serve with roast.

Yield: 10 servings. Approx Per Serving: Cal 403; Prot 37.8 gr; Carbo 9.7 gr; T Fat 22.8 gr; Chol 115.0 mg; Calc 23.5 mg; Potas 637.0 mg; Sod 787.0 mg.

Buffet Mexican Haystacks

Dorothy Graber, Arizona

2	**cups rice**
1	**(29-ounce) can chili beans**
1	**pound lean ground beef**
1	**envelope taco seasoning mix**
1	**pound sharp Cheddar cheese, shredded**
1	**medium head lettuce, shredded**
3	**medium tomatoes, chopped, drained**
6	**medium green onions, sliced**
2	**large avocados, chopped**
2	**medium green peppers, chopped**
1	**cup sliced black olives**
2	**cups salsa**
1	**(16-ounce) package taco chips**

Cook rice using package directions just until tender. Heat beans to serving temperature. Brown ground beef in skillet, stirring until crumbly; drain. Add taco seasoning mix according to package directions. Place hot ingredients in separate serving bowls on buffet table. Add separate dishes of remaining ingredients. Guests serve themselves by layering rice, beans and ground beef mixture on plate and adding remaining ingredients as desired.

Yield: 8 servings. Approx Per Serving: Cal 1065; Prot 43.6 gr; Carbo 98.1 gr; T Fat 58.3 gr; Chol 109.0 mg; Calc 664.0 mg; Potas 1210.0 mg; Sod 1235.0 mg.

Meat Loaf with Ham and Mozzarella

Sandra Mayton, Washington

Preheat oven to 375 degrees. Combine ground beef, cracker crumbs, eggs, catsup and seasonings in bowl; mix well. Shape into ¾-inch thick rectangle on foil. Layer ham slices on ground beef mixture, leaving 1-inch edges. Sprinkle with cheese. Roll to enclose filling; seal edges. Seal foil tightly. Place in baking pan. Bake for 30 minutes. Remove foil carefully. Bake for 30 minutes.

Yield: 10 servings. Approx Per Serving: Cal 566; Prot 46.1 gr; Carbo 14.1 gr; T Fat 35.0 gr; Chol 207.0 mg; Calc 147.0 mg; Potas 642.0 mg; Sod 997.0 mg.

3 **pounds lean ground beef**
4 **ounces crackers, crushed**
2 **eggs, beaten**
¾ **cup catsup**
1 **tablespoon oregano**
 Salt and pepper to taste
2 **(6-ounce) packages thinly sliced ham**
2 **cups shredded mozzarella cheese**

Denver Sandwich Ring

Dianne Busby, Oklahoma

Preheat oven to 425 degrees. Combine baking mix, oil, egg and ¼ cup milk in bowl. Mix until smooth. Stir in ham, green onions and green pepper. Drop by spoonfuls into ring on baking sheet. Bake for 15 to 20 minutes or until brown. Melt butter in saucepan. Blend in flour and salt. Stir in 1½ cups milk gradually. Cook until thickened, stirring constantly. Stir in cheese until melted. Place sandwich ring on serving plate. Spoon sauce over top.

Yield: 6 servings. Approx Per Serving: Cal 802; Prot 24.6 gr; Carbo 49.2 gr; T Fat 56.4 gr; Chol 129.0 mg; Calc 368.0 mg; Potas 416.0 mg; Sod 2010.0 mg.

1½ **cups buttermilk baking mix**
½ **cup oil**
1 **egg**
¼ **cup milk**
1½ **cups chopped cooked ham**
⅓ **cup chopped green onions**
⅓ **cup chopped green pepper**
3 **tablespoons butter or margarine**
3 **tablespoons all-purpose flour**
½ **teaspoon salt**
1½ **cups milk**
1½ **cups shredded Cheddar cheese**

Veal and Mushroom Stew

Phyllis Sanzone, New York

2	**cloves of garlic, minced**
1	**medium onion, chopped**
¼	**cup oil**
2	**pounds veal, cubed**
6	**medium green peppers, cut into strips**
1	**pound mushrooms, sliced**
1	**(28-ounce) can tomatoes, mashed**
3½	**cups water**
2	**bay leaves**
½	**teaspoon sugar**
	Salt and pepper to taste

Sauté garlic and onion in oil in heavy saucepan. Add veal. Cook for 12 to 15 minutes or until brown on all sides, stirring frequently. Add green peppers, mushrooms, tomatoes, water, bay leaves, sugar, salt and pepper; mix well. Bring to a boil; reduce heat. Simmer, covered, for 2 to 3 hours or until veal is tender. Remove bay leaves.

Yield: 6 servings. Approx Per Serving: Cal 432; Prot 53.9 gr; Carbo 16.7 gr; T Fat 17.0 gr; Chol 207.0 mg; Calc 64.9 mg; Potas 1467.0 mg; Sod 351.0 mg.

Plantation Shortcake

Betty J. Miller, Nebraska

1	**(10-ounce) package corn bread mix**
1	**(8¾-ounce) can cream-style corn**
½	**cup shredded Swiss cheese**
2	**eggs, lightly beaten**
2	**tablespoons milk**
2	**teaspoons mustard**
1	**(14-ounce) can artichoke hearts, drained, chopped**
1	**(3-ounce) can chopped mushrooms, drained**
1	**cup shredded Swiss cheese**

Preheat oven to 350 degrees. Prepare corn bread mix using package directions. Add corn, ½ cup cheese, eggs, milk and mustard; mix well. Spread 1 cup batter in greased 8 x 8-inch baking pan. Mix artichokes, mushrooms and 1 cup cheese in bowl. Spoon into prepared pan. Top with remaining batter. Bake for 40 minutes or until brown. Cut into squares. Spoon Plantation Sauce over top.

Yield: 6 servings. Approx Per Serving: Cal 458; Prot 27.2 gr; Carbo 36.7 gr; T Fat 22.9 gr; Chol 169.0 mg; Calc 383.0 mg; Potas 539.0 mg; Sod 1038.0 mg.

Plantation Sauce

2	**tablespoons butter or margarine**
2	**tablespoons all-purpose flour**
¾	**cup chicken broth**
¾	**cup half and half**
2	**egg yolks, beaten**
1	**cup chopped cooked chicken**
1	**cup chopped cooked ham**

Melt butter in saucepan. Blend in flour. Stir in chicken broth and half and half gradually. Cook until thickened, stirring constantly. Stir a small amount of hot mixture into beaten egg yolks; stir egg yolks into hot mixture. Add chicken and ham; mix well. Heat to serving temperature.

Nutritional information not available.

Oriental Chicken with Peaches

Carol Ann Robinson, British Columbia, Canada

Drain peaches, reserving ½ cup liquid. Coat filets with flour. Brown in oil in skillet; remove and set aside. Sauté mushrooms and green pepper in drippings for 1 minute. Add filets. Pour mixture of onion, soy sauce, vinegar and reserved peach liquid over filets. Simmer, covered, for 20 minutes or until tender. Add peaches. Cook for 5 minutes longer. Remove filets to serving plate. Stir mixture of cornstarch and water into pan drippings. Cook until thickened, stirring constantly. Pour over filets. Sprinkle with almonds.

Yield: 6 servings. Approx Per Serving: Cal 505; Prot 58.1 gr; Carbo 26.8 gr; T Fat 17.8 gr; Chol 146.0 mg; Calc 45.1 mg; Potas 561.0 mg; Sod 468.0 mg.

1 *(16-ounce) can sliced peaches*
6 *large chicken breast filets*
½ *cup all-purpose flour*
¼ *cup oil*
1 *cup sliced mushrooms*
1 *small green pepper, chopped*
2 *tablespoons chopped onion*
2 *tablespoons soy sauce*
2 *tablespoons vinegar*
1 *tablespoon cornstarch*
1 *tablespoon water*
⅓ *cup slivered almonds*

Asparagus and Crab Meat Royale

Trudy England, Florida

Preheat oven to 350 degrees. Steam asparagus spears in saucepan for 10 minutes or until tender; drain. Reserve 8 spears; slice remaining asparagus into 1-inch pieces. Chill in refrigerator if desired. Beat eggs in mixer bowl. Add cottage cheese, mayonnaise, almonds, pimento, lime juice, Tabasco sauce and seasonings; mix well. Fold in crab meat and sliced asparagus. Spoon into buttered round 2-quart baking dish. Arrange reserved asparagus spears in spoke design on top. Place cheese wedges between spokes. Sprinkle with paprika. Bake 30 minutes.

Yield: 8 servings. Approx Per Serving: Cal 275; Prot 25.9 gr; Carbo 8.4 gr; T Fat 15.6 gr; Chol 145.0 mg; Calc 223.0 mg; Potas 489.0 mg; Sod 923.0 mg.

1 *pound medium asparagus, trimmed*
2 *eggs*
2 *cups cottage cheese*
½ *cup mayonnaise*
¼ *cup slivered almonds*
1 *tablespoon chopped pimento*
1 *tablespoon lime juice*
   Tabasco sauce to taste
½ *teaspoon tarragon*
1 *teaspoon salt*
¼ *teaspoon pepper*
1 *pound crab meat*
8 *thin Cheddar cheese wedges*
   Paprika to taste

Baked Halibut

Dorothy Kelly, California

1	**medium onion, thinly sliced**
2	**pounds halibut fillets**
1½	**cups sliced mushrooms**
⅓	**cup chopped tomato**
¼	**cup chopped green pepper**
¼	**cup chopped parsley**
½	**cup dry white wine**
2	**tablespoons lemon juice**
¼	**teaspoon dillweed**
⅛	**teaspoon pepper**

Preheat oven to 350 degrees. Layer onion and halibut fillets in baking dish. Sprinkle with mushrooms, tomato, green pepper and parsley. Mix wine, lemon juice and seasonings in bowl. Drizzle over vegetables. Bake for 30 minutes or until fish flakes easily.

Yield: 6 servings. Approx Per Serving: Cal 196; Prot 32.3 gr; Carbo 3.7 gr; T Fat 3.7 gr; Chol 48.4 mg; Calc 83.3 mg; Potas 837.0 mg; Sod 85.6 mg.

Scrambled Egg Crêpes

Joan Stockman, Nebraska

16	**eggs, beaten**
½	**cup milk**
2	**tablespoons chopped chives**
1	**teaspoon salt**
16	**crêpes**
2	**cups milk**
2	**tablespoons cornstarch**
1	**teaspoon dry mustard**
½	**teaspoon salt**
	Pepper to taste
½	**cup shredded Monterey Jack cheese**
3	**tablespoons chopped chives**

Preheat oven to 375 degrees. Combine first 4 ingredients in bowl; mix well. Pour into nonstick skillet. Cook over low heat until set, stirring frequently. Spoon ¼ cup scrambled eggs onto each crêpe; roll to enclose filling. Place seam side down in 9 x 13-inch baking dish. Blend 2 cups milk, cornstarch, dry mustard, ½ teaspoon salt and pepper in saucepan. Cook until thickened, stirring constantly. Simmer for 2 minutes longer, stirring constantly. Stir in cheese. Spoon over crêpes. Bake, covered, for 15 minutes. Garnish with chopped chives.

Yield: 8 servings. Approx Per Serving: Cal 365; Prot 20.8 gr; Carbo 20.2 gr; T Fat 21.9 gr; Chol 651.0 mg; Calc 295.6 mg; Potas 323.8 mg; Sod 667.8 mg.

Asparagus Amandine

Preheat oven to 350 degrees. Cook asparagus, covered, in a small amount of water in saucepan for 10 minutes or until tender; drain. Layer asparagus, bean sprouts and onion rings ½ at a time in buttered 2-quart baking dish. Mix soup and soy sauce in bowl. Spoon over layers. Sprinkle with almonds. Bake for 25 minutes or until bubbly.

Yield: 6 servings. Approx Per Serving: Cal 358; Prot 11.5 gr; Carbo 28.2 gr; T Fat 24.5 gr; Chol 11.1 mg; Calc 136.0 mg; Potas 543.0 mg; Sod 933.0 mg.

1	*pound fresh asparagus spears*
12	*ounces fresh bean sprouts*
2	*(3-ounce) cans French-fried onion rings*
2	*(10-ounce) cans cream of mushroom soup*
2	*teaspoons soy sauce*
1	*cup slivered almonds*

Green Beans with Radishes

Trim green beans. Cook in a small amount of water in saucepan until tender-crisp; drain. Sauté green onion in butter in skillet. Stir in lemon juice, seasoned salt, soy sauce and radishes. Stir-fry for 2 minutes. Add beans. Stir-fry until heated through. Add almonds. Serve at once.

Yield: 6 servings. Approx Per Serving: Cal 133; Prot 3.2 gr; Carbo 9.7 gr; T Fat 10.3 gr; Chol 20.7 mg; Calc 61.2 mg; Potas 304.0 mg; Sod 220.0 mg.

1½	*pounds fresh green beans*
1	*tablespoon chopped green onion*
¼	*cup butter or margarine*
1	*teaspoon lemon juice*
¼	*teaspoon seasoned salt*
1	*teaspoon soy sauce*
¼	*cup sliced radishes*
2	*tablespoons toasted slivered almonds*

Vidalia Onion Bake

Marion Beightol, Florida

Preheat oven to 350 degrees. Mix cracker crumbs and melted butter in bowl. Press over bottom and side of pie plate to form crust. Sauté onions in 2 tablespoons butter in skillet just until tender. Spoon into prepared pie plate. Beat milk, eggs, salt and pepper in bowl until smooth. Pour over onions. Sprinkle with cheese and paprika. Bake for 30 minutes. Cut into wedges. Serve at once.

Yield: 6 servings. Approx Per Serving: Cal 602; Prot 10.6 gr; Carbo 59.4 gr; T Fat 44.8 gr; Chol 143.0 mg; Calc 180.0 mg; Potas 257.0 mg; Sod 960.0 mg.

2	*cups crushed bacon-flavored crackers*
6	*tablespoons melted butter or margarine*
2	*cups thinly sliced Vidalia onions*
2	*tablespoons butter or margarine*
¾	*cup milk*
2	*eggs*
	Salt and pepper to taste
⅓	*cup shredded Cheddar cheese*
	Paprika to taste

Spinach and Bulgur Casserole

Audrey Spaulding, Colorado

1 **cup bulgur**
2 **cups water**
1 **pound spinach, chopped**
1 **(17-ounce) can chicken bouillon**
3 **eggs, beaten**
1 **small tomato, chopped**
½ **cup yogurt**
1½ **cups shredded Cheddar cheese**

Preheat oven to 350 degrees. Combine bulgur and water in saucepan. Cook for 15 minutes or until water is absorbed. Cook spinach in a small amount of water in saucepan for 10 minutes; drain. Combine bulgur, spinach, chicken bouillon, eggs, tomato and yogurt in bowl; mix well. Spoon into 9x13-inch baking dish. Top with cheese. Bake for 25 minutes.

Yield: 6 servings. Approx Per Serving: Cal 300; Prot 17.9 gr; Carbo 27.3 gr; T Fat 14.0 gr; Chol 170.0 mg; Calc 329.0 mg; Potas 707.0 mg; Sod 537.0 mg.

Pasta alla Pomodoro

¼ **cup chopped onion**
1 **clove of garlic, minced**
¼ **cup olive oil**
1 **(28-ounce) can tomatoes**
6 **fresh basil leaves**
Salt and pepper to taste
12 **ounces fettucini**
Parmesan cheese

Sauté onion and garlic in olive oil in skillet until tender. Drain and chop tomatoes, reserving liquid. Add tomatoes, tomato liquid and seasonings to skillet. Simmer, uncovered, for 15 to 20 minutes, stirring occasionally. Cook fettucini according to package directions; drain well. Place in large serving bowl. Add hot sauce; toss lightly. Sprinkle with cheese.

Yield: 6 servings. Approx Per Serving: Cal 533; Prot 7.4 gr; Carbo 53.9 gr; T Fat 9.6 gr; Chol 0.0 mg; Calc 43.4 mg; Potas 336.0 mg; Sod 216.0 mg.

Hashed Brown Potato Pie

Robyn Mosher, Michigan

1 **(16-ounce) package instant hashed brown potatoes with onions**
¼ **cup butter or margarine**
6 **eggs, beaten**
6 **tablespoons milk**
½ **cup shredded Cheddar cheese**

Brown potatoes in butter in skillet over hot coals. Combine eggs, milk and cheese in bowl; mix well. Pour over potatoes. Cook, tightly covered, for 5 to 8 minutes or until set.

Yield: 6 servings. Approx Per Serving: Cal 359; Prot 11.4 gr; Carbo 22.8 gr; T Fat 25.6 gr; Chol 307.0 mg; Calc 126.0 mg; Potas 427.0 mg; Sod 224.0 mg.

Dijon Garlic Bread

Dorothy Lucas, Oregon

Preheat oven to 400 degrees. Combine butter, garlic salt, mustard and cheese in bowl; mix well. Cut loaf lengthwise. Spread with butter mixture; sprinkle with paprika. Wrap in foil and store in refrigerator or freezer if desired. Place unwrapped loaf on baking sheet. Toast for 10 minutes or until golden. Cut diagonally into serving pieces.

Yield: 6 servings. Approx Per Serving: Cal 439; Prot 9.0 gr; Carbo 38.7 gr; T Fat 27.2 gr; Chol 64.7 mg; Calc 143.0 mg; Potas 86.8 mg; Sod 938.0 mg.

¾   **cup butter or margarine, softened**
½   **teaspoon garlic salt**
2   **tablespoons Dijon-style mustard**
¼   **cup Parmesan cheese**
1   **(16-ounce) loaf French bread**
    Paprika to taste

Strawberry and Banana Loaf

Jean Roberts, Oregon

Preheat oven to 325 degrees. Cream butter and sugar in mixer bowl until light and fluffy. Blend in eggs and salt. Mix sour cream, baking powder and soda in bowl. Blend into creamed mixture. Add bananas, flour, pecans and vanilla; mix well. Fold in strawberries. Pour into greased and floured 5 x 9-inch loaf pan. Bake for 1½ hours or until loaf tests done. Remove to wire rack to cool.

Yield: 12 servings. Approx Per Serving: Cal 329; Prot 3.8 gr; Carbo 47.0 gr; T Fat 14.9 gr; Chol 68.5 mg; Calc 23.4 mg; Potas 156.0 mg; Sod 172.0 mg.

½   **cup butter or margarine, softened**
1⅔   **cups sugar**
2   **eggs**
¼   **teaspoon salt**
¼   **cup sour cream**
½   **teaspoon baking powder**
½   **teaspoon soda**
1   **cup mashed bananas**
1¾   **cups all-purpose flour**
¾   **cup chopped pecans**
1   **teaspoon vanilla extract**
¾   **cup sliced strawberries**

Gingered Fresh Fruit Bowl

Mary Satterwhite, Kansas

Combine marmalade, water and ginger in small bowl; mix well. Let stand for several minutes. Layer cherries, pineapple, cantaloupe and strawberries in glass bowl. Sprinkle banana with lemon juice. Layer banana slices over strawberries. Drizzle with marmalade mixture. Chill until serving time. Garnish with fresh mint.

Yield: 8 servings. Approx Per Serving: Cal 143; Prot 1.6 gr; Carbo 35.5 gr; T Fat 0.9 gr; Chol 0.0 mg; Calc 24.3 mg; Potas 438.0 mg; Sod 8.5 mg.

½   **cup orange marmalade**
¼   **cup hot water**
1½   **teaspoons finely chopped candied ginger**
2   **cups Bing cherry halves**
1½   **cups fresh pineapple chunks**
3   **cups cantaloupe balls**
2   **cups fresh strawberries**
1   **medium banana, sliced**
1   **tablespoon lemon juice**
      Fresh mint leaves

June

Asparagus Roll-Ups

Mary Mille, Tennessee

20	**large fresh asparagus spears**
2	**tablespoons water**
8	**ounces cream cheese, softened**
2	**ounces bleu cheese, crumbled**
10	**slices bread**
2	**tablespoons melted butter or margarine**
¼	**cup Parmesan cheese**

Microwave asparagus with water in covered glass dish on High for 7 minutes or just until tender; drain. Blend cream cheese and bleu cheese in bowl until smooth. Trim crusts from bread; cut slices into halves. Flatten each half with rolling pin. Spread with cheese mixture. Place asparagus spear on each slice; roll to enclose asparagus. Place seam side down on lightly greased baking sheet. Brush with melted butter; sprinkle with Parmesan cheese. Chill in refrigerator if desired. Broil until light brown. Drain on paper towel. Serve hot or cold.

Yield: 20 servings. Approx Per Serving: Cal 105; Prot 3.5 gr; Carbo 7.8 gr; T Fat 6.8 gr; Chol 18.4 mg; Calc 59.1 mg; Potas 78.4 mg; Sod 174.0 mg.

Ginger Dip

Elaine Bass, Georgia

Combine mayonnaise, sour cream and soy sauce in bowl; mix well. Stir in green onions, parsley, water chestnuts, ginger and garlic. Chill until serving time. Serve with crackers or chips.

Yield: 32 tablespoons. Approx Per Tablespoon: Cal 45; Prot 0.4 gr; Carbo 2.4 gr; T Fat 4.0 gr; Chol 5.1 mg; Calc 10.4 mg; Potas 16.0 mg; Sod 88.3 mg.

1 *cup mayonnaise*
1 *cup sour cream*
1 *tablespoon soy sauce*
¼ *cup minced green onions*
¼ *cup minced parsley*
¼ *cup chopped water chestnuts*
2 *tablespoons chopped candied ginger*
2 *cloves of garlic, minced*

Fresh Fruit with Yogurt Dip

Sarah Preston, Kentucky

Blend cream cheese and yogurt in bowl. Add lemon rind, vanilla and sugar; mix well. Chill in refrigerator. Spoon into serving bowl. Serve with fruit for dipping.

Yield: 32 tablespoons. Approx Per Tablespoon: Cal 34; Prot 0.8 gr; Carbo 1.7 gr; T Fat 2.7 gr; Chol 8.7 mg; Calc 14.4 mg; Potas 19.5 mg; Sod 24.2 mg.

8 *ounces cream cheese, softened*
1 *cup yogurt*
1 *teaspoon grated lemon rind*
1 *teaspoon vanilla extract*
3 *tablespoons sugar*
 Apple wedges
 Fresh pineapple chunks
 Strawberries

Spiced Beets

Miriam Slaybaugh, Pennsylvania

Cook beets in boiling water in saucepan until tender; drain. Cool and peel. Combine vinegar and sugar in saucepan. Bring to a boil. Add salt, hot pepper, cloves, allspice and cinnamon; mix well. Add beets. Bring to a boil. Spoon into hot sterilized jars; seal with 2-piece lids. Let stand for several days before serving.

Yield: 8 cups. Approx Per Cup: Cal 252; Prot 1.6 gr; Carbo 64.7 gr; T Fat 0.2 gr; Chol 0.0 mg; Calc 31.2 mg; Potas 301.0 mg; Sod 734.0 mg.

8 *cups tiny whole beets*
1½ *cups vinegar*
2 *cups sugar*
1 *teaspoon salt*
1 *small hot pepper, chopped*
10 *whole cloves*
10 *whole allspice*
3 *(1-inch) cinnamon sticks*

Cream of Cauliflower Soup

5 cups chopped cauliflower
1 cup chopped leek
¼ cup butter or margarine
2 cups chicken broth
¼ teaspoon chervil
¼ teaspoon marjoram
¼ teaspoon fines herbes
1 bay leaf
⅛ teaspoon salt
⅛ teaspoon pepper
1½ cups light cream
Leek slices

Sauté cauliflower and 1 cup leek in butter in 3-quart saucepan over low heat for 15 minutes or until almost tender. Add chicken broth and seasonings; mix well. Cook, covered, over medium heat for 10 minutes or until vegetables are tender. Process ½ at a time in blender container until smooth. Combine with cream in saucepan. Heat just to serving temperature; do not boil. Remove bay leaf. Ladle into soup bowls. Garnish with leek slices.

Yield: 8 servings. Approx Per Serving: Cal 143; Prot 4.1 gr; Carbo 7.1 gr; T Fat 11.5 gr; Chol 32.5 mg; Calc 77.0 mg; Potas 359.0 mg; Sod 319.0 mg.

Spring Green Salad

Carol Hall, California

1 large Vidalia onion
2 cups sugar
½ cup wine vinegar
2 teaspoons salt
1 teaspoon celery seed
1 teaspoon dry mustard
⅛ teaspoon pepper
1 teaspoon Beau Monde seasoning
⅛ teaspoon marjoram
⅛ teaspoon sweet basil
2 cups oil
1 large head iceberg lettuce, cut into wedges

Grate onion. Mix onion and onion juice with sugar in mixer bowl. Let stand for several minutes. Combine vinegar and seasonings in small bowl. Let stand for several minutes. Add seasoning mixture to onion mixture. Beat until well mixed. Add oil in fine stream, beating constantly until thick. Store in airtight container in refrigerator. Serve over lettuce wedges.

Yield: 6 servings. Approx Per Serving: Cal 201; Prot 2.9 gr; Carbo 20.2 gr; T Fat 13.6 gr; Chol 17.0 mg; Calc 60.8 mg; Potas 551.0 mg; Sod 34.1 mg.

Curried Beef

Nancy Sedarat, Texas

Slice steak into ⅛x2-inch strips. Coat with mixture of flour, salt and pepper. Brown steak, garlic and onions in oil in skillet, stirring frequently; drain. Add curry powder and water. Simmer, covered, for 30 minutes, stirring occasionally. Stir in tomato sauce and lemon juice. Simmer, covered, for 20 minutes or until steak is tender. Cook rice according to package directions. Combine rice and peas in serving dish. Spoon curried beef over top.

Yield: 6 servings. Approx Per Serving: Cal 542; Prot 35.2 gr; Carbo 40.8 gr; T Fat 25.7 gr; Chol 94.7 mg; Calc 42.0 mg; Potas 851.0 mg; Sod 501.0 mg.

1½	**pounds round steak**
3	**tablespoons all-purpose flour**
	Salt and pepper to taste
1	**clove of garlic, crushed**
1	**small onion, chopped**
2	**tablespoons oil**
1	**teaspoon curry powder**
¾	**cup water**
1	**(15-ounce) can tomato sauce**
2	**teaspoons lemon juice**
1	**cup rice**
2	**cups fresh green peas**

Meatballs in Potato Boats

Preheat oven to 450 degrees. Oil potatoes lightly. Bake for 45 minutes or until tender. Combine ground beef and next 3 ingredients in bowl; mix well. Shape into tiny meatballs. Place in shallow baking dish. Bake for 15 minutes or until cooked through; drain. Combine beef bouillon, 3 tablespoons catsup and chutney in bowl; mix well. Mix with meatballs. Cut potatoes horizontally into halves. Scoop out potato pulp, leaving ¼-inch shells. Mash pulp with cream, seasoned salt and cheese in bowl. Spoon a small amount into each potato shell. Fill shells with meatball mixture. Spoon remaining potato mixture over meatballs. Broil until brown.

Yield: 4 servings. Approx Per Serving: Cal 572; Prot 30.0 gr; Carbo 62.1 gr; T Fat 21.7 gr; Chol 89.1 mg; Calc 152.0 mg; Potas 1254.0 mg; Sod 1051.0 mg.

4	**large baking potatoes**
¾	**pound lean ground beef**
¾	**cup soft bread crumbs**
⅓	**cup dry white wine**
2	**tablespoons catsup**
⅓	**cup beef bouillon**
3	**tablespoons catsup**
1	**tablespoon chutney**
½	**cup light cream**
1	**teaspoon seasoned salt**
¼	**cup Parmesan cheese**

Honeyed Pork Oriental

Constance Cooper, Ohio

2	*pounds pork shoulder steaks*
2	*tablespoons oil*
1	*envelope brown gravy mix*
¾	*cup water*
¼	*cup honey*
3	*tablespoons soy sauce*
2	*tablespoons red wine vinegar*
1	*teaspoon ginger*
½	*teaspoon garlic salt*
4	*carrots, thinly sliced*
1	*medium onion, cut in wedges*
1	*medium green pepper, cut in squares*

Cut pork steaks into 1-inch pieces. Brown in oil in large skillet for 15 minutes, stirring frequently; drain. Combine gravy mix, water, honey, soy sauce, vinegar, ginger and garlic salt in bowl; mix well. Add to skillet. Cook, covered, for 20 minutes. Add carrots. Cook for 10 minutes. Add onion and green pepper. Cook for 10 minutes longer or until pork is tender.

Yield: 6 servings. Approx Per Serving: Cal 612; Prot 50.6 gr; Carbo 45.1 gr; T Fat 25.8 gr; Chol 172.0 mg; Calc 45.0 mg; Potas 874.0 mg; Sod 1068.0 mg.

Spaghetti Carbonara

Beth Steiner, Maryland

1	*(16-ounce) package spaghetti*
1	*egg, beaten*
¼	*cup cream*
1½	*cups chopped cooked ham*
2	*cups shredded provolone cheese*
1	*tablespoon margarine*
½	*cup Parmesan cheese*
¼	*cup minced fresh parsley*
¼	*cup chopped green onions*
¼	*cup crumbled crisp-fried bacon*

Cook spaghetti according to package directions until just tender; drain. Return to pan; place over low heat. Add mixture of egg and cream; stir gently. Add ham, provolone cheese, margarine and ½ cup Parmesan cheese. Heat to serving temperature, stirring constantly. Place on serving platter. Sprinkle with parsley, green onions and bacon. Serve with additional Parmesan cheese and freshly ground pepper.

Yield: 8 servings. Approx Per Serving: Cal 422; Prot 23.2 gr; Carbo 44.1 gr; T Fat 16.2 gr; Chol 75.3 mg; Calc 307.0 mg; Potas 298.0 mg; Sod 676.0 mg.

Chicken Roco

Jacqueline Leary, New York

Preheat oven to 375 degrees. Cut cheese into 8 sticks. Wrap chicken breast around each stick. Dip into beaten egg; roll in crumbs to coat. Brown on all sides in butter in skillet; remove from skillet. Sauté onion, mushrooms and green pepper in pan drippings. Add bouillon, flour, salt and pepper; mix well. Stir in water. Cook until thickened, stirring constantly. Remove from heat. Stir in rice. Pour into 9 x 13-inch baking dish. Arrange chicken rolls on top. Bake for 30 minutes.

Yield: 8 servings. Approx Per Serving: Cal 600; Prot 49.7 gr; Carbo 37.3 gr; T Fat 26.7 gr; Chol 223.0 mg; Calc 310.0 mg; Potas 430.0 mg; Sod 608.0 mg.

10	**ounces Cheddar cheese**
8	**chicken breast filets**
2	**eggs, beaten**
1	**cup dry bread crumbs**
⅓	**cup butter or margarine**
½	**cup chopped onion**
½	**cup sliced fresh mushrooms**
½	**cup chopped green pepper**
1	**teaspoon instant chicken bouillon**
2	**tablespoons all-purpose flour** **Salt and pepper to taste**
1	**cup water**
4	**cups cooked rice**

Sweet and Sour Chicken

Juliana Jones, Texas

Slice chicken filets into strips. Sauté chicken, carrots and garlic in shortening in skillet for 5 minutes. Add cucumber, tomatoes, onion and chicken broth. Simmer, covered, for 5 minutes. Add mixture of flour, sugar, soy sauce and vinegar. Cook until thickened, stirring constantly.

Yield: 6 servings. Approx Per Serving: Cal 239; Prot 26.0 gr; Carbo 15.8 gr; T Fat 8.13 gr; Chol 63.8 mg; Calc 42.1 mg; Potas 564.0 mg; Sod 824.0 mg.

4	**chicken breast filets**
2	**large carrots, sliced**
3	**cloves of garlic, crushed**
2	**tablespoons shortening**
1	**large cucumber, chopped**
3	**small tomatoes, cut into wedges**
1	**large onion, cut into wedges**
½	**cup chicken broth**
1	**tablespoon all-purpose flour**
2	**tablespoons sugar**
¼	**cup soy sauce**
¼	**cup vinegar**

Seafood Kabobs

Kathy Webb, Illinois

1 **pound large shrimp, peeled**
1 **pound large scallops**
3 **medium green peppers, cut into 1-inch pieces**
3 **cups fresh pineapple chunks**
12 **ounces mushroom caps**
¼ **cup melted butter or margarine**
¼ **cup lemon juice**
¼ **cup soy sauce**
1 **tablespoon chopped parsley**

Combine shrimp, scallops, green peppers, pineapple chunks and mushroom caps in shallow dish. Mix butter, lemon juice, soy sauce and parsley in bowl. Pour over seafood mixture. Marinate, covered, in refrigerator for 2 hours. Drain, reserving marinade. Alternate ingredients on 6 skewers. Place on grill 4 inches from medium-hot coals. Grill for 15 minutes, turning occasionally and brushing with reserved marinade.

Yield: 6 servings. Approx Per Serving: Cal 233;
Prot 35.6 gr; Carbo 19.1 gr; T Fat 2.43 gr;
Chol 181.0 mg; Calc 66.2 mg;
Potas 865.0 mg; Sod 1010.0 mg.

Sour Cream Enchiladas

Kathy McDonough, California

2 **cups sour cream**
1 **cup chopped green onions**
2 **cups shredded Cheddar cheese**
2 **cups shredded Monterey Jack cheese**
1 **(4-ounce) can chopped black olives, drained**
  Oil for frying
12 **corn tortillas**
1 **(10-ounce) can enchilada sauce**
2 **cups shredded Monterey Jack cheese**

Preheat oven to 350 degrees. Combine sour cream, green onions, mixture of 2 cups each Cheddar and Monterey Jack cheese and olives in bowl; mix well. Heat ½ inch oil in small skillet over high heat. Fry tortillas 1 at a time in hot oil for 15 seconds or until softened. Drain briefly on paper towels. Dip into enchilada sauce. Place heaping spoonful sour cream mixture on each tortilla; roll to enclose filling. Place seam side down in 9 x 13-inch baking dish. Sprinkle with remaining 2 cups Monterey Jack cheese. Bake enchiladas for 20 minutes.

Yield: 6 servings. Approx Per Serving: Cal 811;
Prot 35.9 gr; Carbo 39.2 gr; T Fat 59.5 gr;
Chol 143.0 mg; Calc 1040.0 mg;
Potas 341.0 mg; Sod 1297.0 mg.

Sesame Green Beans

Linda Deyette, Vermont

Trim green beans. Slice French-style. Cook in a small amount of water in 2-quart saucepan just until tender; drain. Add remaining ingredients; mix lightly. Spoon into serving dish.

Yield: 4 servings. Approx Per Serving: Cal 65; Prot 2.3 gr; Carbo 8.3 gr; T Fat 3.4 gr; Chol 7.8 mg; Calc 50.4 mg; Potas 242.0 mg; Sod 36.0 mg.

1 **pound fresh green beans**
1 **tablespoon butter**
   or margarine
1 **teaspoon sesame seed**
3 **drops hot pepper sauce**

Grilled Vidalia Onions

Nell Absher, Georgia

Place each onion on square of heavy-duty foil. Make crosswise slits in tops of onions. Place 1 teaspoon butter, 1 bouillon cube and salt and pepper to taste on each onion; seal foil. Place on grill 4 inches from medium coals. Cook for 45 minutes or until tender.

Yield: 4 servings. Approx Per Serving: Cal 75; Prot 2.0 gr; Carbo 7.3 gr; T Fat 4.6 gr; Chol 11.0 mg; Calc 25.1 mg; Potas 152.0 mg; Sod 1053.0 mg.

4 **medium Vidalia onions**
4 **teaspoons butter or margarine**
4 **beef bouillon cubes**
   Salt and pepper to taste

Foiled Potatoes

Marlene Mallon, Kansas

Cut potatoes into halves crosswise. Cut slices ¾ inch apart to but not through bottom. Mix butter, cheese, chives, garlic powder and pepper in small bowl. Place a small amount of butter mixture and 1 onion slice in each slit. Wrap potatoes in foil. Place on grill 4 inches from hot coals. Cook for 45 minutes or until potatoes are tender.

Note: May bake at 400 degrees for 45 minutes.

Yield: 4 servings. Approx Per Serving: Cal 258; Prot 5.4 gr; Carbo 52.5 gr; T Fat 3.5 gr; Chol 8.8 mg; Calc 43.3 mg; Potas 877.0 mg; Sod 64.2 mg.

4 **large baking potatoes**
1 **tablespoon butter or**
   margarine, softened
1 **tablespoon Parmesan cheese**
1 **teaspoon chopped chives**
⅛ **teaspoon garlic powder**
½ **teaspoon pepper**
1 **medium onion, thinly sliced**

Escarole Priazzo

Donna Lucente-Surber, Maryland

½	package (½ tablespoon) dry yeast
1	cup warm (115-degree) water
2⅔	cups unbleached flour
	Salt and freshly ground pepper to taste
2	tablespoons (or more) olive oil
3	pounds escarole
½	cup olive oil
4	cloves of garlic, chopped
½	cup pine nuts
1½	cups pitted black olives
1	tablespoon capers
¼	cup raisins
	Salt to taste

Dissolve yeast in water in bowl. Add flour, salt, pepper and 2 tablespoons olive oil; mix well. Knead on floured surface until smooth and elastic, adding additional olive oil if necessary. Place in greased bowl, turning to grease surface. Let rise, covered, in warm place for 30 to 40 minutes or until doubled in bulk. Preheat oven to 375 degrees. Sauté escarole ⅓ at a time in ½ cup olive oil in skillet for 10 minutes. Cook over high heat for several minutes if necessary to remove remaining liquid. Drain and chop escarole. Combine with remaining ingredients; mix well. Divide dough into 2 portions, 1 slightly larger than the other. Roll larger portion into 12-inch circle on floured surface. Fit into greased 10-inch pizza pan. Fill with escarole mixture. Cover with remaining dough; seal edges. Bake for 45 minutes or until brown and slightly puffed.

Yield: 8 servings. Approx Per Serving: Cal 456; Prot 9.1 gr; Carbo 44.2 gr; T Fat 30.7 gr; Chol 0.0 mg; Calc 150.0 mg; Potas 679.0 mg; Sod 361.0 mg.

Linguine Florentine

4	cups fresh spinach
1	cup fresh parsley
¾	cup Parmesan cheese
½	cup walnuts
¾	cup olive oil
1	clove of garlic
½	teaspoon salt
¼	teaspoon pepper
12	ounces linguine
	Parmesan cheese

Combine spinach, parsley, ¾ cup Parmesan cheese, walnuts, olive oil, garlic, salt and pepper in blender or food processor container. Process until smooth. Cook linguine according to package directions; drain well. Place in large serving bowl. Add spinach mixture; toss until coated. Sprinkle with additional Parmesan cheese. Serve at once.

Yield: 6 servings. Approx Per Serving: Cal 570; Prot 14.1 gr; Carbo 47.0 gr; T Fat 37.1 gr; Chol 7.9 mg; Calc 211.0 mg; Potas 449.0 mg; Sod 224.0 mg.

Blueberry Streusel Muffins

Dorothy Rhoden, Georgia

Preheat oven to 425 degrees. Beat eggs in mixer bowl until thick and lemon-colored. Add sour cream and milk; mix well. Stir in oil. Sift 2 cups flour, baking powder, soda, sugar and salt together. Add to egg mixture; stir just until moistened. Fold in blueberries. Fill buttered muffin cups ¾ full. Cut margarine into mixture of brown sugar, ¼ cup flour and cinnamon in bowl until crumbly. Sprinkle over muffins. Bake for 15 to 20 minutes or until golden. Serve hot or cold.

Yield: 18 servings. Approx Per Serving: Cal 168; Prot 2.8 gr; Carbo 21.6 gr; T Fat 7.9 gr; Chol 36.7 mg; Calc 38.3 mg; Potas 78.4 mg; Sod 154.0 mg.

2	*eggs*
1	*cup sour cream*
⅓	*cup milk*
¼	*cup oil*
2	*cups sifted all-purpose flour*
2	*teaspoons baking powder*
½	*teaspoon soda*
3	*tablespoons sugar*
½	*teaspoon salt*
1½	*cups blueberries*
2	*tablespoons margarine*
½	*cup packed light brown sugar*
¼	*cup all-purpose flour*
1	*teaspoon cinnamon*

Gingerbread Pancakes with Fruit Sauce

Karen Boyce, Utah

Combine fruit and pudding mix in large plastic zip-lock bag; seal. Squeeze gently until well mixed. Let stand for 5 minutes. Prepare gingerbread mix according to package directions, reducing liquid by 1 to 2 tablespoons. Pour onto hot greased skillet. Bake until light brown on both sides. Serve pancakes with fruit topping.

Yield: 6 servings. Nutritional information not available.

1	*(16-ounce) can fruit cocktail*
1	*(20-ounce) can pineapple chunks*
1	*(11-ounce) can mandarin oranges, drained*
2	*large bananas, sliced*
1	*(3-ounce) package lemon instant pudding mix*
1	*(14-ounce) package gingerbread mix*

Sour Cream Banana Bread

Miriam Welch, California

²⁄₃	**cup butter or margarine, softened**
1⅓	**cups sugar**
2	**eggs**
1½	**cups mashed bananas**
2¾	**cups all-purpose flour, sifted**
1	**teaspoon baking powder**
1	**teaspoon soda**
½	**teaspoon salt**
½	**cup sour cream**
1	**cup chopped walnuts**

Preheat oven to 350 degrees. Cream butter and sugar in mixer bowl until light and fluffy. Blend in eggs. Fold in bananas. Add mixture of dry ingredients alternately with sour cream, mixing just until moistened after each addition. Stir in walnuts. Spoon into greased 5 x 9-inch loaf pan. Bake for 1 hour and 15 minutes or until bread tests done. Cool in pan for 20 minutes. Remove to wire rack to cool completely. Store, wrapped in plastic wrap, in refrigerator for up to 2 weeks.

Yield: 12 servings. Approx Per Serving: Cal 394; Prot 5.8 gr; Carbo 50.5 gr; T Fat 19.8 gr; Chol 77.7 mg; Calc 39.7 mg; Potas 215.0 mg; Sod 290.0 mg.

Jalapeño Hush Puppies

Marna Shofner, Texas

1½	**cups white cornmeal**
½	**cup sifted all-purpose flour**
2½	**teaspoons baking powder**
1½	**teaspoons salt**
½	**teaspoon pepper**
1	**cup milk**
1	**egg, beaten**
3	**tablespoons oil**
⅓	**cup finely chopped onion**
¼	**cup finely chopped jalapeño pepper**
	Oil for deep frying

Combine dry ingredients in bowl. Add milk, egg and 3 tablespoons oil; mix well. Stir in onion and jalapeño pepper. Heat oil to 350 degrees in deep saucepan. Drop batter by spoonfuls into oil. Deep-fry for 3 minutes or until golden brown, turning once. Drain on paper towel.

Yield: 30 servings. Approx Per Serving: Cal 50; Prot 1.3 gr; Carbo 6.6 gr; T Fat 2.1 gr; Chol 10.2 mg; Calc 17.3 mg; Potas 36.9 mg; Sod 156.0 mg.

Fruit Compote

¾	**cup Karo light corn syrup**
½	**cup orange juice**
2	**tablespoons very thin strips lemon rind**
¼	**cup lemon juice**
8	**cups mixed fresh fruit**

Blend corn syrup, orange juice, lemon rind and lemon juice in large bowl. Add fruit; toss lightly. Chill covered, in refrigerator for several hours.

Yield: 12 servings. Approx Per Serving: Cal 63; Prot 0.1 gr; Carbo 16.9 gr; T Fat 0.0 gr; Chol 0.0 mg; Calc 10.4 mg; Potas 29.4 mg; Sod 9.4 mg. Information does not include fruit.

Spice Cake with Butterscotch Meringue

Preheat oven to 350 degrees. Cream butter and 2 cups brown sugar in mixer bowl until light and fluffy. Blend in beaten egg yolks and vanilla. Sift flour with baking powder, spices and salt. Stir soda into buttermilk. Add dry ingredients to creamed mixture alternately with buttermilk, beginning and ending with dry ingredients and mixing well after each addition. Spoon into greased 9 x 13-inch cake pan. Beat egg whites in bowl until stiff peaks form. Add 1 cup brown sugar gradually, beating constantly. Spread over cake batter, sealing to sides of pan. Sprinkle with filberts. Bake for 45 minutes or until toothpick inserted in center comes out clean.

Yield: 15 servings. Approx Per Serving: Cal 359;
          Prot 3.5 gr; Carbo 59.4 gr; T Fat 12.7 gr;
          Chol 61.9 mg; Calc 82.2 mg;
          Potas 229.0 mg; Sod 239.0 mg.

¾   *cup butter or margarine, softened*
2   *cups packed brown sugar*
2   *egg yolks, beaten*
1   *teaspoon vanilla extract*
2⅔   *cups cake flour*
1   *teaspoon baking powder*
1   *teaspoon cinnamon*
1   *teaspoon cloves*
¼   *teaspoon salt*
1   *teaspoon soda*
1¼   *cups buttermilk*
2   *egg whites*
1   *cup packed brown sugar*
½   *cup chopped filberts (hazelnuts)*

Strawberry Cheese Pie

Elizabeth Cooley, Texas

Combine 1 cup strawberries, ½ cup sugar, cornstarch, lemon juice, salt and water in blender container. Process until smooth. Pour into small saucepan. Cook until thickened, stirring constantly. Cool to room temperature. Whip ⅔ cup whipping cream, cottage cheese and almond flavoring in mixer bowl until very thick. Spread in pie shell. Spoon ⅔ of the strawberry glaze over cottage cheese mixture. Cut remaining strawberries into halves. Arrange cut side down in single layer over top; mound any remaining berries in center. Spoon remaining glaze over top. Chill for 5 to 6 hours or until firm. Whip ⅓ cup whipping cream in mixer bowl until soft peaks form. Spoon over strawberries.

Yield: 6 servings. Approx Per Serving: Cal 404;
          Prot 5.5 gr; Carbo 39.7 gr; T Fat 25.8 gr;
          Chol 56.9 mg; Calc 55.2 mg;
          Potas 228.0 mg; Sod 333.0 mg.

1   *quart fresh strawberries*
½   *cup sugar*
1   *tablespoon cornstarch*
1   *tablespoon lemon juice*
     Pinch of salt
½   *cup water*
⅔   *cup whipping cream*
½   *cup cream-style cottage cheese*
⅛   *teaspoon almond extract*
1   *baked 9-inch pie shell*
⅓   *cup whipping cream*

Summer

*I*n memory my childhood Summers have a wonderful air of freedom about them. Summer was time to do nothing more than stretch out under a shady tree with a good book, run through the sprinkler or snap beans into a big pot for dinner, or hike to the corner for nickel Fudgesicles.

In Summer the earth offers us some of her best and most beautiful efforts for the table—food so lovely and delicious that it requires only the simplest preparation. Who has not, while preparing a salad for dinner, stopped to admire the intricacy and beauty of fresh-from-the-garden lettuce?

Vegetables often are the bases of wonderful entreés in Summer, especially in combination with pasta. The variety is limited only by your imagination, but I'm fond of fettucini tossed with steamed red and yellow peppers, broccoli, fresh Parmesan, butter, a dash of cream, and freshly ground pepper. Summer vegetable soup is easy to prepare and makes a light lunch entrée or a refreshing first-course dinner dish.

Fruit, not to be outdone, is in its glory, too, in these warm weather months. Fruit is always wonderful served chilled all by itself at any meal. But, a simple dressing of plain yogurt, honey and sesame seed turns plain fruit into a great brunch dish. These jewels in nature's crown are also gorgeous on a fruit plate or in the luscious summer desserts in this book.

One of the most attractive aspects of this most informal of seasons is the easy entertaining we enjoy. Summer is the season for family reunions, company picnics, Fourth of July block parties, ice cream "socials," and, of course, the all-American barbecue cookout.

These days nearly everyone cooks out in some form or other. It's a good bet that the hamburger is the most cooked-out food in this country, followed by hot dogs, steak, chicken and ribs. You'll find recipes for barbecued chicken and ribs. In keeping with the trend toward lighter menus, kabobs combine tasty tidbits of meat and assorted top-of-the-season vegetables.

Incidentally, as you enjoy the season's bounty, now is the time to think ahead a bit. Whatever your family's tastes and your own canning abilities, there's something you might consider "putting up." Not only do they look wonderful on your pantry shelves, they're a taste of Summer in those months ahead when we need it the most.

FRESH VEGETABLE STEW

1 1/2 cups chopped onions	2 teaspoons salt
1 cup sliced celery	12 cups bite-sized mixed fresh green beans, red and green bell peppers, zucchini, eggplant, potatoes, summer squash, mushrooms and kale
2 cloves of garlic, crushed	
2 tablespoons olive oil	
1 (19-ounce) can cannellini	
1 (19-ounce) can chick peas	
3 cups chopped fresh tomatoes	4 cups steamed brown rice
1 tablespoon Italian seasoning	Parmesan cheese

□ Sauté onions, celery and garlic in olive oil in large saucepan for 5 minutes or until tender.

□ Drain cannellini and chick peas, reserving liquid. Add enough water to reserved liquid to measure 2 1/2 cups.

□ Add to sauce pan with tomatoes, salt and Italian seasoning.

□ Bring to a boil; reduce heat.

□ Simmer, covered, for 15 minutes. Add fresh vegetables.

□ Simmer, covered, for 8 minutes or until almost tender, stirring occasionally.

□ Stir in cannellini and chick peas. Heat to serving temperature. Serve over steamed brown rice.

□ Garnish with Parmesan cheese.

□ Yield: 8 servings.

PASTA PRIMAVERA SALAD

8 ounces shell macaroni	1 cup sliced fresh mushrooms
2 cups cherry tomato halves	1/2 cup chopped onion
1 cup broccoli flowerets	1 cup thinly sliced zucchini
2 tablespoons minced fresh parsley	1/2 cup Italian salad dressing

□ Cook macaroni using package directions; rinse with cold water and drain well.

□ Combine macaroni, vegetables and salad dressing in bowl; toss lightly.

□ Chill until serving time.

□ Yield: 4 servings.

CONFETTI SALAD

8 ounces pasta rings	1/2 cup thinly sliced radishes
4 ounces Cheddar cheese, cubed	1/4 cup chopped parsley
1 cup chopped cauliflower	1 cup creamy cucumber salad dressing
1/2 cup chopped green bell pepper	

□ Cook pasta rings using package directions; rinse with cold water and drain well.

□ Combine pasta rings with cheese, vegetables and salad dressing in bowl; toss lightly.

□ Chill until serving time.

□ Yield: 4 servings.

Summer Foods

July	August	September	
GREEN BEANS	LIMA BEANS		**Vegetables**
CORN			
	CUCUMBERS		
	BEETS		
	KOHLRABI		
SNOW PEAS			
	OKRA	CAULIFLOWER	
EGGPLANT			
BELL PEPPERS			
SUMMER SQUASH			
TOMATOES			
APRICOTS		POMEGRANATES	**Fruits**
	BLACKBERRIES		
		BLUEBERRIES	
		RASPBERRIES	
	CHERRIES		
GRAPES			
	KIWIFRUIT		
	LEMONS/LIMES		
		MANGOS	
		NECTARINES	
		PEACHES	
BARTLETT PEARS			
	PLUMS		
		MELONS	
	FIGS		
		CHICKEN (BROILER-FRYERS)	**Meats**
		CHICKEN (ROASTERS)	
		COD	
		OYSTERS	

July

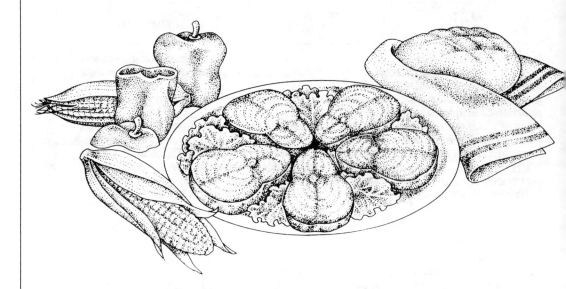

Garden Salad Loaf

Sara Brown, Illinois

2	**medium green peppers, cut into thin strips**
4	**medium green onions, chopped**
10	**large radishes, thinly sliced**
2	**medium carrots, thinly sliced**
4	**small tomatoes, cut into thin wedges**
¾	**cup French salad dressing**
2	**envelopes unflavored gelatin**
½	**cup red wine vinegar**
2	**tablespoons lemon juice**
¼	**cup sugar**
1	**teaspoon salt**
2⅔	**cups boiling water**
2	**cups finely shredded lettuce**
1	**cup torn spinach**
6	**thick tomato wedges**

Combine green peppers, green onions, radishes, carrots and 4 tomatoes in bowl. Add French dressing; mix well. Let stand for 15 minutes or longer. Soften gelatin in vinegar and lemon juice in bowl. Add sugar, salt and boiling water; stir until gelatin and sugar are dissolved. Chill until partially set. Drain vegetable mixture well. Fold marinated vegetables and greens into gelatin mixture. Pour into oiled 4x8-inch loaf pan. Chill until set. Unmold onto serving plate. Garnish with thick tomato wedges. Cut into slices.

Yield: 6 servings. Approx Per Serving: Cal 253; Prot 4.2 gr; Carbo 21.5 gr; T Fat 18.1 gr; Chol 0.0 mg; Calc 46.3 mg; Potas 482.0 mg; Sod 753.0 mg.

Summer Dip with Vegetables

Marilyn Vohs, Kansas

Combine eggs, vinegar and sugar in saucepan; mix well. Cook over low heat until thickened, stirring constantly. Remove from heat. Stir in butter and onion. Add cream cheese. Cook over low heat until cream cheese is melted, stirring to mix well. Spoon into serving dish. Chill in refrigerator. Cut vegetables into bite-sized pieces. Place dip in center of serving plate. Arrange vegetables around dip.

Yield: 12 servings. Approx Per Serving: Cal 126; Prot 4.1 gr; Carbo 8.1 gr; T Fat 9.1 gr; Chol 91.7 mg; Calc 45.5 mg; Potas 273.0 mg; Sod 98.4 mg.

3   *eggs, beaten*
3   *tablespoons white vinegar*
3   *tablespoons sugar*
1   *tablespoon butter or margarine*
1   *tablespoon grated onion*
8   *ounces cream cheese*
1   *medium cucumber*
2   *medium carrots*
2   *medium stalks celery*
1   *small zucchini*
2   *medium stalks broccoli*
½   *medium head cauliflower*

Cold Crawfish Cocktail with Cajun Sauce

Rinse crawfish. Combine crawfish, rock salt and water to cover in bowl. Let stand for 1 hour or longer. Combine 10 cups cold water, salt, onion, sugar, wine and dill in saucepan. Drain and rinse crawfish. Add to saucepan. Bring to a boil over high heat; reduce heat. Simmer for 10 minutes; remove from heat. Let stand in broth until cool. Strain broth. Place crawfish in bowl; add broth to cover. Chill until serving time. Drain and peel crawfish. Line serving dishes with romaine. Spoon Cajun Cocktail Sauce into center. Arrange crawfish around cocktail sauce.

Yield: 4 servings. Approx Per Serving: Cal 473; Prot 27.9 gr; Carbo 43.4 gr; T Fat 19.9 gr; Chol 177.0 mg; Calc 109.0 mg; Potas 1177.0 mg; Sod 2168.0 mg.

3   *dozen crawfish*
½   *cup rock salt*
10   *cups cold water*
1   *teaspoon salt*
1   *medium onion, coarsely chopped*
1   *teaspoon sugar*
½   *cup wine*
½   *cup coarsely chopped fresh dill*
1   *medium head romaine*

Cajun Cocktail Sauce

Combine olive oil, vinegar, dry mustard, salt and white pepper in covered jar. Shake, covered, to mix well. Combine with remaining ingredients in bowl; mix well. Chill, covered, until serving time.

⅓   *cup olive oil*
5   *teaspoons vinegar*
    Dry mustard, salt and white pepper to taste
2   *cups catsup*
¼   *cup lemon juice*
¼   *cup horseradish*
3   *tablespoons Worcestershire sauce*
1   *tablespoon Tabasco sauce*

Spinach and Cheese Squares

½   **cup finely chopped onions**
¼   **cup chopped scallions**
¼   **cup olive oil**
2   **pounds fresh spinach**
2   **tablespoons dillweed**
¼   **cup minced parsley**
⅓   **cup milk**
8   **ounces feta cheese, crumbled**
4   **eggs, lightly beaten**
8   **sheets phyllo dough**
1   **cup melted margarine**
8   **sheets phyllo dough**

Preheat oven to 300 degrees. Sauté onion and scallions in olive oil in heavy 10-inch skillet. Add spinach. Cook, covered, for 5 minutes. Stir in dillweed and parsley. Cook for 10 minutes or until liquid is absorbed, stirring frequently. Combine with milk in bowl. Cool to room temperature. Mix in cheese and eggs. Keep phyllo dough covered until ready to use. Brush 8 sheets phyllo with melted margarine. Layer in buttered 7 x 12-inch baking dish, fitting well into corners. Spoon spinach mixture into prepared dish. Brush remaining melted margarine over remaining phyllo dough. Layer over top. Trim edges. Bake for 1 hour or until golden brown. Cut into squares.

Yield: 12 servings. Nutritional information not available.

Hearty Garden Soup

Alma Walkem, Ohio

2   **large onions, chopped**
4   **cloves of garlic, chopped**
¼   **cup butter or margarine**
2   **cups chopped celery**
3   **medium zucchini, chopped**
2   **cups chopped tomatoes**
2   **cups tomato juice**
1   **large green pepper, chopped**
1   **large red sweet pepper,**
     chopped
     Basil, marjoram and rosemary
     to taste
1   **(6-ounce) can tomato paste**
4   **medium carrots, sliced**
2   **cups chopped broccoli**
2   **cups chopped cauliflower**

Sauté onions and garlic in butter in 6-quart saucepan until tender. Stir in celery and zucchini. Cook, covered, over low heat for 10 minutes. Add tomatoes, juice, peppers and seasonings. Simmer, covered, for 1 hour, stirring occasionally. Add tomato paste, carrots, broccoli, cauliflower and water to make of desired consistency. Simmer, covered, for 30 minutes or until vegetables are tender.

Yield: 16 servings. Approx Per Serving: Cal 76; Prot 2.5 gr; Carbo 11.2 gr; T Fat 3.3 gr; Chol 7.8 mg; Calc 39.0 mg; Potas 526.0 mg; Sod 169.0 mg.

Fruity Bagels

Charlene Gomez, New Mexico

Peel and slice peaches, bananas and kiwifruit. Sprinkle peach and banana slices with lemon juice. Split bagels; place on baking sheet. Toast until light brown. Spread bagels with cream cheese. Sprinkle with cinnamon and cloves. Add fruit slices. Arrange on serving plate.

Yield: 10 servings. Approx Per Serving: Cal 207; Prot 5.7 gr; Carbo 27.7 gr; T Fat 8.6 gr; Chol 24.8 mg; Calc 34.8 mg; Potas 238.0 mg; Sod 218.0 mg.

2 **large peaches**
2 **medium bananas**
2 **medium kiwifruit**
2 **tablespoons lemon juice**
5 **large bagels**
8 **ounces cream cheese, softened**
 Cinnamon and cloves to taste

Pita Sproutwiches

Sylvia Rouse, Wisconsin

Cut pita rounds into halves; open to form pockets. Spread 1 side of each pocket with avocado; spread other side with mayonnaise. Fill with onions, tomato slices and cheese slices. Top with alfalfa sprouts and shredded carrots. Sprinkle with soy sauce. Arrange on serving plate.

Yield: 10 servings. Approx Per Serving: Cal 324; Prot 13.0 gr; Carbo 28.5 gr; T Fat 18.5 gr; Chol 29.0 mg; Calc 317.0 mg; Potas 484.0 mg; Sod 342.0 mg.

5 **pita bread rounds**
2 **medium avocados, mashed**
½ **cup mayonnaise**
2 **small onions, chopped**
2 **medium tomatoes, thinly sliced**
10 **slices Swiss cheese**
2 **cups alfalfa sprouts**
2 **cups shredded carrots**
 Soy sauce to taste

Summer Melon Delight

Peel and slice honeydew, cantaloupe and kiwifruit. Place lettuce in salad bowl. Arrange melons on lettuce. Layer kiwifruit over melon slices. Sprinkle with cheese. Serve with French dressing if desired.

Yield: 4 servings. Approx Per Serving: Cal 401; Prot 10.6 gr; Carbo 35.2 gr; T Fat 26.2 gr; Chol 26.0 mg; Calc 318.0 mg; Potas 975.0 mg; Sod 470.0 mg.

½ **medium honeydew melon**
½ **medium cantaloupe**
4 **large kiwifruit**
½ **medium head lettuce, torn**
1 **cup shredded Swiss cheese**
½ **cup French salad dressing**

Curried Rice and Lamb Salad

Debby Didawick, Virginia

1	**cup long grain rice**
½	**cup cooked fresh green peas**
½	**cup sliced fresh mushrooms**
2	**teaspoons curry powder**
2	**hard-boiled eggs, chopped**
1	**cup chopped cooked lamb**
½	**cup mayonnaise**
½	**cup sour cream**
2	**tablespoons minced parsley**
6	**medium tomatoes**
6	**large lettuce leaves**

Cook rice using package directions for firm rice. Add peas, mushrooms and curry powder; mix well. Cool. Add eggs, lamb and mixture of mayonnaise, sour cream and parsley; toss lightly. Chill until serving time. Cut tops from tomatoes; scoop out pulp. Invert on paper towels to drain. Place on lettuce-lined salad plates. Fill with salad.

Yield: 6 servings. Approx Per Serving: Cal 394;
Prot 17.4 gr; Carbo 34.4 gr; T Fat 20.1 gr;
Chol 142.0 mg; Calc 51.2 mg;
Potas 315.0 mg; Sod 736.0 mg.

Beef Kabobs

Jean MacWilliam, Florida

½	**cup oil**
1	**tablespoon wine vinegar**
2	**tablespoons lemon juice**
2	**tablespoons chopped onion**
1	**teaspoon chili powder**
½	**teaspoon poultry seasoning**
½	**teaspoon oregano**
½	**teaspoon ginger**
	Garlic salt, salt
	and pepper to taste
1½	**pounds lean beef cubes**
8	**large mushrooms**
8	**large cherry tomatoes**
1	**large onion, cut into wedges**
1	**large green pepper, cut into strips**

Combine oil, vinegar, lemon juice, chopped onion and seasonings in bowl; mix well. Add beef cubes. Marinate in refrigerator overnight. Drain, reserving marinade. Alternate beef cubes and vegetables on skewers. Place on grill 4 inches from medium coals. Grill for 5 minutes on each side or to desired degree of doneness, basting with reserved marinade.

Yield: 4 servings. Approx Per Serving: Cal 622;
Prot 50.0 gr; Carbo 8.3 gr; T Fat 43.0 gr;
Chol 130.0 mg; Calc 32.7 mg;
Potas 938.0 mg; Sod 126.0 mg.

Crock•Pot Barbecued Brisket

Cut brisket crosswise into 6 portions; place in Crock•Pot. Sauté onion in butter in skillet until golden. Add remaining ingredients; mix well. Simmer for 15 minutes. Pour over brisket in Crock•Pot. Cook on Low for 10 to 12 hours.

Yield: 6 servings. Approx Per Serving: Cal 413; Prot 44.5 gr; Carbo 20.6 gr; T Fat 16.4 gr; Chol 135.1 mg; Calc 41.3 mg; Potas 931.0 mg; Sod 711.0 mg.

1 *(2-pound) beef brisket*
1 *large onion, minced*
2 *tablespoons butter or margarine*
2 *tablespoons vinegar*
2 *tablespoons brown sugar*
¼ *cup lemon juice*
1 *cup catsup*
3 *tablespoons Worcestershire sauce*
1 *tablespoon mustard*
1 *cup water*
Salt and cayenne pepper to taste

Mock Reuben Pie

Jan Hinze, Nebraska

Preheat oven to 350 degrees. Combine ground beef, oats, egg, ½ cup salad dressing and seasonings in bowl; mix well. Press over bottom and side of 9-inch pie plate. Bake for 25 minutes; drain. Mix sauerkraut and cheese lightly in bowl. Spoon into ground beef shell. Bake for 15 minutes longer. Cut into wedges. Spoon remaining ½ cup salad dressing over wedges.

Yield: 6 servings. Approx Per Serving: Cal 566; Prot 32.9 gr; Carbo 16.9 gr; T Fat 41.1 gr; Chol 157.0 mg; Calc 408.0 mg; Potas 486.0 mg; Sod 960.0 mg.

1 *pound lean ground beef*
⅔ *cup oats*
1 *egg, beaten*
½ *cup Thousand Island salad dressing*
⅛ *teaspoon garlic powder*
Salt and pepper to taste
1 *(16-ounce) can sauerkraut, drained*
2 *cups shredded Swiss cheese*
½ *cup Thousand Island salad dressing*

Chicken Loaves Elegante

4	ounces mushrooms, sliced
12	chicken breast filets
1½	pounds sliced bacon
	Salt, thyme and lemon pepper to taste
1	(4-ounce) jar chopped pimento
1	(4-ounce) jar stuffed green olives, sliced
1	(4-ounce) jar pitted black olives, sliced
1	cup fresh celery leaves

Preheat oven to 375 degrees. Sauté mushrooms in skillet until tender; drain. Flatten chicken filets between waxed paper. Arrange half the bacon slices diagonally and overlapping slightly in 9 x 13-inch baking pan. Arrange 3 of the flattened filets down center. Sprinkle with salt, thyme and lemon pepper. Add layers of half the mushrooms, pimento, olives and celery leaves. Top with 3 filets. Fold bacon slices over top, securing with toothpicks. Repeat with remaining ingredients. Chill in refrigerator if desired. Bake for 45 minutes. Cut each loaf into 6 slices. Serve with choice of sauces.

Yield: 12 servings. Approx Per Serving: Cal 608; Prot 48.0 gr; Carbo 2.0 gr; T Fat 44.9 gr; Chol 140.0 mg; Calc 43.0 mg; Potas 664.0 mg; Sod 1303.0 mg.

Cheese Sauce

6	tablespoons melted margarine
6	tablespoons all-purpose flour
1½	cups chicken broth
½	teaspoon salt
¼	teaspoon pepper
1	cup shredded Cheddar cheese
¼	cup Sherry

Blend margarine and flour in saucepan. Stir in broth gradually. Cook until thickened, stirring constantly. Add remaining ingredients. Cook until cheese melts, stirring constantly.

Yield: 32 tablespoons. Approx Per Tablespoon: Cal 42; Prot 1.3 gr; Carbo 1.2 gr; T Fat 3.4 gr; Chol 3.8 mg; Calc 27.4 mg; Potas 17.3 mg; Sod 117.0 mg.

Simple Hollandaise Sauce

6	egg yolks
1	cup melted margarine
¼	cup fresh lemon juice
	Salt to taste

Place egg yolks in blender container. Process for several seconds. Add margarine and lemon juice gradually, processing constantly. Season with salt to taste.

Yield: 24 tablespoons. Approx Per Tablespoon: Cal 84; Prot 0.8 gr; Carbo 0.3 gr; T Fat 9.0 gr; Chol 68.0 mg; Calc 9.5 mg; Potas 10.9 mg; Sod 91.2 mg.

Vegetable Pasta Eté

Cheri Cabal, Texas

Peel tomatoes and cut into wedges. Slice onions and zucchini. Cook noodles according to package directions; keep warm. Sauté onions and garlic in oil and 2 tablespoons margarine in skillet. Add tomatoes, zucchini and oregano. Cook just until tender-crisp. Drain noodles. Combine noodles, vegetables, cheese, cream and 2 tablespoons margarine in serving bowl; toss to mix well.

Yield: 8 servings. Approx Per Serving: Cal 422; Prot 10.9 gr; Carbo 48.7 gr; T Fat 21.0 gr; Chol 39.0 mg; Calc 146.0 mg; Potas 813.0 mg; Sod 753.0 mg.

3   *medium tomatoes*
3   *medium onions*
3   *medium zucchini*
1   *(16-ounce) package whole wheat noodles*
1   *clove of garlic, minced*
2   *tablespoons olive oil*
2   *tablespoons margarine*
    Oregano to taste
¾   *cup Parmesan cheese*
1   *cup light cream*
2   *tablespoons margarine*

Corn in Foil

Joyce Barbach, New York

Cream ½ cup butter with horseradish, mustard, salt and pepper in mixer bowl until fluffy. Remove husks from corn. Place corn on square of foil. Spread corn with butter mixture. Wrap loosely in foil; seal tightly. Cook corn over hot coals for 20 minutes or until tender. Mix ¼ cup butter with parsley. Open foil packets. Drizzle parsley-butter over corn.

Yield: 4 servings. Approx Per Serving: Cal 391; Prot 3.1 gr; Carbo 19.8 gr; T Fat 35.7 gr; Chol 93.2 mg; Calc 15.7 mg; Potas 212.0 mg; Sod 353.0 mg.

½   *cup butter or margarine, softened*
1   *teaspoon horseradish*
1   *tablespoon mustard*
    Salt and freshly ground pepper to taste
4   *ears sweet corn*
¼   *cup melted butter or margarine*
1   *tablespoon chopped parsley*

Zucchini and Cheese Turnovers

Cynthia Goudy, Louisiana

1	*cup chopped zucchini*
¼	*cup chopped onion*
½	*cup Parmesan cheese*
½	*cup shredded Cheddar cheese*
2	*tablespoons all-purpose flour*
¼	*teaspoon thyme*
	Marjoram to taste
¼	*teaspoon salt*
1	*cup cottage cheese, drained*
1	*(2-ounce) can chopped mushrooms, drained*
1	*egg, beaten*
1	*recipe Whole Wheat Pastry*
1	*teaspoon sesame seed*

Preheat oven to 400 degrees. Cook zucchini and onion in a small amount of water in saucepan for 5 minutes or just until tender. Drain well. Mix Parmesan cheese, Cheddar cheese, flour, thyme, marjoram and ¼ teaspoon salt in bowl. Add zucchini, cottage cheese and mushrooms; mix well. Stir in 2 tablespoons egg. Roll pastry into two 9-inch circles on floured surface. Place on baking sheets. Spoon zucchini mixture onto half of each circle. Fold over dough to enclose filling; moisten and seal edges. Brush with remaining egg. Sprinkle with sesame seed. Cut steam vents. Bake for 25 to 30 minutes or until brown. Cool for 10 minutes.

Yield: 4 servings. Approx Per Serving: Cal 486; Prot 22.1 gr; Carbo 38.9 gr; T Fat 27.4 gr; Chol 93.7 mg; Calc 285.0 mg; Potas 277.0 mg; Sod 627.0 mg.

Whole Wheat Pastry

¾	*cup whole wheat flour*
¾	*cup all-purpose flour*
¼	*teaspoon salt*
⅓	*cup shortening*
¼	*cup (about) cold water*

Mix whole wheat flour, all-purpose flour and salt in bowl. Cut in shortening until crumbly. Sprinkle with water, 1 tablespoon at a time, tossing lightly with fork after each addition. Shape into ball.

Heavenly Onion Casserole

Mary Ann Springer, Pennsylvania

1	*large sweet onion, sliced*
½	*cup butter or margarine*
1	*(10-ounce) can cream of chicken soup*
¾	*cup milk*
⅛	*teaspoon pepper*
3	*slices firm white bread, crumbled*
2	*cups shredded Cheddar cheese*

Preheat oven to 350 degrees. Sauté onion in butter in skillet until tender; do not brown. Mix soup, milk and pepper in bowl. Stir in bread, 1½ cups cheese and sautéed onion; mix well. Pour into casserole. Chill for several hours if desired. Sprinkle with remaining ½ cup cheese. Bake for 30 minutes or until bubbly and golden.

Yield: 6 servings. Approx Per Serving: Cal 396; Prot 13.3 gr; Carbo 14.2 gr; T Fat 32.2 gr; Chol 89.0 mg; Calc 346.0 mg; Potas 173.0 mg; Sod 819.0 mg.

Twice Baked Potatoes

Brenda McNeeley, Missouri

Preheat oven to 425 degrees. Scrub potatoes well; prick with fork. Bake for 40 to 60 minutes or until cooked through. Split potatoes. Scoop out pulp; reserve shell. Mash potato pulp in bowl. Add butter, sour cream and enough milk to make of desired consistency. Mixture should be medium-stiff. Add cheese, chives and salt and pepper to taste. Spoon into potato shells. Arrange potatoes in shallow baking dish. Top with crumbled bacon and sprinkle of paprika. Bake for 15 to 20 minutes or until golden brown.

12	medium baking potatoes
1½	cups butter or margarine
3	cups sour cream
½	cup (about) milk
3	cups shredded Cheddar cheese
¾	cup chopped chives
	Salt and pepper to taste
24	slices crisp-fried bacon, crumbled
	Paprika to taste

Yield: 12 servings. Approx Per Serving: Cal 740; Prot 18.0 gr; Carbo 54.5 gr; T Fat 51.2 gr; Chol 129.0 mg; Calc 312.0 mg; Potas 1043.0 mg; Sod 622.0 mg.

Barbecued Bread

Sandra Mori, Maryland

Preheat oven to 400 degrees. Sauté onion and garlic in butter in skillet until golden. Add chili sauce and next 5 seasonings; mix well. Simmer for 30 minutes or until of desired consistency. Cut loaf into 1-inch slices to but not through bottom. Place on large sheet heavy-duty foil. Spread slices with sauce; sprinkle with cheese. Seal in foil. Refrigerate for several hours if desired. Bake for 15 minutes. Open foil. Bake for 5 minutes longer.

½	cup chopped onion
1	clove of garlic, crushed
2	tablespoons butter or margarine
½	cup chili sauce
1	tablespoon Worcestershire sauce
2	tablespoons vinegar
2	teaspoons brown sugar
½	teaspoon celery salt
1	teaspoon prepared mustard
1	(16-ounce) loaf French bread
½	cup Parmesan cheese

Yield: 8 servings. Approx Per Serving: Cal 239; Prot 8.1 gr; Carbo 35.7 gr; T Fat 6.7 gr; Chol 11.7 mg; Calc 145.0 mg; Potas 162.0 mg; Sod 836.0 mg.

Saucy Pear Muffins

Beverly Tudor, Texas

3	**medium pears**
1	**egg**
2	**tablespoons oil**
2	**cups unbleached flour**
2	**teaspoons baking powder**
1	**teaspoon soda**
½	**teaspoon nutmeg**
1	**cup chopped pecans**

Preheat oven to 350 degrees. Peel and chop pears. Purée in blender container. Measure 1½ cups purée. Combine pear purée, egg and oil in mixer bowl; beat until smooth. Add mixture of dry ingredients gradually, mixing well after each addition. Stir in pecans. Spoon into greased muffin cups. Sprinkle with additional nutmeg. Bake for 15 minutes. Serve muffins hot or cold.

Yield: 12 servings. Approx Per Serving: Cal 188; Prot 3.5 gr; Carbo 22.9 gr; T Fat 9.8 gr; Chol 22.8 mg; Calc 23.4 mg; Potas 115.0 mg; Sod 130.0 mg.

Grilled Bananas

8	**large green-tipped bananas**
¼	**cup melted butter or margarine**
½	**teaspoon Tabasco sauce**

Peel ½-inch strip from each banana, leaving remaining peel intact. Pierce exposed banana with fork. Brush mixture of butter and Tabasco sauce over peeled surface. Grill peeled side up over hot coals for 15 minutes or just until tender.

Yield: 8 servings. Approx Per Serving: Cal 156; Prot 1.3 gr; Carbo 26.7 gr; T Fat 6.3 gr; Chol 15.5 mg; Calc 8.7 mg; Potas 453.0 mg; Sod 51.3 mg.

Blueberry Cheesecake

½	**cup butter or margarine, softened**
¼	**cup sugar**
1¼	**cups sifted all-purpose flour**
8	**ounces cream cheese, softened**
1½	**cups cold milk**
1	**(3-ounce) package vanilla instant pudding mix**
2	**teaspoons grated lemon rind**
2	**cups blueberries**
4	**teaspoons cornstarch**
3	**tablespoons sugar**
½	**cup water**

Preheat oven to 325 degrees. Blend butter and ¼ cup sugar in bowl. Add flour; mix until crumbly. Knead to form soft dough. Press into 9-inch springform pan. Prick bottom with fork. Bake for 35 minutes or until light brown. Beat cream cheese in mixer bowl until light. Blend in ½ cup milk gradually. Add remaining milk, pudding mix and lemon rind. Beat at low speed for 1 minute or just until mixed. Pour into crust. Chill until firm. Crush ¾ cup blueberries in saucepan. Add cornstarch, 3 tablespoons sugar and water. Cook until thickened, stirring constantly. Stir in remaining blueberries. Cool for 15 minutes. Spread over chilled layer. Chill in refrigerator. Place on serving plate. Remove side of pan.

Yield: 8 servings. Approx Per Serving: Cal 401; Prot 5.9 gr; Carbo 43.7 gr; T Fat 23.3 gr; Chol 68.2 mg; Calc 80.5 mg; Potas 149.0 mg; Sod 274.0 mg.

Backyard Spice Cake

Preheat oven to 350 degrees. Cream margarine and brown sugar in mixer bowl until light and fluffy. Blend in eggs and ½ teaspoon vanilla. Sift dry ingredients together. Mash 2 bananas in measuring cup. Add enough milk to measure ⅔ cup; mix well. Add sifted dry ingredients to creamed mixture alternately with banana mixture, mixing well after each addition. Stir in peanuts. Spoon into greased and floured 8 x 8-inch cake pan. Bake for 40 minutes or until cake tests done. Cool in pan for 10 minutes. Remove to wire rack to cool completely. Place on serving plate. Beat peanut butter and ½ teaspoon vanilla in mixer bowl until light. Add confectioners' sugar and 1 tablespoon milk; mix until smooth. Add enough remaining milk to make of spreading consistency. Spread over cake. Arrange banana slices on top just before serving.

Yield: 8 servings. Approx Per Serving: Cal 418;
Prot 8.3 gr; Carbo 65.3 gr; T Fat 15.3 gr;
Chol 69.7 mg; Calc 55.8 mg;
Potas 396.0 mg; Sod 216.0 mg.

¼	*cup margarine, softened*
¾	*cup packed light brown sugar*
2	*eggs*
½	*teaspoon vanilla extract*
1¼	*cups sifted all-purpose flour*
1	*teaspoon baking powder*
½	*teaspoon soda*
½	*teaspoon cinnamon*
¼	*teaspoon cloves*
¼	*teaspoon nutmeg*
2	*bananas*
2	*tablespoons (about) milk*
½	*cup unsalted peanuts*
3	*tablespoons creamy peanut butter*
½	*teaspoon vanilla extract*
1½	*cups confectioners' sugar*
2½	*tablespoons (about) milk*
1	*banana, sliced*

Frozen Strawberry and Peach Pie

Combine ½ cup strawberries, peaches and ½ cup corn syrup in blender container. Process at high speed for 30 seconds or until smooth. Beat cream in bowl until soft peaks form. Add ¼ cup corn syrup gradually, beating constantly until stiff peaks form. Fold in fruit mixture. Spoon into pie shell. Freeze until firm. Let stand at room temperature for 10 minutes. Garnish with whipped cream and whole strawberries.

Yield: 8 servings. Approx Per Serving: Cal 454;
Prot 2.9 gr; Carbo 52.4 gr; T Fat 27.5 gr;
Chol 61.1 mg; Calc 58.6 mg;
Potas 153.0 mg; Sod 270.0 mg.

½	*cup sliced strawberries*
½	*cup sliced peeled peaches*
½	*cup Karo light corn syrup*
1	*cup whipping cream*
¼	*cup Karo light corn syrup*
1	*9-inch graham cracker pie shell*
1	*cup whipped cream*
8	*whole strawberries*

August

Marinated Mushrooms

Janet Stratton, Maryland

½ **cup minced green pepper**
¼ **cup minced onion**
½ **cup minced celery**
¼ **cup shredded carrot**
1 **(12-ounce) bottle of Italian dressing**
2 **pounds fresh mushrooms**
1 **lemon, cut into wedges**
Salt to taste

Combine green pepper, onion, celery and carrot in bowl. Add dressing; mix well. Combine mushrooms, lemon wedges and salt with water to cover in saucepan. Bring to a boil. Cook for 3 minutes; drain. Add mushrooms to marinade; mix well. Marinate in refrigerator for 24 hours to 8 weeks.

Yield: 8 servings. Approx Per Serving: Cal 235;
Prot 2.9 gr; Carbo 11.6 gr; T Fat 26.1 gr;
Chol 0.0 mg; Calc 17.0 mg;
Potas 490.0 mg; Sod 221.0 mg.

Chili Relleno Soufflé

Kathy McDonoyl, California

Roast, peel and seed chilies. Rinse and pat dry. Preheat oven to 325 degrees. Combine flour, salt, pepper and egg yolks in bowl. Fold gently into stiffly beaten egg whites. Pour half the mixture into greased 9 x 13-inch baking pan. Arrange chilies in single layer in prepared pan. Sprinkle with mixture of cheeses. Spread remaining batter over top. Bake for 25 minutes or until puffed and golden brown. Cut into squares. Serve with salsa if desired.

12	*large green chilies*
1	*tablespoon all-purpose flour*
¼	*teaspoon salt*
	Pepper to taste
6	*eggs, separated*
1	*cup shredded Cheddar cheese*
1	*cup shredded Monterey Jack cheese*

Yield: 48 servings. Approx Per Serving: Cal 33; Prot 2.2 gr; Carbo 1.3 gr; T Fat 2.2 gr; Chol 38.9 mg; Calc 40.2 mg; Potas 50.7 mg; Sod 47.7 mg.

Pepper Relish

Della Dewey, Ohio

Grind vegetables coarsely. Sprinkle with salt. Let stand for 5 minutes. Drain and squeeze dry. Combine vegetables with remaining ingredients in saucepan. Bring to a boil. Boil for 10 minutes. Ladle into hot sterilized pint jars; seal with 2-piece lids. Store in refrigerator.

12	*large green peppers*
12	*large sweet red peppers*
6	*large onions*
2	*tablespoons salt*
2	*cups vinegar*
2	*cups sugar*
1	*teaspoon celery seed*
1	*teaspoon mustard seed*

Yield: 32 servings. Approx Per Serving: Cal 74; Prot 0.8 gr; Carbo 18.5 gr; T Fat 0.3 gr; Chol 0.0 mg; Calc 15.4 mg; Potas 171.0 mg; Sod 402.0 mg.

Hot Gazpacho

Combine tomatoes, vegetable juice, cucumbers, scallions, vinegar, garlic powder, sugar and salt in large saucepan. Bring to a boil; reduce heat. Simmer, covered, for 5 minutes or until tomatoes are tender. Ladle into serving bowls. Sprinkle croutons on top.

5	*cups chopped Florida tomatoes*
1	*(46-ounce) can vegetable juice cocktail*
2	*cups chopped peeled cucumbers*
3	*tablespoons chopped scallions*
3	*tablespoons red wine vinegar*
½	*teaspoon garlic powder*
½	*teaspoon sugar*
½	*teaspoon salt*
¾	*cup croutons*

Yield: 6 servings. Approx Per Serving: Cal 92; Prot 3.4 gr; Carbo 21.2 gr; T Fat 0.7 gr; Chol 0.0 mg; Calc 47.3 mg; Potas 807.0 mg; Sod 1034.0 mg.

Chicken Salad Sandwiches

2 **cups finely chopped cooked chicken breasts**
1 **cup drained crushed pineapple**
2 **tablespoons chutney**
1 **cup chopped celery**
1 **cup chopped scallions**
1 **cup chopped water chestnuts**
½ **cup toasted slivered almonds**
½ **cup sour cream**
1 **cup mayonnaise**
   Curry powder to taste
20 **slices sprouted wheat bread**

Combine chicken, pineapple, chutney, celery, scallions, water chestnuts and almonds in serving bowl. Combine sour cream, mayonnaise and curry powder in small bowl; mix well. Chill chicken mixture and mayonnaise mixture for 2 hours or longer. Stir dressing into salad; mix well. Spread on half the bread slices; top with remaining slices. Arrange sandwiches on serving plate. Cut into halves.

Yield: 10 servings. Approx Per Serving: Cal 406; Prot 18.1 gr; Carbo 46.8 gr; T Fat 18.1 gr; Chol 34.7 mg; Calc 104.0 mg; Potas 368.0 mg; Sod 662.0 mg.

Mediterranean Pitas

Diane Jacobs, Florida

2 **cloves of garlic, minced**
2 **teaspoons olive oil**
1½ **tablespoons lemon juice**
1 **tablespoon corn oil**
1 **cup cooked bulgur**
2 **cups chopped watercress**
3 **cups chopped parsley**
1 **cup thinly sliced celery**
1 **cup drained chopped tomato**
½ **cup chopped onion**
2 **cups alfalfa sprouts**
10 **pita bread rounds, split**

Sauté garlic in olive oil in skillet. Cool. Add lemon juice and corn oil. Combine bulgur, watercress, parsley, celery, tomato, onion and alfalfa sprouts in bowl. Add garlic mixture; toss lightly. Serve in pita bread.

Yield: 10 servings. Approx Per Serving: Cal 228; Prot 8.4 gr; Carbo 41.2 gr; T Fat 3.4 gr; Chol 0.0 mg; Calc 94.2 mg; Potas 299.0 mg; Sod 362.0 mg.

Midnight Roast Beef Sandwiches

Cheryl Hart, Iowa

1 **(4-pound) chuck roast**
3 **beef bouillon cubes**
3 **cups hot water**
3 **tablespoons sugar**
2 **teaspoons minced garlic**
1 **teaspoon basil**
1 **teaspoon oregano**
1 **teaspoon salt**
½ **teaspoon pepper**

Preheat oven to 350 degrees. Place roast in roasting pan. Combine remaining ingredients in bowl; mix until bouillon is dissolved. Pour over roast. Bake, covered, for 3 hours. Let stand for 10 minutes. Cut into thin slices. Serve with pan gravy. Store leftovers in refrigerator for up to 5 days. Serve hot or cold in sandwiches.

Yield: 10 servings. Approx Per Serving: Cal 713; Prot 46.4 gr; Carbo 4.4 gr; T Fat 55.4 gr; Chol 186.0 mg; Calc 27.2 mg; Potas 416.0 mg; Sod 632.0 mg.

Grape Ring with Pimento Dressing

Evelyn Voorhes, Ohio

Cut grapes into halves. Dissolve gelatin in boiling water in bowl. Add frozen grape juice and grapes; stir until grape juice melts. Chill until partially set. Stir in nuts. Pour into ring mold. Chill until firm. Unmold onto serving plate. Blend cream cheese spread and marshmallow creme in bowl. Spoon into center of ring.

Yield: 12 servings. Approx Per Serving: Cal 205; Prot 5.2 gr; Carbo 30.2 gr; T Fat 8.0 gr; Chol 13.5 mg; Calc 95.5 mg; Potas 104.0 mg; Sod 253.0 mg.

2   *cups seedless red grapes*
2   *(3-ounce) packages grape gelatin*
2   *cups boiling water*
1   *(6-ounce) can frozen grape juice concentrate*
½   *cup chopped nuts*
1   *(6-ounce) jar pimento cream cheese spread*
5   *tablespoons marshmallow creme*

New Moon Salad

Camie Donaldson, California

Cut cantaloupes into thin wedges; peel. Combine sour cream, bleu cheese, green onions and lemon juice in bowl. Arrange cantaloupe on serving plates. Spoon sour cream mixture over top.

Yield: 6 servings. Approx Per Serving: Cal 180; Prot 4.9 gr; Carbo 17.2 gr; T Fat 11.3 gr; Chol 24.0 mg; Calc 117.0 mg; Potas 643.0 mg; Sod 168.0 mg.

2   *large cantaloupes*
1   *cup sour cream*
¼   *cup crumbled bleu cheese*
¼   *cup chopped green onions*
1   *tablespoon lemon juice*

Salmon Salad

Mary Ann O'Sullivan, Louisiana

Cut potatoes into wedges. Cook in a small amount of water in saucepan until tender; drain. Cut tomatoes into wedges. Spoon salmon into center of large serving platter. Arrange potatoes around salmon. Place eggs and tomatoes on potato wedges. Combine remaining ingredients in bowl. Spoon over salmon and vegetables.

Yield: 6 servings. Approx Per Serving: Cal 356; Prot 26.1 gr; Carbo 11.0 gr; T Fat 24.8 gr; Chol 251.0 mg; Calc 58.5 mg; Potas 558.0 mg; Sod 523.0 mg.

4   *medium potatoes, peeled*
2   *ripe tomatoes*
2   *cups flaked, cooked salmon*
4   *hard-boiled eggs, sliced*
½   *cup chopped celery*
½   *cup chopped green onions*
¼   *cup sliced black olives*
¼   *cup sliced green olives*
¼   *cup Italian salad dressing*
¼   *cup mayonnaise*
¼   *cup chopped parsley*

Garden Potato Salad

2	**pounds new red potatoes**
1	**cup (1-inch pieces) green beans**
½	**cup canned corn**
½	**cup shredded carrots**
¼	**cup plain yogurt**
¼	**cup cottage cheese**
2	**teaspoons milk**
½	**teaspoon cider vinegar**
½	**teaspoon onion powder**
¼	**teaspoon tarragon**
¼	**teaspoon salt**
	Pinch of pepper

Cook potatoes in water to cover in saucepan until tender; drain. Rinse in cold water; drain. Cut potatoes into quarters. Cook green beans in 1-inch boiling water in saucepan for 2 to 3 minutes or until tender-crisp; drain. Combine potatoes, beans, corn and carrots in salad bowl. Combine remaining ingredients in blender container. Process at high speed until smooth. Pour over salad; mix lightly. Chill, covered, for 2 hours or longer.

Yield: 8 servings. Approx Per Serving: Cal 151; Prot 4.3 gr; Carbo 32.8 gr; T Fat 0.8 gr; Chol 2.1 mg; Calc 33.0 mg; Potas 559.0 mg; Sod 133.0 mg.

Spanish Salad

½	**cup chopped onion**
2	**teaspoons minced garlic**
2	**teaspoons Dijon-style mustard**
1	**teaspoon grated lemon rind**
¼	**cup lemon juice**
¼	**teaspoon oregano**
1	**teaspoon salt**
¼	**teaspoon pepper**
¾	**cup oil**
1	**cup soft bread crumbs**
2	**cups green pepper strips**
3	**cups shredded cabbage**
2	**cups chopped cucumber**
4	**cups chopped tomatoes**
1	**cup chopped celery**
¼	**cup chopped parsley**

Combine onion, garlic, mustard, lemon rind, lemon juice, oregano, salt and pepper in blender container. Process until smooth. Add oil in fine stream, processing until creamy. Layer bread crumbs, green pepper, cabbage, cucumber, tomatoes, celery and dressing ½ at a time in 3-quart straight-sided glass dish. Chill, covered, for several hours. Sprinkle parsley over top.

Yield: 8 servings. Approx Per Serving: Cal 242; Prot 2.5 gr; Carbo 13.3 gr; T Fat 21.2 gr; Chol 0.0 mg; Calc 47.4 mg; Potas 462.0 mg; Sod 339.0 mg.

Zucchini and Grapefruit Salad

3	**envelopes unflavored gelatin**
1½	**cups grapefruit juice**
⅔	**cup sugar**
½	**cup tarragon vinegar**
1½	**cups grapefruit juice**
1½	**cups shredded zucchini**
¾	**cup chopped green pepper**
⅓	**cup sliced green onions**
1	**cup grapefruit sections**

Soften gelatin in 1½ cups grapefruit juice in saucepan. Add sugar. Heat until gelatin and sugar dissolve, stirring constantly. Add vinegar and 1½ cups grapefruit juice. Chill until thickened, stirring occasionally. Fold in vegetables and grapefruit sections. Pour into mold. Chill until firm. Unmold onto serving plate.

Yield: 10 servings. Approx Per Serving: Cal 102; Prot 2.7 gr; Carbo 23.8 gr; T Fat 0.2 gr; Chol 0.0 mg; Calc 15.9 mg; Potas 235.0 mg; Sod 3.8 mg.

Grilled Beef Burgers

Gina Spence, Wisconsin

Combine ground beef, croutons, mustard, egg and tomato in bowl; mix lightly. Shape into patties. Grill over hot coals to desired degree of doneness. Serve on hard rolls.

Yield: 8 servings. Approx Per Serving: Cal 494; Prot 34.8 gr; Carbo 34.0 gr; T Fat 24.6 gr; Chol 133.0 mg; Calc 51.8 mg; Potas 447.0 mg; Sod 557.0 mg.

2	**pounds lean ground beef**
1	**cup garlic croutons**
¼	**cup Dijon-style mustard**
1	**egg, beaten**
1	**large tomato, finely chopped**
8	**hard rolls, split**

Barbecued Spareribs

Sharon Moulson, British Columbia, Canada

Preheat oven to 350 degrees. Place ribs in large roasting pan. Sprinkle with seasonings to taste. Add water. Cover tightly with foil. Bake for 30 minutes. Bake, uncovered, for 15 minutes longer. Drain. Refrigerate if desired. Combine barbecue sauce, honey, soy sauce and onion in saucepan. Heat until well mixed, stirring constantly. Separate ribs into serving portions. Place on grill over hot coals. Cook until tender and glazed, turning and basting frequently with sauce.

Yield: 8 servings. Approx Per Serving: Cal 925; Prot 67.5 gr; Carbo 20.1 gr; T Fat 65.0 gr; Chol 257.5 mg; Calc 107.5 mg; Potas 741.5 mg; Sod 584.0 mg.

5	**pounds spareribs**
	Salt, pepper and garlic powder to taste
½	**cup water**
½	**cup barbecue sauce**
½	**cup honey**
2	**tablespoons soy sauce**
½	**cup minced onion**

Chicken and Beef Kabobs

Kathy Nelson, Ohio

Cut chicken and beef into 1-inch cubes. Cut peppers into large pieces. Thread chicken, beef and vegetables alternately onto skewers. Marinate in mixture of remaining ingredients in refrigerator for several hours. Drain, reserving marinade. Grill over hot coals for 3 to 4 minutes on each side, basting frequently with marinade.

Yield: 8 servings. Approx Per Serving: Cal 452; Prot 45.2 gr; Carbo 3.6 gr; T Fat 26.2 gr; Chol 127.0 mg; Calc 25.8 mg; Potas 603.0 mg; Sod 1140.0 mg.

4	**chicken breast filets**
1½	**pounds sirloin**
2	**medium green peppers**
16	**medium mushrooms**
½	**cup soy sauce**
⅔	**cup white wine**
¼	**cup oil**
1½	**teaspoons mixed herbs**
1	**teaspoon grated gingerroot**
2	**cloves of garlic, minced**
½	**teaspoon onion powder**

Sweet and Sour Bass

Kim Graves, Illinois

6	pounds fresh water bass fillets
⅔	cup flour
1	teaspoon salt
	Oil for frying
1	cup packed brown sugar
1	cup vinegar
2	tablespoons soy sauce
½	teaspoon salt
¾	cup water
7	teaspoons cornstarch
¼	cup water
1	large green pepper, chopped
½	cup chopped onion
2	medium tomatoes, chopped, drained

Preheat oven to 250 degrees. Coat fillets with mixture of flour and 1 teaspoon salt. Fry in ¼ inch hot oil in skillet over medium heat until golden brown. Place on rack in baking pan. Keep warm in oven. Mix brown sugar, vinegar, soy sauce and ½ teaspoon salt in saucepan. Stir in ¾ cup water. Bring to a boil. Stir in cornstarch dissolved in ¼ cup water. Cook until thickened, stirring constantly. Add green pepper and onion. Cook for 3 minutes. Add tomatoes. Heat to serving temperature. Serve over bass.

Yield: 8 servings. Approx Per Serving: Cal 596; Prot 83.6 gr; Carbo 42.1 gr; T Fat 13.9 gr; Chol 272.0 mg; Calc 329.0 mg; Potas 1581.0 mg; Sod 928.0 mg.

Eggplant Creole

2	cups chopped peeled eggplant
1½	tablespoons butter or margarine
1½	tablespoons all-purpose flour
1	cup chopped peeled tomato
½	cup chopped green pepper
½	cup chopped onion
1½	teaspoons light brown sugar
½	bay leaf
2	whole cloves
½	teaspoon salt
½	cup bread crumbs
2	tablespoons Parmesan cheese

Preheat oven to 350 degrees. Cook eggplant in a small amount of boiling salted water in saucepan for 10 minutes; drain. Place in buttered 8 x 8-inch baking dish. Melt butter in skillet. Blend in flour. Cook over low heat until light brown, stirring constantly. Stir in tomato, green pepper, onion, brown sugar, bay leaf, cloves and salt. Cook for 5 minutes, stirring constantly. Remove bay leaf and cloves. Pour over eggplant. Top with mixture of bread crumbs and cheese. Bake for 30 minutes.

Yield: 4 servings. Approx Per Serving: Cal 144; Prot 4.2 gr; Carbo 19.6 gr; T Fat 6.0 gr; Chol 14.2 mg; Calc 78.5 mg; Potas 270.0 mg; Sod 449.0 mg.

Garden Casserole

Faye Williams, Missouri

Preheat oven to 350 degrees. Drain cooked vegetables well. Combine in bowl; mix lightly. Blend cream sauce with catsup. Stir in seasonings, parsley and chives. Alternate layers of vegetable mixture and sauce in greased 2-quart casserole. Chill for several hours if desired. Top with mixture of crumbs and cheese. Bake for 30 minutes or until bubbly.

Yield: 6 servings. Approx Per Serving: Cal 232; Prot 7.7 gr; Carbo 21.7 gr; T Fat 13.5 gr; Chol 21.3 mg; Calc 201.0 mg; Potas 495.0 mg; Sod 811.0 mg.

1	*cup cooked chopped celery*
1	*cup cooked fresh green beans*
1	*cup cooked chopped potatoes*
1	*cup cooked chopped carrots*
1	*cup cooked chopped cauliflower*
2	*cups medium cream sauce*
1	*tablespoon catsup*
1	*teaspoon salt*
1/4	*teaspoon pepper*
1/4	*teaspoon thyme*
1	*tablespoon minced parsley*
1	*tablespoon minced chives*
1/2	*cup cracker crumbs*
1/2	*cup shredded sharp Cheddar cheese*

Summer Squash Ring

Preheat oven to 350 degrees. Slice squash; reserve 8 thin slices. Cook remaining squash in a small amount of water in saucepan until tender; drain well. Mash and drain well. Measure 3 cups squash. Combine with eggs, butter, seasonings and crumbs; mix well. Arrange squash slices in oiled 1-quart ring mold. Spoon squash mixture into mold. Place in pan of hot water. Bake for 25 minutes or until set. Invert onto serving plate. Fill center with peas.

Yield: 6 servings. Approx Per Serving: Cal 244; Prot 10.4 gr; Carbo 27.5 gr; T Fat 11.7 gr; Chol 158.0 mg; Calc 115.0 mg; Potas 777.0 mg; Sod 135.0 mg.

6	*medium yellow squash*
3	*eggs, beaten*
1/4	*cup melted butter or margarine*
	Salt, pepper and cayenne pepper to taste
1/4	*cup dry bread crumbs*
3	*cups cooked fresh peas, drained*

Rice Jardin

Cathy Martin, Ohio

3	**medium tomatoes**
¾	**cup chopped onion**
1½	**pounds zucchini, thinly sliced**
2	**tablespoons margarine**
2	**cups cooked fresh corn**
3	**cups cooked brown rice**
	Salt and pepper to taste
¼	**teaspoon oregano**

Cut tomatoes into wedges. Sauté onion and zucchini in margarine in skillet until tender. Stir in corn, tomatoes, rice and seasonings. Simmer, covered, for 15 minutes.

Yield: 8 servings. Approx Per Serving: Cal 183; Prot 4.8 gr; Carbo 34.5 gr; T Fat 4.1 gr; Chol 0.0 mg; Calc 30.9 mg; Potas 484.0 mg; Sod 46.5 mg.

Pan de Relleno

4	**large fresh green chilies**
1	**cup buttermilk baking mix**
1	**(15-ounce) can cream-style corn**
1	**egg, beaten**
½	**cup milk**
2	**tablespoons melted margarine**
1	**tablespoon sugar**
2	**cups shredded Monterey Jack cheese**

Roast, peel, seed and chop chilies. Preheat oven to 350 degrees. Combine baking mix, corn, egg, milk, margarine and sugar in bowl; mix well. Pour half the batter into greased 2-quart baking dish. Add layers of green chilies and cheese. Pour remaining batter over top. Bake for 30 minutes or until golden brown. Let stand for 5 minutes; cut into squares.

Yield: 6 servings. Approx Per Serving: Cal 454; Prot 15.8 gr; Carbo 47.1 gr; T Fat 23.2 gr; Chol 83.0 mg; Calc 366.0 mg; Potas 328.0 mg; Sod 1000.0 mg.

Whole Wheat Biscuits

2	**cups whole wheat flour**
2	**teaspoons baking powder**
¼	**teaspoon salt**
3	**tablespoons shortening**
½	**cup milk**

Preheat oven to 450 degrees. Mix dry ingredients in bowl. Cut in shortening until crumbly. Add milk. Roll ½ inch thick on lightly floured surface; cut with biscuit cutter. Arrange on lightly greased baking sheet. Bake for 10 minutes.

Yield: 18 servings. Approx Per Serving: Cal 68; Prot 2.0 gr; Carbo 9.9 gr; T Fat 2.6 gr; Chol 0.9 mg; Calc 19.3 mg; Potas 59.0 mg; Sod 69.4 mg.

Dessertwiches

Donna McBride, Texas

Cut waffles into halves. Mix marmalade and pecans in bowl. Spread mixture of marmalade and pecans on half the waffles. Place on serving plates. Top each with ice cream, remaining marmalade mixture and remaining waffles.

Yield: 10 servings. Approx Per Serving: Cal 225; Prot 4.2 gr; Carbo 27.8 gr; T Fat 11.0 gr; Chol 43.6 mg; Calc 100.0 mg; Potas 187.0 mg; Sod 288.0 mg.

10 **small frozen waffles, toasted**
1 **(12-ounce) jar marmalade**
¼ **cup chopped pecans**
1 **quart vanilla ice cream, sliced**

Easy Fruit Tartlets

Prepare pudding mix according to package directions using 1½ cups milk. Spoon into tartlet shells. Arrange fruit over pudding. Chill in refrigerator. Prepare gelatin using package directions. Chill until thickened. Spoon over fruit. Chill until set. Garnish with whipped topping.

Yield: 8 servings. Approx Per Serving: Cal 403; Prot 5.4 gr; Carbo 45.2 gr; T Fat 17.5 gr; Chol 6.2 mg; Calc 59.4 mg; Potas 137.0 mg; Sod 403.0 mg.

1 **(3-ounce) package lemon instant pudding mix**
1½ **cups milk**
8 **baked 3-inch tartlet shells**
1 **cup strawberry halves**
1 **cup blueberries**
1 **(3-ounce) package apricot gelatin**
1 **cup whipped topping**

Raspberry Float

Lois Roberts, Montana

Microwave 2 cups water in 4-cup glass measure on High for 4 minutes or until boiling. Combine gelatin, sugar and boiling water in pitcher. Add 2 cups cold water, lime juice, orange juice and lemonade. Cool. Add ginger ale and raspberries just before serving; mix gently. Pour over ice in frosted glasses.

Yield: 8 servings. Approx Per Serving: Cal 195; Prot 2.1 gr; Carbo 48.8 gr; T Fat 0.2 gr; Chol 0.0 mg; Calc 13.0 mg; Potas 121.0 mg; Sod 55.9 mg.

4 **cups water**
1½ **(3-ounce) packages raspberry gelatin**
¾ **cup sugar**
¼ **cup lime juice**
1 **cup orange juice**
1 **cup lemonade**
2 **cups ginger ale**
2 **cups raspberries**

September

Sicilian Eggplant Relish

Lois Perruccio, Connecticut

2	**cups chopped celery**
½	**cup olive oil**
6	**cups chopped peeled eggplant**
1	**large onion, chopped**
2	**tablespoons olive oil**
1	**tablespoon sugar**
⅓	**cup wine vinegar**
2	**tablespoons tomato paste**
1	**cup water**
12	**large green olives, chopped**
1	**tablespoon chopped parsley**
1	**tablespoon capers**
	Salt and pepper to taste

Sauté celery in ½ cup olive oil in skillet for 7 minutes. Remove with slotted spoon. Add eggplant to skillet. Sauté for 10 minutes or until golden. Remove with slotted spoon; drain on paper towel. Add onion and 2 tablespoons olive oil to skillet. Sauté until soft; do not brown. Add sugar, vinegar, tomato paste and water. Simmer, covered, for 15 to 20 minutes. Stir in eggplant, celery, olives, parsley, capers, salt and pepper. Simmer, covered, for 10 minutes. Cool. Store in covered container in refrigerator for up to 10 days. Serve cold on antipasto tray or with roasted meats or chicken.

Yield: 40 servings. Approx Per Serving: Cal 39; Prot 0.3 gr; Carbo 1.9 gr; T Fat 3.6 gr; Chol 0.0 mg; Calc 8.8 mg; Potas 60.5 mg; Sod 34.5 mg.

Cheese Puffs

Ruby Trostle, Pennsylvania

Combine butter, cream cheese and Cheddar cheese in double boiler pan. Heat over hot water until melted; mix well. Beat egg white in mixer bowl until stiff peaks form. Fold in cheese mixture. Cut loaf into 1-inch slices; trim crusts. Cut bread into 1-inch cubes. Dip into cheese mixture; place on baking sheet. Freeze until firm. Store in plastic bags in freezer. Preheat oven to 350 degrees. Place frozen cubes on baking sheet. Bake for 15 minutes. Serve hot.

½ **cup butter or margarine**
4 **ounces cream cheese**
1 **cup shredded Cheddar cheese**
1 **egg white**
1 **loaf French bread**

Yield: 48 servings. Approx Per Serving: Cal 62; Prot 1.7 gr; Carbo 4.9 gr; T Fat 3.9 gr; Chol 10.2 mg; Calc 30.1 mg; Potas 15.3 mg; Sod 93.6 mg.

Cantaloupe Pickles

Cecilia Kelsey, Washington

Peel and seed cantaloupes. Slice lengthwise into thin wedges. Combine with salted water to cover in bowl. Let stand for 1 hour. Tie pickling spices in cheesecloth bag. Combine with sugar, vinegar and ½ cup cold water in saucepan. Bring to a boil, stirring until sugar is dissolved. Cook for 15 minutes. Drain cantaloupe wedges; rinse with cold water. Combine with hot syrup in bowl. Let stand for 24 hours. Drain syrup into saucepan. Bring to a boil. Pour over cantaloupe. Let stand for 24 hours. Repeat process 2 more times. Pour syrup into saucepan. Cook until syrup is thick. Pack cantaloupe wedges into hot sterilized jars. Add hot syrup, leaving ½-inch headspace; seal with 2-piece lids. Process in boiling water bath for 10 minutes.

2 **firm cantaloupes**
3 **tablespoons pickling spices**
3 **cups sugar**
1 **cup vinegar**
½ **cup cold water**

Yield: 3 pints. Approx Per Pint: Cal 905; Prot 3.1 gr; Carbo 233.0 gr; T Fat 1.0 gr; Chol 0.0 mg; Calc 46.3 mg; Potas 1187.0 mg; Sod 37.7 mg.

Garden Minestrone

3	tablespoons tomato paste
2	tablespoons olive oil
4	cups water
2	tablespoons instant beef bouillon
3	tablespoons dried onions
¼	teaspoon garlic powder
2	teaspoons salt
½	cup chopped carrots
½	cup chopped celery
1	teaspoon chopped parsley
½	teaspoon Italian seasoning
1	cup cut green beans
1	cup peas
1	cup lima beans
¼	cup chopped zucchini
½	cup chopped spinach
½	cup elbow macaroni
	Grated Romano cheese

Combine tomato paste, olive oil, water, beef bouillon, dried onions, garlic powder and salt in stockpot. Bring to a boil. Simmer for 10 to 15 minutes. Add carrots, celery, parsley and Italian seasoning. Simmer for 20 minutes. Add green beans, peas, lima beans, zucchini and spinach. Simmer until vegetables are tender-crisp. Add macaroni. Simmer just until macaroni and vegetables are tender. Ladle into soup bowls. Sprinkle with cheese.

Yield: 6 servings. Approx Per Serving: Cal 197; Prot 7.2 gr; Carbo 31.5 gr; T Fat 5.2 gr; Chol 0.2 mg; Calc 51.9 mg; Potas 525.0 mg; Sod 1079.0 mg.

Brunch Pleasers

Paul Fabens, Texas

5	cups sliced fresh mushrooms
¾	cup chopped green pepper
1¼	cups butter or margarine
¾	cup all-purpose flour
3	tablespoons Worcestershire sauce
	Hot pepper sauce to taste
1½	teaspoons salt
½	teaspoon pepper
7	cups milk
12	hard-boiled eggs
12	English muffins, split, toasted
	Parsley sprigs

Sauté mushrooms and green peppers in ¼ cup butter in saucepan. Drain and set aside. Melt remaining 1 cup butter in saucepan. Blend in flour, Worcestershire sauce, hot pepper sauce, salt and pepper. Stir in milk gradually. Cook over low heat until thickened, stirring constantly. Chop egg whites. Stir egg whites and sautéed vegetables into sauce. Cook over low heat until heated through. Arrange English muffins on serving plates. Spoon sauce over muffins. Grate egg yolks over top. Garnish with parsley.

Yield: 12 servings. Approx Per Serving: Cal 514; Prot 17.0 gr; Carbo 41.3 gr; T Fat 30.8 gr; Chol 345.0 mg; Calc 289.0 mg; Potas 750.0 mg; Sod 969.0 mg.

Homemade Pimento Cheese Sandwiches

Ida Walker, North Carolina

Combine cheese, butter, mayonnaise, pimento, milk, onion, vinegar, Worcestershire sauce and seasonings in blender or food processor container. Process until well mixed. Add enough sour cream to make of desired consistency. Store in covered container in refrigerator. Spread on half the bread slices; top with remaining slices. Cut sandwiches as desired. Arrange on serving plate.

Yield: 10 servings. Approx Per Serving: Cal 475; Prot 19.1 gr; Carbo 37.6 gr; T Fat 29.2 gr; Chol 68.7 mg; Calc 400.0 mg; Potas 207.0 mg; Sod 870.0 mg.

1 **pound Cheddar cheese, shredded**
¼ **cup melted butter or margarine**
½ **cup mayonnaise**
2 **(4-ounce) jars chopped pimento, drained**
2 **tablespoons milk**
1 **tablespoon minced onion**
1 **tablespoon vinegar**
1 **tablespoon Worcestershire sauce**
  Garlic salt, salt and pepper to taste
½ **cup (about) sour cream**
20 **slices whole wheat bread**

Pita Treats

Pam Matlock, Kansas

Combine soup mix, sour cream, water chestnuts and green onions in bowl. Drain spinach; squeeze dry. Add to sour cream mixture. Chill for several hours. Cut pita rounds into halves; open halves to form pockets. Spoon spinach filling into pockets. Cut each half into 4 wedges. Arrange on serving plate.

Yield: 64 servings. Approx Per Serving: Cal 44; Prot 1.4 gr; Carbo 6.0 gr; T Fat 1.7 gr; Chol 3.3 mg; Calc 22.2 mg; Potas 46.6 mg; Sod 140.0 mg.

1 **package dry vegetable soup mix**
2 **cups sour cream**
1 **(8-ounce) can water chestnuts, chopped**
3 **medium green onions, chopped**
1 **(10-ounce) package frozen chopped spinach, thawed**
8 **pita bread rounds**

Fruit Medley Plate

Mrs. Frank Skinner, Alabama

3	**large peaches**
3	**large pears**
2	**tablespoons lemon juice**
	Lettuce leaves
12	**pineapple spears**
12	**small grape clusters**
2	**large oranges, peeled, sectioned**
2	**large bananas, sliced**

Peel peaches and pears. Cut into halves; discard pits and cores. Sprinkle with lemon juice. Place 1 peach half and 1 pear half on each lettuce-lined serving plate. Arrange pineapple, grapes, orange sections and bananas around pear and peach halves. Drizzle with Honey Dressing.

Yield: 6 servings. Approx Per Serving: Cal 330; Prot 2.7 gr; Carbo 68.5 gr; T Fat 8.6 gr; Chol 0.0 mg; Calc 53.8 mg; Potas 787.4 mg; Sod 21.5 mg.

Honey Dressing

¼	**cup sugar**
1	**teaspoon dry mustard**
1	**teaspoon paprika**
1	**teaspoon celery seed**
¼	**teaspoon salt**
⅓	**cup vinegar**
⅓	**cup honey**
1	**tablespoon lemon juice**
½	**teaspoon grated onion**
1	**cup oil**

Mix sugar, dry mustard, paprika, celery seed and salt in bowl. Add vinegar, honey, lemon juice and onion. Add oil gradually, beating constantly. Store in refrigerator.

Yield: 32 tablespoons. Approx Per Tablespoon: Cal 67; Prot 0.0 gr; Carbo 1.9 gr; T Fat 6.8 gr; Chol 0.0 mg; Calc 1.6 mg; Potas 8.4 mg; Sod 17.0 mg.

Melon Basket

1	**small oval watermelon**
2	**cups cantaloupe balls**
2	**cups honeydew melon balls**
2	**cups fresh pineapple chunks**
2	**cups fresh raspberries or strawberries**
1	**cup plain yogurt**
2	**tablespoons lemon juice**
½	**teaspoon poppy seed**

Carve watermelon into basket, leaving handle. Scoop out 4 cups watermelon balls. Remove remaining watermelon pulp; drain basket shell. Combine watermelon balls with remaining fruit in bowl. Mix yogurt, lemon juice and poppy seed in small serving bowl. Chill watermelon basket, fruit and dressing until serving time. Spoon fruit into watermelon basket. Serve with yogurt-poppy seed dressing.

Yield: 6 servings. Approx Per Serving: Cal 79; Prot 4.3 gr; Carbo 14.4 gr; T Fat 1.0 gr; Chol 2.5 mg; Calc 48.1 mg; Potas 408.0 mg; Sod 242.0 mg.

Tuna Salad Floridian

Cook potatoes in water to cover in saucepan until tender; drain. Rinse with cold water; drain and slice. Chill in refrigerator. Combine olive oil, vinegar, mustard, garlic, salt and pepper in jar; cover and shake. Line serving platter with romaine. Spoon tuna into center. Arrange eggs, green pepper rings, cucumbers, tomato wedges and potato slices around tuna. Garnish with olives. Drizzle dressing over salad.

Yield: 8 servings. Approx Per Serving: Cal 436
Prot 20.4 gr; Carbo 7.4 gr; T Fat 36.8 gr;
Chol 214.0 mg; Calc 54.7 mg;
Potas 425.0 mg; Sod 639.0 mg.

2	*pounds red new potatoes*
1	*cup olive oil*
6	*tablespoons red wine vinegar*
4	*teaspoons Dijon-style mustard*
1	*teaspoon minced garlic*
¾	*teaspoon salt*
¼	*teaspoon pepper*
1	*head romaine*
2	*(7-ounce) cans tuna, drained*
6	*hard-boiled eggs, sliced*
1½	*cups green pepper rings*
1½	*cups sliced cucumbers*
2	*tomatoes, cut into wedges*
½	*cup green olives*

Carnitas

Preheat oven to 350 degrees. Wrap tortillas in foil. Heat for 10 to 15 minutes. Brown beef and garlic in oil in skillet. Stir in chili sauce and hot pepper sauce. Combine avocado and remaining ingredients in bowl; mix lightly. Spoon beef mixture and avocado mixture onto hot tortillas. Fold to enclose filling. Arrange on serving plate.

Yield: 10 servings. Approx Per Serving: Cal 293;
Prot 17.7 gr; Carbo 25.7 gr; T Fat 14.2 gr;
Chol 48.0 mg; Calc 35.8 mg;
Potas 383.0 mg; Sod 459.0 mg.

10	*flour tortillas*
1	*pound beef chuck steak, cubed*
1	*clove of garlic, minced*
1	*tablespoon oil*
½	*cup chili sauce*
	Hot pepper sauce to taste
1	*large avocado, chopped*
1	*medium tomato, finely chopped*
¼	*cup chopped green chilies*
1	*teaspoon lemon juice*
½	*teaspoon cumin*
½	*teaspoon salt*

Ground Beef and Spaghetti Squash Casserole

1	*(3½-pound) spaghetti squash*
4	*quarts water*
1	*pound ground beef*
1	*medium onion, chopped*
1	*(15-ounce) jar spaghetti sauce*
1	*teaspoon basil*
¼	*teaspoon oregano*
¼	*teaspoon thyme*
⅛	*teaspoon pepper*
1	*cup shredded sharp Cheddar cheese*
1	*cup shredded mozzarella cheese*
1	*cup large curd cottage cheese*

Preheat oven to 350 degrees. Cook whole spaghetti squash in water in covered saucepan for 20 to 30 minutes or until tender. Drain and cool. Cook ground beef with onion in skillet, stirring until ground beef is crumbly; drain. Stir in spaghetti sauce and seasonings. Simmer, covered, for 15 minutes. Mix cheeses in bowl. Cut squash in half lengthwise; discard seed. Scrape with fork to separate squash into strands. Layer squash, ground beef mixture and cheeses ⅓ at a time in 9 x 13-inch baking dish. Chill in refrigerator if desired. Bake for 45 minutes or until bubbly.

Yield: 6 servings. Approx Per Serving: Cal 536; Prot 35.0 gr; Carbo 32.0 gr; T Fat 30.1 gr; Chol 106.0 mg; Calc 347.0 mg; Potas 915.0 mg; Sod 797.0 mg.

Hunter's Pork Chops

Tracy Paquin, Maryland

4	*(¾-inch thick) loin pork chops*
1	*tablespoon oil*
2	*medium green peppers, cut into strips*
1	*medium onion, chopped*
8	*ounces mushrooms, cut into halves*
1	*(8-ounce) bottle of sweet-spicy French dressing*
½	*teaspoon sugar*
½	*teaspoon salt*
⅛	*teaspoon pepper*
¼	*cup water*
1	*medium tomato, chopped*

Brown pork chops on both sides in oil in 12-inch skillet; remove chops. Sauté green peppers, onion and mushrooms in pan drippings until tender-crisp. Add French dressing, sugar, seasonings and water; mix well. Add pork chops. Simmer, covered, for 45 minutes or until pork chops are tender. Skim. Add tomato. Heat to serving temperature.

Yield: 4 servings. Approx Per Serving: Cal 781; Prot 38.3 gr; Carbo 11.7 gr; T Fat 64.8 gr; Chol 126.0 mg; Calc 27.9 mg; Potas 878.0 mg; Sod 1031.0 mg.

Chicken Veronique

Lorraine Smith, Maryland

Preheat oven to 325 degrees. Rinse filets and pat dry. Flatten with meat mallet. Prepare wild rice according to package directions. Combine with cream cheese, Brandy, ½ teaspoon salt and white pepper in bowl; mix well. Spoon stuffing onto filets. Roll to enclose filling; secure with skewers. Place on rack in shallow roasting pan. Brush generously with 2 tablespoons melted butter. Bake for 1 hour and 15 minutes, basting occasionally with pan juices. Blend 2 tablespoons melted butter, flour and lemon juice in saucepan. Stir in chicken stock gradually. Cook until thickened, stirring constantly. Stir a small amount of hot mixture into beaten egg yolks; stir egg yolks into hot mixture. Cook just until sauce begins to bubble, stirring constantly. Stir in salt and pepper to taste and grapes. Arrange stuffed filets on serving plate; spoon sauce over top.

Yield: 8 servings. Approx Per Serving: Cal 433; Prot 40.4 gr; Carbo 28.3 gr; T Fat 15.4 gr; Chol 187.0 mg; Calc 43.0 mg; Potas 450.0 mg; Sod 440.0 mg.

8	**chicken breast filets**
1½	**cups wild rice**
2	**ounces strawberry-flavored whipped cream cheese**
½	**cup Brandy**
½	**teaspoon salt**
	Dash of white pepper
4	**tablespoons melted butter or margarine**
2	**tablespoons all-purpose flour**
1½	**teaspoons lemon juice**
1½	**cups chicken stock**
2	**egg yolks**
	Salt and pepper to taste
2	**cups seedless green grapes**

Southern Catfish

Rudy Villanueva, Texas

Rinse catfish and pat dry. Season with salt and pepper. Dip into milk, flour, eggs and bread crumbs in order listed. Chill for 30 minutes. Melt butter with oil in skillet. Brown fish on both sides in butter and oil. Drain on paper towel. Place on warm platter. Sauté peanuts in pan drippings until golden brown. Add lemon juice, stirring to deglaze skillet. Pour peanuts and pan juices over catfish. Sprinkle with parsley. Garnish with lemon wedges.

Yield: 6 servings. Approx Per Serving: Cal 576; Prot 40.2 gr; Carbo 25.5 gr; T Fat 35.0 gr; Chol 225.0 mg; Calc 134.0 mg; Potas 805.0 mg; Sod 360.0 mg.

6	**catfish**
	Salt and pepper to taste
½	**cup milk**
½	**cup all-purpose flour**
2	**eggs, beaten**
1	**cup bread crumbs**
6	**tablespoons butter or margarine**
3	**tablespoons oil**
½	**cup peanuts**
	Juice of 3 lemons
3	**tablespoons chopped parsley**
	Lemon wedges

Fresh Vegetable Frittata

Barbara Judge, Florida

4	**medium tomatoes, peeled, chopped**
1	**cup chopped green onions**
2	**medium zucchini, thinly sliced**
12	**soda crackers, crushed**
5	**eggs, beaten**
	Salt and pepper to taste
1	**teaspoon oregano**
3	**tablespoons oil**
¼	**cup dry white wine**
¼	**cup Parmesan cheese**

Preheat oven to 300 degrees. Combine vegetables and cracker crumbs in bowl; toss lightly. Beat eggs with seasonings, oil and wine. Add to vegetable mixture; mix lightly. Pour into greased 9-inch deep-dish pie plate. Sprinkle with Parmesan cheese. Bake for 55 minutes or until knife inserted near center comes out clean. Serve warm or at room temperature.

Yield: 6 servings. Approx Per Serving: Cal 200; Prot 8.2 gr; Carbo 10.8 gr; T Fat 13.3 gr; Chol 233.0 mg; Calc 94.8 mg; Potas 392.0 mg; Sod 207.0 mg.

Corn and Tomato Casserole

Paula Throckmorton, Illinois

3	**cups bread cubes**
3	**tablespoons melted butter or margarine**
2	**cups cooked fresh corn**
2½	**cups chopped fresh tomatoes**
½	**cup chopped onion**
	Salt and pepper to taste
½	**cup shredded Cheddar cheese**

Preheat oven to 375 degrees. Toss bread cubes with butter. Reserve 1 cup buttered bread cubes. Alternate layers of remaining bread cubes, corn, tomatoes and onion in 1½-quart casserole. Sprinkle with salt and pepper. Top with mixture of reserved bread cubes and cheese. Bake for 30 minutes or until bubbly.

Yield: 6 servings. Approx Per Serving: Cal 227; Prot 6.9 gr; Carbo 29.1 gr; T Fat 10.7 gr; Chol 25.4 mg; Calc 108.0 mg; Potas 348.0 mg; Sod 238.0 mg.

Rice Soufflé

Shirley Knight, Oregon

1	**cup cold cooked rice**
3	**egg yolks, beaten**
½	**cup milk**
2	**tablespoons melted butter or margarine**
1	**cup shredded Cheddar cheese**
3	**egg whites**
⅛	**teaspoon salt**

Preheat oven to 300 degrees. Combine rice, egg yolks, milk, butter and cheese in bowl; mix well. Beat egg whites with salt in mixer bowl until stiff peaks form. Fold gently into rice mixture. Spoon into greased 8 x 10-inch baking dish. Bake for 30 minutes or until set and brown.

Yield: 4 servings. Approx Per Serving: Cal 298; Prot 13.7 gr; Carbo 14.5 gr; T Fat 20.4 gr; Chol 253.0 mg; Calc 266.0 mg; Potas 130.0 mg; Sod 373.0 mg.

Beignets

Marie Thibideaux, Louisiana

Melt butter in saucepan. Blend in water and flour. Cook over low heat for 5 minutes, stirring constantly; remove from heat. Add eggs 1 at a time. Beat for 3 minutes after each addition. Beat in vanilla. Preheat oil to 365 degrees. Drop batter by teaspoonfuls into hot oil. Deep-fry until golden brown. Drain on paper towel. Dust with confectioners' sugar. Serve warm.

Yield: 4 servings. Approx Per Serving: Cal 144; Prot 7.2 gr; Carbo 8.81 gr; T Fat 8.6 gr; Chol 282.0 mg; Calc 30.6 mg; Potas 76.1 mg; Sod 93.4 mg.

1   **tablespoon butter or margarine**
6   **tablespoons water**
6   **tablespoons all-purpose flour**
4   **eggs**
1   **teaspoon vanilla extract**
    Oil for deep frying
    Confectioners' sugar

Blueberry Corn Bread

Evelyn Roberts, Rhode Island

Preheat oven to 375 degrees. Combine first 5 ingredients in bowl; mix well. Beat egg with melted butter and milk. Add to cornmeal mixture; stir just until moistened. Pour into greased 8x8-inch baking pan. Sprinkle blueberries on top. Bake for 20 to 25 minutes or until golden brown. Serve warm.

Yield: 8 servings. Approx Per Serving: Cal 299; Prot 4.9 gr; Carbo 37.8 gr; T Fat 14.0 gr; Chol 69.4 mg; Calc 394.0 mg; Potas 152.0 mg; Sod 2227.0 mg.

1   **cup sifted all-purpose flour**
¼   **cup sugar**
1   **tablespoon baking powder**
½   **teaspoon salt**
1   **cup cornmeal**
1   **egg, beaten**
½   **cup melted butter or margarine**
1   **cup milk**
¾   **cup blueberries**

Chocolate Pastry Torte

Helen Marquiss, Maryland

Preheat oven to 425 degrees. Combine chocolate, sugar, water and coffee powder in saucepan. Cook over low heat until blended, stirring constantly. Stir in vanilla. Cool to room temperature. Combine flour and salt in bowl. Cut in shortening until crumbly. Add ¾ cup chocolate mixture; mix well with fork. Divide into 6 portions. Press each portion into 8-inch cake pan to within 1 inch of side. Bake for 5 minutes. Cool. Whip cream in bowl until soft peaks form. Fold in remaining chocolate mixture. Spread on pastry circles. Stack on serving plate. Chill for 8 hours.

Yield: 12 servings. Approx Per Serving: Cal 467; Prot 6.6 gr; Carbo 30.9 gr; T Fat 38.4 gr; Chol 54.5 mg; Calc 38.7 mg; Potas 135.0 mg; Sod 194.5 mg.

8   **ounces sweet chocolate**
½   **cup sugar**
½   **cup water**
1½   **teaspoons instant coffee powder**
1   **teaspoon vanilla extract**
1½   **cups all-purpose flour**
1   **teaspoon salt**
1   **cup shortening**
2   **cups whipping cream**

Fall

*A*s long as I can remember, Fall has been my favorite season. From the very sound of the word "autumn" to the crunch of leaves underfoot and the smell of woodsmoke from neighborhood chimneys, everything about this season is invigorating. By the end of Summer, I'm ready for the change of tempo the Fall brings.

To me the deepening reds, yellows, and browns of the trees are the cue for one of the year's happiest times. I like the energy of Fall, when school shoes are still shiny and when excited discussions break out over popcorn in our living room on election night. Long walks, given up for most of August in our part of the country, become a daily pleasure again as do incomparable Fall picnics in the park.

This season of special times with family and friends presents the cook with both pleasures and challenges. It's a season when we can flex our culinary muscles. In a matter of weeks, you may very well devise an imaginative and hearty lunch before the game, produce a treat for Halloween trick-or-treaters, turn out hundreds of cookies and dozens of jars of relish for Christmas gift-giving, and spend days on end cooking full-tilt to get ready for the ultimate Thanksgiving feast.

Sweet potatoes, cranberries, turkey, and other native American foods of the season have been Thanksgiving cornerstones for years. A suggested menu from *American Kitchen* magazine for Thanksgiving 1896 included cream of chestnuts, croutons, fricassee of oysters, olives, salted peanuts, roast turkey, giblet stuffing, cranberry sauce, mashed potatoes, diced turnips, new cider, lemon milk sherbet, roast duck, Brussels sprouts, plum jelly, apple and celery salad, cheese, water thin wafers, plum pudding, hard sauce, mince pie, squash pie, fruit, nuts, confectionery, and coffee. And all this, mind you, before the invention of the microwave, the freezer or the self-cleaning oven.

Few of us today would attempt a feast of these epic proportions, our holiday meals are still the most elaborate we prepare all year. They are one of our best gifts to those we care about, an expression of love for family and friends.

Whatever your style of entertaining this season, the key for all of us in these busy days is to enjoy all fall has to offer—the deepening cool of the weather, the foods of this harvest season, and each other.

PHOTOGRAPHS FOR THESE RECIPES ON COVER AND PAGE 36.

HARVEST RICE

1 pound sausage	1/2 cup raisins
3 cups cooked rice	1 tablespoon light
1 tart red apple,	brown sugar
chopped	1/2 teaspoon salt
1/2 cup chopped	1/4 teaspoon allspice
onion	1/4 teaspoon
1/2 cup chopped	cinnamon
celery	1/8 teaspoon pepper

☐ Preheat oven to 350 degrees.
☐ Cook sausage in skillet until brown and crumbly; drain well.
☐ Combine with rice, apple, onion, celery, raisins, brown sugar and seasonings in bowl; mix well.
☐ Spoon into well-buttered 2-quart baking dish.
☐ Bake for 25 minutes.
☐ Yield: 8 servings.

BREAST OF TURKEY EN CROUTE

1/2 cup chopped	1/2 cup shredded
onion	carrots
1/4 cup butter	1/4 cup chopped
1 cup brown rice	parsley
1 1/2 cups chicken	1 (6-pound) turkey
broth	breast
1 cup orange juice	1 cup orange juice
1/2 cup sliced celery	1/4 teaspoon
1/2 teaspoon salt	cinnamon
1/4 teaspoon	1/4 teaspoon
cinnamon	cardamom
1/4 teaspoon	1/8 teaspoon cloves
cardamom	1 (17-ounce)
1/8 teaspoon cloves	package frozen
8 prunes, chopped	puff pastry,
3/4 cup chopped	thawed
walnuts	1 egg, beaten

☐ Preheat oven to 350 degrees.
☐ Sauté onion in butter in skillet.
☐ Add rice. Sauté until golden brown.
☐ Stir in broth, 1 cup orange juice, celery and next 4 seasonings. Simmer, covered, for 40 minutes.
☐ Add prunes, walnuts, carrots and parsley; mix well.
☐ Bone turkey breast carefully; do not separate the two halves.

☐ Place boned side up on flat surface. Fold back thick part of each side of breast to resemble page of book.
☐ Spread about 3/4 cup stuffing on each side; replace breast meat. Spoon 1/2 cup stuffing down center of breast.
☐ Fold sides of breast together to resemble unboned breast; secure with string. Place in shallow baking pan.
☐ Pour mixture of 1 cup orange juice and remaining seasonings over turkey.
☐ Bake for 1 hour, basting frequently with pan juices. Cool for 10 minutes. Spread remaining stuffing over turkey.
☐ Place turkey on one 7x10-inch rectangle puff pastry; fold edges over turkey. Cover with 12x15-inch rectangle puff pastry; tuck edges under.
☐ Cut leaves and acorns from remaining puff pastry. Brush pastry shell with egg; arrange leaves on shell.
☐ Brush with egg. Bake at 400 degrees for 35 minutes or until golden brown.
☐ Cool for 10 minutes before slicing.
☐ Yield: 8 servings.

ORANGE AND CRANBERRY SQUASH

1 orange, peeled	3/4 cup sugar
3 cups fresh	2 tablespoons
cranberries	chopped candied
1 cup orange juice	ginger
1/2 cup chopped	4 small acorn squash
onion	

☐ Preheat oven to 400 degrees. Process orange in blender.
☐ Combine with cranberries, orange juice, onion, sugar and ginger in medium saucepan.
☐ Cook for 20 minutes or until thickened, stirring frequently.
☐ Cut squash into halves; discard seed.
☐ Cut off small piece from bottom to form base. Place cavity side down in shallow baking dish. Add 1/2 inch water.
☐ Bake for 25 minutes.
☐ Turn cavity side up; fill with cranberry mixture.
☐ Bake for 10 minutes longer.
☐ Yield: 8 servings.

Fall Foods

	October	November	December	
BEETS				Vegetables
BROCCOLI				
BRUSSELS SPROUTS				
CAULIFLOWER				
ENDIVE				
COLLARD GREENS				
KALE				
LEEKS				
PARSNIPS				
PUMPKINS				
RUTABAGAS				
SALSIFY				
SWEET POTATOES				
WINTER SQUASH				
TURNIPS				
APPLES				Fruits
COCONUTS				
CRANBERRIES				
FIGS				
GRAPES		GRAPEFRUIT		
ORANGES				
WINTER PEARS				
PERSIMMONS				
POMEGRANATES				
TANGELOS				
TANGERINES				
KIWIFRUIT				
PLUMS	KUMQUATS			
BEEF				Meats
CHICKEN (ROASTERS)				
CHICKEN (STEWERS)				
COD				
OYSTERS				
PORK				
TURKEY				

October

Hibachi Treats

Marla Major, Ohio

1	*(16-ounce) package frankfurters*
1	*pound cooked ham*
1	*(12-ounce) package fresh mushrooms*
4	*cups fresh pineapple cubes*
1	*(16-ounce) can small onions, drained*
1	*(16-ounce) package smoked cocktail sausages*
1	*cup chili sauce*
1	*cup catsup*
1	*teaspoon prepared mustard*
2	*tablespoons lemon juice*
2	*drops of steak sauce*
⅛	*teaspoon garlic salt*
1	*teaspoon brown sugar*

Preheat coals in hibachi until very hot. Cut each frankfurter into 4 pieces. Cut ham into 1-inch cubes. Remove stems from mushrooms. Thread frankfurters, ham, mushrooms, pineapple, onions and sausages onto skewers. Cook over hot coals for 10 minutes or until heated through, turning occasionally. Combine chili sauce, catsup, mustard, lemon juice, steak sauce, garlic salt and brown sugar in bowl; mix well. Arrange skewers on serving platter with sauce in center.

Yield: 10 servings. Approx Per Serving: Cal 498; Prot 25.8 gr; Carbo 28.0 gr; T Fat 31.8 gr; Chol 69.3 mg; Calc 52.0 mg; Potas 818.0 mg; Sod 2424.0 mg.

Bouillabaise

Marilyn McDowell, Washington

Sauté onion, green onions, green pepper and garlic in oil in large saucepan for 5 minutes. Add parsley, tomato paste, tomato sauce, water and seasonings; mix well. Simmer, covered, for 1 hour. Cut fillets into pieces. Add to sauce. Simmer for 10 to 15 minutes or until fish flakes easily. Remove bay leaf. Ladle into serving bowls.

Yield: 8 servings. Approx Per Serving: Cal 264;
Prot 32.3 gr; Carbo 10.0 gr; T Fat 10.5 gr;
Chol 73.1 mg; Calc 63.9 mg;
Potas 1142.0 mg; Sod 280.0 mg.

1   **cup sliced onion**
1   **bunch green onions, chopped**
1   **medium green pepper, chopped**
2   **cloves of garlic, crushed**
⅓   **cup oil**
⅓   **cup chopped parsley**
1   **(6-ounce) can tomato paste**
1   **(8-ounce) can tomato sauce**
4   **cups water**
½   **bay leaf**
⅛   **teaspoon rosemary**
⅛   **teaspoon thyme**
    Salt and pepper to taste
3   **pounds butterfish fillets**

Hot Meatball Sandwiches

Marie Allen, Maine

Preheat oven to 350 degrees. Combine ground beef, ½ cup onion, bread crumbs, milk and minced garlic in bowl; mix well. Shape into small balls. Place in baking pan. Bake for 30 minutes; drain. Sauté ½ cup onion and chopped garlic in oil in skillet. Add tomatoes, tomato purée, cheese, wine, sugar and seasonings. Simmer for 30 minutes. Combine meatballs and sauce in Crock•Pot. Heat on Low until serving time. Serve on rolls.

Yield: 8 servings. Approx Per Serving: Cal 897;
Prot 44.3 gr; Carbo 96.8 gr; T Fat 38.1 gr;
Chol 102.0 mg; Calc 232.0 mg;
Potas 1232.0 mg; Sod 1202.0 mg.

2   **pounds lean ground beef**
½   **cup finely chopped onion**
½   **cup fresh bread crumbs**
¼   **cup milk**
2   **cloves of garlic, minced**
½   **cup chopped onion**
1   **clove of garlic, chopped**
¼   **cup oil**
2   **(28-ounce) cans tomatoes**
2   **cups tomato purée**
¼   **cup Parmesan cheese**
¼   **cup wine**
2   **tablespoons sugar**
1   **tablespoon basil**
    Salt and pepper to taste
8   **large Italian rolls**

Seafoam Salad

1 (3-ounce) package lime gelatin
1 cup boiling water
1 (8-ounce) can juice-pack crushed pineapple
1 cup cream-style cottage cheese
1 teaspoon horseradish
½ cup mayonnaise
½ cup chopped walnuts
6 lettuce leaves
6 maraschino cherries

Dissolve gelatin in boiling water in bowl. Drain pineapple, reserving juice. Stir reserved juice into gelatin. Chill until partially set. Beat until frothy. Fold in pineapple, cottage cheese, horseradish, mayonnaise and walnuts. Pour into 8 x 8-inch dish. Chill until set. Cut into squares. Serve on lettuce leaf. Garnish with cherry.

Yield: 6 servings. Approx Per Serving: Cal 258; Prot 7.7 gr; Carbo 27.2 gr; T Fat 14.3 gr; Chol 10.2 mg; Calc 42.5 mg; Potas 165.0 mg; Sod 328.0 mg.

Chicken and Macaroni Salad

Gail Thompson, Tennessee

3 cups chopped cooked chicken breasts
1 stalk celery, thinly sliced
1 small onion, minced
1 large cucumber, chopped
4 cups cooked macaroni, chilled
¼ cup sliced black olives
¾ cup mayonnaise
1 tablespoon horseradish
Salt and pepper to taste
8 medium avocados

Combine first 6 ingredients in bowl; toss to mix. Blend mayonnaise, horseradish, salt and pepper in small bowl. Add to chicken mixture; toss until coated. Chill until serving time. Serve on avocado halves on lettuce-lined plates.

Yield: 8 servings. Approx Per Serving: Cal 614; Prot 24.1 gr; Carbo 42.1 gr; T Fat 42.0 gr; Chol 49.9 mg; Calc 56.6 mg; Potas 1472.0 mg; Sod 264.0 mg.

Cabbage Salad Supreme

1 (2-pound) cabbage
2 cups drained pineapple chunks
1 (8-ounce) can sliced water chestnuts, drained
1 (11-ounce) can mandarin oranges, drained
1 cup raisins, plumped
1 cup chopped walnuts
¾ cup mayonnaise
1½ teaspoons sugar
2 tablespoons pineapple juice

Shred or finely chop cabbage. Combine with fruit and walnuts in bowl. Blend mayonnaise and remaining ingredients in small bowl. Pour over cabbage mixture. Chill until serving time.

Yield: 8 servings. Approx Per Serving: Cal 345; Prot 5.0 gr; Carbo 50.2 gr; T Fat 17.0 gr; Chol 5.6 mg; Calc 91.9 mg; Potas 651.0 mg; Sod 185.0 mg.

Vermicelli Salad

Karen Stager, Texas

Break vermicelli into 2-inch pieces. Cook using package directions; rinse and drain. Combine with oil, lemon juice and seasoned salt in bowl. Marinate, tightly covered, in refrigerator overnight. Drain well. Add olives, pimento, green onions, celery, green pepper and mayonnaise; mix well. Spoon into serving bowl.

Yield: 8 servings. Approx Per Serving: Cal 434; Prot 8.0 gr; Carbo 50.7 gr; T Fat 23.6 gr; Chol 3.8 mg; Calc 50.1 mg; Potas 248.0 mg; Sod 262.0 mg.

1	*(16-ounce) package vermicelli*
½	*cup oil*
½	*cup lemon juice*
	Seasoned salt to taste
1	*cup chopped black olives*
1	*(4-ounce) jar chopped pimento, drained*
1	*cup chopped green onions*
1	*cup chopped celery*
1	*cup chopped green pepper*
½	*cup mayonnaise*

Herbed Roast Beef

Preheat oven to 325 degrees. Place roast in roasting pan. Combine mustard, parsley, garlic, chives and seasonings in small bowl; mix into paste. Spread on roast. Roast for 20 minutes per pound or to desired degree of doneness. Place on serving plate. Slice thinly. Serve hot or cold.

Yield: 8 servings. Approx Per Serving: Cal 326; Prot 48.9 gr; Carbo 0.3 gr; T Fat 12.8 gr; Chol 138.0 mg; Calc 14.1 mg; Potas 660.0 mg; Sod 401.0 mg.

1	*(3-pound) eye-of-round roast*
1	*tablespoon Dijon-style mustard*
1	*tablespoon chopped parsley*
1	*clove of garlic, minced*
1	*tablespoon chopped chives*
1	*teaspoon mixed thyme, marjoram and rosemary*
1	*teaspoon salt*

Hearty Steak Pie

Joan Jacobs, Illinois

Cut steak into bite-sized pieces. Brown steak and onion in oil in skillet. Add wine, tomato sauce, garlic, basil, thyme, 1 teaspoon salt and ¼ teaspoon pepper. Simmer, covered, for 30 minutes. Place in greased 2-quart baking dish. Preheat oven to 375 degrees. Combine mashed potatoes with remaining ingredients; mix well. Spoon around edge of baking dish. Bake for 25 to 30 minutes or until brown.

Yield: 6 servings. Approx Per Serving: Cal 446; Prot 37.3 gr; Carbo 16.9 gr; T Fat 24.0 gr; Chol 144.0 mg; Calc 107.0 mg; Potas 883.0 mg; Sod 1053.0 mg.

1½	*pounds round steak*
½	*cup chopped onion*
2	*tablespoons oil*
½	*cup dry red wine*
1	*(8-ounce) can tomato sauce*
1	*clove of garlic, crushed*
¼	*teaspoon basil*
¼	*teaspoon thyme*
1	*teaspoon salt*
¼	*teaspoon pepper*
2	*cups mashed potatoes*
2	*tablespoons chopped green onions*
1	*egg, beaten*
¼	*cup melted margarine*
⅓	*cup Parmesan cheese*
	Salt and pepper to taste

Italian Meat Loaf

Nancy Youden, Maryland

4	**slices rye bread, torn**
1	**cup water**
1	**pound lean ground beef**
¾	**cup chopped onion**
½	**cup chopped parsley**
3	**tablespoons Parmesan cheese**
1	**egg**
1	**teaspoon salt**
½	**teaspoon pepper**
1	**(8-ounce) can tomato sauce**
1	**teaspoon oregano**

Preheat oven to 375 degrees. Soak bread in water in bowl for several minutes. Add ground beef, onion, parsley, cheese, egg, salt and pepper; mix well. Shape into loaf in greased shallow baking dish. Bake for 30 minutes. Pour mixture of tomato sauce and oregano over loaf. Bake for 20 minutes longer.

Yield: 4 servings. Approx Per Serving: Cal 439; Prot 34.5 gr; Carbo 19.1 gr; T Fat 25.0 gr; Chol 170.0 mg; Calc 120.0 mg; Potas 710.0 mg; Sod 1229.0 mg.

One-Dish Spaghetti

Lister Endsley, Ohio

1	**tablespoon butter**
1	**cup chopped onion**
1	**clove of garlic, minced**
1	**pound lean ground beef**
2	**cups tomato sauce**
1½	**cups water**
1	**teaspoon parsley flakes**
¾	**teaspoon salt**
¼	**teaspoon pepper**
½	**teaspoon oregano**
½	**teaspoon basil**
4	**ounces spaghetti**
	Parmesan cheese

Combine butter, onion, garlic and crumbled ground beef in 2-quart casserole. Microwave on High for 5 to 6 minutes or until cooked through; drain. Add tomato sauce, water and seasonings; mix well. Microwave for 4 minutes. Break spaghetti into casserole; mix well. Microwave, covered, for 15 to 18 minutes or just until spaghetti is tender, stirring 2 or 3 times. Let stand for 5 minutes. Serve with Parmesan cheese.

Yield: 4 servings. Approx Per Serving: Cal 489; Prot 33.8 gr; Carbo 33.3 gr; T Fat 24.9 gr; Chol 106.5 mg; Calc 49.9 mg; Potas 925.5 mg; Sod 1256.5 mg.

Veal Cutlets Fontana

4	**veal cutlets**
¼	**cup all-purpose flour**
2	**tablespoons oil**
1	**tablespoon minced shallot**
½	**cup dry white wine**
1	**small white onion, sliced**
2	**medium tomatoes, chopped**
1	**large green pepper, sliced**
3	**cups chopped fresh mushrooms**
1	**cup whipping cream**
	Salt and pepper to taste

Pound veal cutlets very thin with meat mallet. Coat lightly with flour; shake off excess. Brown lightly in hot oil in skillet. Drain cutlets; keep warm. Add shallot and wine to skillet; deglaze skillet. Add onion, tomatoes, green pepper and mushrooms. Sauté for 5 minutes. Whisk in cream and salt and pepper. Cook until thickened, stirring constantly. Spoon sauce over cutlets.

Yield: 4 servings. Approx Per Serving: Cal 555; Prot 41.5 gr; Carbo 15.2 gr; T Fat 34.5 gr; Chol 237.0 mg; Calc 66.2 mg; Potas 970.0 mg; Sod 129.0 mg.

Sausage Ring with Cheesy Scrambled Eggs

Elaine Pugh, West Virginia

Preheat oven to 350 degrees. Combine sausage, cracker crumbs, 2 eggs, milk and onion in bowl; mix well. Press into lightly oiled 6-cup ring mold. Invert onto rack in shallow baking pan. Bake for 1 hour. Beat 12 eggs with salt, pepper and cheese in bowl. Scramble in butter in large skillet as desired. Unmold sausage ring onto serving platter. Spoon eggs into center. Garnish with sprinkle of paprika. Arrange apricot halves and parsley sprigs around ring.

Yield: 8 servings. Approx Per Serving: Cal 770; Prot 30.1 gr; Carbo 11.1 gr; T Fat 66.5 gr; Chol 591.0 mg; Calc 245.0 mg; Potas 449.0 mg; Sod 1113.0 mg.

2	*pounds pork sausage*
1½	*cups saltine cracker crumbs*
2	*eggs, slightly beaten*
½	*cup milk*
¼	*cup minced onion*
12	*eggs*
	Salt and pepper to taste
1½	*cups shredded Cheddar cheese*
2	*tablespoons butter or margarine*
	Paprika to taste
8	*canned apricot halves*
	Parsley sprigs

Pork Chalupas

Deanna Floch, Idaho

Soak beans according to package directions; drain. Combine roast, beans, water, onions, green chilies, pimento, garlic and seasonings in Crock•Pot. Cook on High for 5 to 6 hours or until roast and beans are tender. Remove and shred roast. Return shredded pork to Crock•Pot; keep warm. Spread layer of corn chips on serving plates. Spoon pork mixture over chips. Top with tomatoes, avocados, green onions, cheese and taco sauce.

Yield: 10 servings. Approx Per Serving: Cal 817; Prot 60.0 gr; Carbo 42.1 gr; T Fat 44.9 gr; Chol 173.0 mg; Calc 302.0 mg; Potas 1163.0 mg; Sod 1501.0 mg.

1	*pound dried pinto beans*
1	*(3-pound) boneless pork roast*
7	*cups water*
½	*cup chopped onion*
1	*(4-ounce) can chopped green chilies*
1	*(2-ounce) can chopped pimento*
2	*cloves of garlic, minced*
1	*tablespoon salt*
2	*tablespoons chili powder*
1	*tablespoon cumin*
1	*teaspoon oregano*
1	*(12-ounce) package corn chips*
3	*large tomatoes, chopped*
3	*medium avocados, chopped*
½	*cup chopped green onions*
2½	*cups shredded Cheddar cheese*
1	*(8-ounce) bottle of taco sauce*

Liver and Rice Casserole

Linda Sterne, South Carolina

1	**cup rice**
1	**pound sliced calves liver**
¼	**cup chopped green pepper**
½	**cup chopped celery**
1	**medium onion, chopped**
2	**tablespoons oil**
1	**(8-ounce) can tomato sauce**
1	**(16-ounce) can tomatoes**
⅛	**teaspoon thyme**
1½	**teaspoons salt**
½	**teaspoon pepper**
½	**cup shredded sharp Cheddar cheese**

Cook rice according to package directions. Preheat oven to 350 degrees. Cut liver into 1-inch pieces. Sauté liver, green pepper, celery and onion in oil in skillet; drain. Add tomato sauce, tomatoes, rice, thyme, salt and pepper. Spoon into greased 1½-quart casserole. Sprinkle with cheese. Bake for 20 to 30 minutes or until bubbly.

Yield: 4 servings. Approx Per Serving: Cal 638; Prot 42.5 gr; Carbo 54.7 gr; T Fat 27.2 gr; Chol 388.0 mg; Calc 186.0 mg; Potas 1147.0 mg; Sod 1564.0 mg.

Chicken Breasts with Crab Meat

6	**chicken breast filets**
	Salt and pepper to taste
2	**tablespoons all-purpose flour**
½	**teaspoon paprika**
2	**tablespoons melted butter or margarine**
¾	**cup chicken broth**
1	**cup chopped onion**
½	**cup chopped celery**
3	**tablespoons butter or margarine**
1	**cup cooked crab meat**
½	**cup herb-seasoned stuffing mix**
3	**tablespoons dry white wine**
1	**envelope Hollandaise sauce mix**
¾	**cup milk**
2	**tablespoons dry white wine**
½	**cup shredded Swiss cheese**

Preheat oven to 375 degrees. Flatten chicken filets with meat mallet. Sprinkle with salt and pepper. Coat with mixture of flour and paprika. Arrange in shallow baking dish. Drizzle with 2 tablespoons butter. Pour chicken broth into baking dish. Sauté onion and celery in 3 tablespoons butter in skillet. Add crab meat, stuffing mix and 3 tablespoons wine; mix well. Spoon into mound on each chicken breast. Bake for 1 hour. Blend Hollandaise sauce mix and milk in saucepan. Cook until thickened, stirring constantly. Stir in 2 tablespoons wine and cheese. Cook until cheese is melted. Place chicken on serving platter. Spoon sauce over top.

Yield: 6 servings. Approx Per Serving: Cal 567; Prot 49.1 gr; Carbo 25.9 gr; T Fat 28.4 gr; Chol 179.0 mg; Calc 253.0 mg; Potas 567.0 mg; Sod 1390.0 mg.

Broccoli with Lemon Sauce

Barb Sanders, Iowa

Preheat oven to 350 degrees. Cook broccoli spears in a small amount of water in saucepan for 7 minutes or until tender-crisp; drain. Arrange in 9 x 13-inch baking dish. Combine cream cheese, milk, lemon rind, lemon juice and seasonings in mixer bowl. Beat until smooth. Spoon over broccoli. Bake for 15 minutes or until bubbly. Sauté almonds in butter in small skillet until golden brown. Sprinkle over broccoli.

Yield: 6 servings. Approx Per Serving: Cal 213; Prot 8.7 gr; Carbo 11.2 gr; T Fat 16.9 gr; Chol 38.2 mg; Calc 133.0 mg; Potas 607.0 mg; Sod 148.0 mg.

2	**pounds fresh broccoli, trimmed**
6	**ounces cream cheese, softened**
6	**tablespoons milk**
1	**teaspoon grated lemon rind**
1	**tablespoon lemon juice**
½	**teaspoon ginger**
½	**teaspoon cardamom**
½	**cup slivered almonds**
1	**tablespoon butter**

Spinach and Beans with Macaroni

Jim Harmon, New Mexico

Sauté onion, garlic and red pepper in oil in skillet for 3 minutes. Add water. Bring to a boil. Stir in macaroni; reserve cheese sauce mix packet. Cook, uncovered, for 7 minutes, stirring occasionally. Add spinach, beans and cheese sauce mix; mix well. Cook for 5 minutes or until heated through. Add cheese; stir gently until cheese melts.

Yield: 6 servings. Approx Per Serving: Cal 390; Prot 19.6 gr; Carbo 40.8 gr; T Fat 17.9 gr; Chol 29.7 mg; Calc 346.0 mg; Potas 431.0 mg; Sod 487.0 mg.

1	**medium onion, chopped**
2	**cloves of garlic, minced**
¼	**teaspoon crushed red pepper**
3	**tablespoons oil**
3	**cups water**
1	**(7-ounce) package macaroni and cheese dinner**
1	**(10-ounce) package frozen chopped spinach, thawed**
2	**cups drained cooked kidney beans**
1½	**cups shredded Cheddar cheese**

Butternut Squash Casserole

Gerda Mullins, Maryland

Cut squash in half lengthwise; discard seed. Place cut side down in glass baking dish. Microwave, covered, on High for 10 minutes per pound or until tender. Scoop out and mash pulp. Measure 3 cups pulp. Combine with butter, sugar, salt and spices in bowl; mix well. Add milk, eggs and vanilla; beat until smooth. Spoon into greased 2-quart casserole. Preheat oven to 325 degrees. Bake for 45 minutes to 1 hour or until knife inserted in center comes out clean.

Yield: 8 servings. Approx Per Serving: Cal 183; Prot 3.3 gr; Carbo 25.0 gr; T Fat 8.4 gr; Chol 120.0 mg; Calc 50.5 mg; Potas 193.0 mg; Sod 216.0 mg.

1	**medium butternut squash**
¼	**cup butter or margarine**
¾	**cup sugar**
½	**teaspoon salt**
¾	**teaspoon cinnamon**
½	**teaspoon nutmeg**
½	**cup milk**
3	**eggs, beaten**
1	**teaspoon vanilla extract**

Old Fashioned Scalloped Tomatoes

¼ **cup chopped onion**
3 **tablespoons butter**
1 **tablespoon light brown sugar**
   Salt and pepper to taste
⅛ **teaspoon nutmeg**
1¾ **cups toasted bread cubes**
3 **cups drained canned tomatoes**

Preheat oven to 350 degrees. Sauté onion in butter in skillet. Add brown sugar, salt, pepper and nutmeg; mix well. Stir in bread cubes. Layer tomatoes and bread mixture alternately in greased 1-quart baking dish, ending with bread mixture. Bake for 30 minutes.

Yield: 6 servings. Approx Per Serving: Cal 120; Prot 2.4 gr; Carbo 14.3 gr; T Fat 6.6 gr; Chol 15.5 mg; Calc 53.4 mg; Potas 299.0 mg; Sod 312.0 mg.

Arroz con Queso

Rosann Seibel, Maryland

1½ **cups brown rice**
½ **cup dried black beans**
3 **cloves of garlic, minced**
1 **cup chopped onion**
2 **tablespoons oil**
1 **(4-ounce) can chopped green chilies**
8 **ounces ricotta cheese**
¼ **cup milk**
3½ **cups shredded Monterey Jack cheese**

Cook rice and black beans according to package directions. Preheat oven to 350 degrees. Sauté garlic and onion in oil in saucepan. Add rice, beans and chilies; mix well. Combine ricotta cheese, milk and 3 cups Monterey Jack cheese in bowl. Alternate layers of rice mixture and cheese mixture in greased 9 x 13-inch baking dish, beginning and ending with rice. Bake for 25 minutes. Sprinkle with remaining ½ cup Monterey Jack cheese. Bake for 5 minutes longer.

Yield: 8 servings. Approx Per Serving: Cal 430; Prot 20.4 gr; Carbo 35.2 gr; T Fat 23.1 gr; Chol 60.7 mg; Calc 459.0 mg; Potas 283.0 mg; Sod 297.0 mg.

Portuguese Corn Bread

Tara DaSilva, Massachusetts

1 **cup water**
1½ **cups yellow cornmeal**
2 **packages (2 tablespoons) dry yeast**
1 **teaspoon salt**
¼ **cup warm (115-degree) water**
1½ **tablespoons oil**
5 **cups self-rising flour**
2¾ **cups water**

Bring 1 cup water to a boil in saucepan. Pour over cornmeal in bowl; mix well. Cool. Dissolve yeast and salt in lukewarm water. Add yeast mixture, oil, flour and 2¾ cups water to cornmeal; mix well. Let rise, covered, in warm place for 2 hours or until doubled in bulk. Spoon into greased and floured 9 x 13-inch baking pan. Preheat oven to 450 degrees. Bake for 45 to 50 minutes or until golden brown.

Yield: 12 servings. Approx Per Serving: Cal 256; Prot 6.8 gr; Carbo 50.4 gr; T Fat 2.9 gr; Chol 0.0 mg; Calc 143.0 mg; Potas 114.0 mg; Sod 741.0 mg.

Cottage Cheese and Fruit Bread

Donna Lou Keller, Nebraska

Preheat oven to 350 degrees. Cream butter and brown sugar in mixer bowl until light and fluffy. Add eggs 1 at a time, mixing well after each addition. Mix in grated rinds and cottage cheese. Add mixture of dry ingredients gradually. Stir in fruit and pecans. Pour into greased loaf pan. Bake at 350 degrees for 45 minutes or until bread tests done. Cool on wire rack.

Yield: 12 servings. Approx Per Serving: Cal 262; Prot 7.1 gr; Carbo 34.1 gr; T Fat 11.4 gr; Chol 65.1 mg; Calc 49.2 mg; Potas 217.0 mg; Sod 326.0 mg.

6 **tablespoons butter or margarine, softened**
½ **cup packed brown sugar**
2 **eggs**
1 **tablespoon grated orange rind**
1 **tablespoon grated lemon rind**
1½ **cups cream-style cottage cheese**
2 **cups all-purpose flour**
2 **teaspoons baking powder**
¾ **teaspoon soda**
¼ **teaspoon salt**
¼ **cup raisins**
¼ **cup chopped dried apples**
¼ **cup chopped dried apricots**
½ **cup chopped pecans**

Honey and Orange Bread

Preheat oven to 325 degrees. Cream shortening in mixer bowl until light. Beat in egg, orange rind, orange juice and honey. Stir in bran flakes. Sift in flour, baking powder, soda and salt; mix well. Spoon into greased 5 x 9-inch loaf pan. Bake for 1 hour and 10 minutes. Remove to wire rack. Cool. Slice thinly. Toast if desired.

Yield: 12 servings. Approx Per Serving: Cal 217; Prot 3.6 gr; Carbo 46.0 gr; T Fat 2.9 gr; Chol 22.8 mg; Calc 23.2 mg; Potas 93.9 mg; Sod 230.0 mg.

2 **tablespoons shortening**
1 **egg**
1½ **tablespoons grated orange rind**
¾ **cup orange juice**
1 **cup honey**
1 **cup 40% bran flakes**
2½ **cups all-purpose flour**
2½ **teaspoons baking powder**
½ **teaspoon soda**
½ **teaspoon salt**

Whole Wheat Griddle Cakes

Maurine Mader, Missouri

Mix flour, brown sugar and salt in bowl. Add milk and egg yolks; mix well. Beat egg whites until stiff peaks form. Fold into batter. Pour ¼ cup at a time onto hot lightly oiled griddle. Bake until golden brown on both sides.

Yield: 4 servings. Approx Per Serving: Cal 366; Prot 15.0 gr; Carbo 61.8 gr; T Fat 8.1 gr; Chol 153.0 mg; Calc 181.0 mg; Potas 465.0 mg; Sod 360.0 mg.

2 **cups whole wheat flour**
¼ **cup packed light brown sugar**
½ **teaspoon salt**
2 **cups milk**
2 **eggs, separated**

Black Magic

Tracey James, Texas

12	**ounces semisweet chocolate chips**
4	**eggs, separated**
¼	**cup sugar**
1	**cup whipping cream**
1	**bakery angel food cake**
½	**cup chopped pecans**

Melt chocolate chips in double boiler pan over hot water. Beat eggs yolks in bowl. Stir a small amount of hot chocolate into beaten egg yolks; stir egg yolks into chocolate. Cool. Beat egg whites until soft peaks form. Add sugar gradually, beating until stiff peaks form. Whip cream in bowl until soft peaks form. Fold gently into egg whites. Fold chocolate mixture gently into egg white mixture. Tear cake into chunks. Fold cake and pecans into chocolate mixture. Spoon into serving dish. Chill for several hours. Spoon into dessert dishes.

Yield: 10 servings. Approx Per Serving: Cal 452; Prot 7.5 gr; Carbo 50.8 gr; T Fat 27.4 gr; Chol 142.0 mg; Calc 76.7 mg; Potas 247.0 mg; Sod 272.0 mg.

Amaretto and Raisin Bundt Cake

Connie Edgeman, Texas

1	**(15-ounce) package pound cake mix**
½	**cup sour cream**
¼	**cup margarine, softened**
½	**cup water**
⅓	**cup Amaretto**
3	**eggs**
2	**cups candied fruit**
1	**cup raisins**
1	**cup chopped pecans**
1½	**cups sugar**
¼	**cup cornstarch**
1½	**cups water**
¼	**cup Amaretto**
¼	**cup margarine**
2	**tablespoons lemon juice**
½	**cup raisins**

Preheat oven to 325 degrees. Combine cake mix, sour cream, ¼ cup margarine, ½ cup water, ⅓ cup Amaretto and eggs in mixer bowl. Beat at low speed until blended. Beat at medium speed for 2 minutes. Fold in candied fruit, 1 cup raisins and pecans. Pour into greased and floured bundt pan. Bake for 1 hour and 10 minutes or until cake tests done. Cool in pan for 25 minutes. Invert onto wire rack to cool completely. Combine sugar and cornstarch in saucepan. Add 1½ cups water and ¼ cup Amaretto gradually. Bring to a boil over medium heat, stirring constantly. Cook for 1 minute, stirring constantly. Add ¼ cup margarine, lemon juice and ½ cup raisins; mix well. Serve warm sauce over cake slices. Store cake and sauce, tightly covered, in refrigerator.

Yield: 16 servings. Nutritional information not available.

Double Chocolate Brownies

Preheat oven to 350 degrees. Cream margarine, sugar and egg in mixer bowl until light and fluffy. Blend in sour cream and vanilla. Add mixture of flour, cocoa and soda; mix well. Stir in 1 cup chocolate chips. Spoon into greased 9x9-inch baking pan. Bake for 30 to 35 minutes or until brownies pull from side of pan. Cool. Sprinkle with nuts and remaining chocolate chips. Cream margarine and cocoa in small mixer bowl until light and fluffy. Add vanilla, confectioners' sugar and milk. Beat until of spreading consistency. Spread frosting over brownies.

Yield: 24 servings. Approx Per Serving: Cal 215;
         Prot 2.1 gr; Carbo 24.7 gr; T Fat 13.6 gr;
         Chol 13.7 mg; Calc 18.3 mg;
         Potas 96.4 mg; Sod 78.5 mg.

½   **cup margarine, softened**
¾   **cup sugar**
1   **egg**
½   **cup sour cream**
1   **teaspoon vanilla extract**
1   **cup all-purpose flour**
¼   **cup cocoa**
¼   **teaspoon soda**
12 **ounces Hershey's miniature chocolate chips**
½   **cup chopped nuts**
3   **tablespoons margarine, softened**
3   **tablespoons cocoa**
½   **teaspoon vanilla extract**
1¼ **cups confectioners' sugar**
2   **tablespoons milk**

Breakfast Shake

Jan Deister, Kansas

Combine all ingredients and 6 ice cubes in blender container. Process until smooth. Pour into glasses. Serve immediately.

Yield: 4 servings. Approx Per Serving: Cal 119;
         Prot 4.0 gr; Carbo 23.5 gr; T Fat 1.6 gr;
         Chol 69.2 mg; Calc 69.6 mg;
         Potas 382.0 mg; Sod 41.8 mg.

1½ **cups orange juice**
1   **banana, sliced**
¼   **cup dry milk powder**
1   **egg**
1   **tablespoon honey**

Sunny Cider

Combine juices in pitcher. Chill in refrigerator. Pour into frosted glasses. Garnish with orange slices if desired.

Yield: 8 servings. Approx Per Serving: Cal 243;
         Prot 1.7 gr; Carbo 60.3 gr; T Fat 0.3 gr;
         Chol 0.0 mg; Calc 51.6 mg;
         Potas 695.0 mg; Sod 15.1 mg.

6   **cups apple juice**
1½ **cups orange juice**
2   **cups pineapple juice**

November

Vegetable Tart Oriental

½ **(8-roll) package refrigerator
    crescent rolls**
3 **ounces cream cheese, softened**
¼ **cup mayonnaise**
1 **teaspoon soy sauce**
1 **cup sliced mushrooms**
½ **cup sliced water chestnuts**
1 **(6-ounce) package frozen
    snow peas, thawed**
5 **cherry tomatoes, cut into
    halves**
¾ **cup water**
1½ **teaspoons instant chicken
    bouillon**
1½ **teaspoons soy sauce**
1 **tablespoon cornstarch**

Preheat oven to 375 degrees. Unroll dough to form rectangle. Press evenly into 6 x 10-inch baking dish, forming 1-inch rim. Bake for 10 minutes or until golden. Cool. Remove from pan; place on serving tray. Blend cream cheese, mayonnaise and 1 teaspoon soy sauce in bowl. Spread over crust. Drain vegetables on paper towel. Arrange over cream cheese layer. Combine water, bouillon, 1½ teaspoons soy sauce and cornstarch in saucepan; mix well. Cook until thickened, stirring constantly. Cook for 2 minutes longer, stirring constantly. Spoon over vegetables. Chill, covered, until set. Cut into squares.

Yield: 8 servings. Approx Per Serving: Cal 148;
         Prot 3.3 gr; Carbo 13.9 gr; T Fat 9.1 gr;
         Chol 13.6 mg; Calc 17.4 mg;
         Potas 162.0 mg; Sod 454.0 mg.

Beef and Bleu Cheese Crêpe Casserole

Pat Johansen, Iowa

Preheat oven to 350 degrees. Brown ground beef with ½ cup onion in skillet, stirring until ground beef is crumbly; drain. Stir in sour cream, cheese, olives and egg. Simmer for 5 minutes, stirring frequently. Season with pepper and paprika to taste. Place heaping tablespoonful in center of each crêpe; roll to enclose filling. Place in greased 9 x 13-inch baking dish. Brush with melted butter. Bake for 15 minutes. Sauté mushrooms and 2 tablespoons onion in 2 tablespoons butter in skillet. Stir in flour. Add milk gradually. Cook until thickened, stirring constantly. Season with salt and pepper to taste. Spoon over crêpes. Bake for 5 minutes longer.

Yield: 8 servings. Approx Per Serving: Cal 406; Prot 20.7 gr; Carbo 13.3 gr; T Fat 30.7 gr; Chol 162.1 mg; Calc 143.8 mg; Potas 386.9 mg; Sod 295.9 mg.

1	**pound ground beef**
½	**cup chopped onion**
1	**cup sour cream**
⅓	**cup crumbled bleu cheese**
½	**cup chopped black olives**
1	**egg, beaten**
	Pepper and paprika to taste
16	**Crêpes**
2	**tablespoons melted butter or margarine**
1	**cup sliced mushrooms**
2	**tablespoons chopped onion**
2	**tablespoons butter or margarine**
2	**tablespoons all-purpose flour**
1	**cup milk**
	Salt and pepper to taste

Crêpes

4	**eggs**
2	**cups all-purpose flour**
2¼	**cups milk**
¼	**cup melted butter or margarine**

Beat eggs with whisk in bowl. Add flour alternately with milk, mixing well after each addition. Beat in butter until smooth. Chill for 1 hour. Spoon about 1½ tablespoons batter into lightly oiled crêpe pan, tilting to coat pan. Bake until light brown on 1 side. Stack between waxed paper.

Yield: 30 crêpes. Approx Per Crêpe: Cal 63; Prot 2.2 gr; Carbo 6.8 gr; T Fat 3.0 gr; Chol 43.1 mg; Calc 24.8 mg; Potas 40.9 mg; Sod 29.9 mg.

Italian Sausage Polenta Pie

Jean Morzenti, California

1½	**pounds sweet Italian sausage**
1	**cup sliced onion**
1	**clove of garlic, crushed**
1	**(16-ounce) can tomatoes**
1	**(8-ounce) can tomato sauce**
½	**teaspoon sugar**
¼	**teaspoon basil**
½	**teaspoon oregano**
¾	**teaspoon salt**
⅛	**teaspoon pepper**
1½	**cups yellow cornmeal**
¾	**teaspoon salt**
3	**cups boiling water**
1	**cup shredded sharp Cheddar cheese**

Cut sausage into 3-inch pieces. Brown on all sides in skillet. Reduce heat. Cook for 15 minutes, turning occasionally. Drain on paper towel; reserve 1 tablespoon drippings. Sauté onion and garlic in reserved drippings in skillet for 5 minutes. Reserve 3 sausage sections. Slice remaining sausage. Add sliced sausage, tomatoes, tomato sauce, sugar, basil, oregano, ¾ teaspoon salt and pepper to sautéed onion. Bring to a boil; reduce heat. Simmer for 25 minutes. Preheat oven to 375 degrees. Stir cornmeal and ¾ teaspoon salt into boiling water in saucepan. Cook for 2 minutes, stirring constantly. Cool for 5 minutes. Layer cornmeal mixture, sausage mixture and cheese ½ at a time in greased 2½-quart casserole. Split reserved sausages lengthwise. Arrange over layers. Bake, covered, for 25 minutes. Bake, uncovered, for 5 minutes.

Yield: 8 servings. Approx Per Serving: Cal 493; Prot 23.4 gr; Carbo 7.3 gr; T Fat 31.7 gr; Chol 84.2 mg; Calc 159.0 mg; Potas 613.0 mg; Sod 1851.0 mg.

Venison Chili

Sharon Vogel, Illinois

2½	**pounds ground venison**
¼	**cup oil**
1	**large onion, chopped**
2	**cloves of garlic, minced**
1	**large green pepper, chopped**
5	**tablespoons chili powder**
2	**teaspoons sugar**
3½	**cups canned whole tomatoes**
1	**cup tomato sauce**
1	**cup water**
½	**teaspoon salt**
2	**teaspoons cayenne pepper**
2	**cups cooked kidney beans**

Brown venison in oil in heavy saucepan, stirring until crumbly. Add onion, garlic and green pepper. Cook for 5 minutes, stirring constantly; drain. Add chili powder, sugar, tomatoes, tomato sauce, water, salt and cayenne pepper. Simmer for 1½ hours. Stir in kidney beans. Heat to serving temperature.

Yield: 8 servings. Approx Per Serving: Cal 383; Prot 48.0 gr; Carbo 22.8 gr; T Fat 11.4 gr; Chol 92.1 mg; Calc 93.8 mg; Potas 1148.0 mg; Sod 638.0 mg.

Chicken Potpie

Place chicken, sliced onion, celery tops and parsley in saucepan. Add rosemary, salt, peppercorns, bay leaf and water. Simmer, covered, for 1 hour and 30 minutes or until chicken is tender. Strain, skim and reserve stock. Bone chicken. Cook carrots and small onions in 4 cups stock in covered saucepan for 20 minutes. Add peas. Combine flour, seasoned salt, pepper and ½ cup milk in bowl; mix well. Stir into vegetables. Bring to a boil, stirring constantly; reduce heat. Cook for 8 minutes, stirring constantly. Preheat oven to 425 degrees. Combine baking mix, egg and ½ cup milk in bowl; mix well. Knead 10 times on floured surface. Roll ¼ inch thick. Cut with biscuit cutter. Pour vegetables into 3-quart casserole. Add hot chicken. Dip biscuit tops into melted butter. Place biscuits, buttered side up, on casserole. Bake for 20 minutes or until biscuits are brown.

Yield: 12 servings. Approx Per Serving: Cal 891; Prot 59.0 gr; Carbo 105.0 gr; T Fat 26.0 gr; Chol 147.0 mg; Calc 228.0 mg; Potas 1287.0 mg; Sod 1862.3 mg.

1	*(5-pound) chicken, cut up*
1	*large onion, sliced*
3	*celery tops*
3	*sprigs of parsley*
¼	*teaspoon rosemary*
2½	*teaspoons salt*
10	*black peppercorns*
1	*bay leaf*
2	*cups water*
1	*pound baby carrots, peeled*
1	*pound small onions, peeled*
1	*(10-pound) package frozen peas*
½	*cup all-purpose flour*
1	*teaspoon seasoned salt*
⅛	*teaspoon pepper*
½	*cup milk*
2	*cups buttermilk baking mix*
1	*egg, beaten*
½	*cup milk*
½	*cup melted butter or margarine*

Turkey Soufflé

Dorothy McDougall, Minnesota

Combine rice, turkey, onion, celery, pimento, eggs, bread crumbs, broth, 1½ cups milk, poultry seasoning and salt in bowl; mix well. Spoon into 9 x 13-inch baking dish. Refrigerate, covered, overnight. Preheat oven to 350 degrees. Bake for 50 to 55 minutes or until brown and bubbly. Combine soup, ¼ cup milk and sour cream in saucepan. Cook until heated through, stirring constantly; do not boil. Cut soufflé into squares. Serve with mushroom sauce.

Yield: 6 servings. Approx Per Serving: Cal 523; Prot 40.2 gr; Carbo 35.1 gr; T Fat 23.7 gr; Chol 281.0 mg; Calc 223.0 mg; Potas 669.0 mg; Sod 1134.0 mg.

1½	*cups cooked rice*
4	*cups chopped cooked turkey*
¾	*cup chopped onion*
¾	*cup chopped celery*
¼	*cup chopped pimento*
4	*eggs, slightly beaten*
3	*cups soft bread crumbs*
1½	*cups chicken broth*
1½	*cups milk*
¾	*teaspoon poultry seasoning*
¾	*teaspoon salt*
1	*(10-ounce) can cream of mushroom soup*
¼	*cup milk*
1	*cup sour cream*

Roast Turkey with Chestnut Stuffing

1	**pound blanched chestnuts**
1	**(1-pound) loaf day-old bread**
	Milk
1	**medium onion**
2	**cups chopped celery**
14	**pitted green olives**
1	**pound pork sausage**
1	**cup chopped parsley**
¼	**teaspoon thyme**
¼	**teaspoon marjoram**
2	**teaspoons salt**
1	**teaspoon pepper**
1	**(10-pound) oven-ready turkey**
½	**cup apple cider**
2	**tablespoons water**
1	**cup apple cider**
3	**tablespoons melted butter**
	or margarine

Preheat oven to 325 degrees. Spread chestnuts on baking sheet. Roast until skins loosen. Remove and discard skins; cut chestnuts into halves. Crumble bread into large bowl. Add enough milk to moisten. Let stand for several minutes. Grind onion, celery and olives. Add to bread mixture with chestnuts, sausage, parsley and seasonings; mix well. Spoon into turkey. Place turkey in roasting pan. Moisten cheesecloth with ½ cup cider mixed with water. Cover turkey with cheesecloth. Insert meat thermometer through cheesecloth. Bake for 3½ to 4 hours or to 185 degrees on meat thermometer, basting frequently with mixture of 1 cup cider and butter. Let stand for 15 to 30 minutes before carving.

Yield: 8 servings. Approx Per Serving: Cal 1020; Prot 99.7 gr; Carbo 64.2 gr; T Fat 37.8 gr; Chol 271.0 mg; Calc 268.0 mg; Potas 1634.0 mg; Sod 1829.0 mg.

Crab Meat Casserole

Carol Banks, Kentucky

8	**slices bread**
4	**eggs, beaten**
3	**cups milk**
2	**cups crab meat**
1	**medium onion,**
	finely chopped
1	**cup chopped celery**
1	**medium green pepper,**
	finely chopped
½	**cup mayonnaise**
1	**(10-ounce) can cream of**
	mushroom soup
1	**cup shredded Cheddar cheese**
	Paprika to taste

Trim crusts from bread, reserving crusts. Cut 4 slices into cubes. Place bread cubes and reserved crusts in 9x13-inch baking dish. Beat eggs with milk in bowl. Add crab meat, onion, celery, green pepper and mayonnaise; mix well. Pour into prepared baking dish. Top with remaining bread slices. Chill for 6 hours to overnight. Preheat oven to 325 degrees. Bake casserole for 15 minutes. Spread soup over top. Sprinkle with cheese and paprika. Bake for 45 minutes.

Yield: 8 servings. Approx Per Serving: Cal 377; Prot 21.1 gr; Carbo 29.5 gr; T Fat 20.2 gr; Chol 198.0 mg; Calc 295.0 mg; Potas 480.0 mg; Sod 900.0 mg.

Hawaiian Halibut Steaks

Rolla Chambers, Alberta, Canada

Preheat oven to 450 degrees. Arrange fillets in lightly oiled baking dish. Brush with mixture of soy sauce and lemon juice. Sprinkle with sliced green onions, green pepper and tomato. Bake, covered, for 10 minutes or until fish flakes easily. Drain pineapple, reserving juice. Blend reserved juice with cornstarch in saucepan. Cook until thickened, stirring constantly. Add pineapple, Worcestershire sauce, garlic powder and ginger; mix well. Pour over fillets. Bake for 5 minutes longer. Serve with rice.

Yield: 6 servings. Approx Per Serving: Cal 167; Prot 24.5 gr; Carbo 10.2 gr; T Fat 3.0 gr; Chol 36.3 mg; Calc 66.9 mg; Potas 683.0 mg; Sod 338.0 mg.

1½	**pounds halibut steaks**
1½	**tablespoons soy sauce**
1½	**tablespoons lemon juice**
4	**medium green onions, sliced**
¾	**cups chopped green pepper**
1	**medium tomato, chopped**
2	**cups pineapple chunks**
2	**teaspoons cornstarch**
2	**teaspoons Worcestershire sauce**
	Garlic powder and ginger to taste

Brunch Soufflé

Frankie Michealson, Maryland

Trim crusts from bread. Arrange 1 layer bread in buttered 9 x 13-inch baking dish. Combine drained spinach, 2 tablespoons chopped onion, Cheddar cheese and lemon juice in bowl; mix well. Pour over bread. Arrange second layer of bread, mozzarella cheese, tomatoes, mushrooms, ½ cup onion and remaining bread over spinach. Combine eggs, milk, oregano and garlic salt in bowl; mix well. Pour over layers. Top with Parmesan cheese. Chill, covered, in refrigerator overnight. Preheat oven to 325 degrees. Bake for 1½ hours or until set.

Yield: 10 servings. Approx Per Serving: Cal 291; Prot 16.0 gr; Carbo 24.7 gr; T Fat 14.3 gr; Chol 173.0 mg; Calc 362.0 mg; Potas 392.0 mg; Sod 459.0 mg.

12	**thin bread slices**
1½	**(10-ounce) packages frozen chopped spinach, thawed**
2	**tablespoons chopped onion**
1¼	**cups shredded Cheddar cheese**
1	**tablespoon lemon juice**
1½	**cups shredded mozzarella cheese**
1	**(12-ounce) can sliced tomatoes, drained**
1	**cup sliced mushrooms**
½	**cup chopped onion**
5	**eggs, beaten**
3	**cups milk**
	Oregano and garlic salt to taste
	Parmesan cheese

Onion and Wheat Germ Quiche

Lois L. Flick, California

1	**egg**
1	**cup sour cream**
½	**cup minced parsley**
½	**teaspoon tarragon**
¼	**teaspoon salt**
1	**medium onion, thinly sliced**
¼	**cup butter or margarine**
½	**cup wheat germ**
¼	**cup dry white wine**
1	**partially baked Wheat Germ Pie Crust**
½	**cup shredded Monterey Jack cheese**
¼	**cup chopped almonds Parsley sprigs**

Preheat oven to 375 degrees. Beat egg with sour cream in bowl. Stir in parsley, tarragon and salt. Sauté onion in butter in skillet for 4 to 5 minutes. Stir in wheat germ, wine and sour cream mixture. Spoon into pie shell. Sprinkle with cheese and almonds. Bake for 25 minutes or until set. Garnish with fresh parsley sprigs.

Yield: 6 servings. Approx Per Serving: Cal 396; Prot 10.1 gr; Carbo 19.4 gr; T Fat 31.2 gr; Chol 112.7 mg; Calc 162.6 mg; Potas 282.5 mg; Sod 304.8 mg.

Wheat Germ Pie Crust

¼	**cup butter or margarine**
⅔	**cup all-purpose flour**
¼	**cup wheat germ**
4	**to 6 teaspoons water**

Preheat oven to 425 degrees. Cut butter into flour in bowl until crumbly. Mix in wheat germ. Sprinkle with water 1 teaspoon at a time, tossing with fork after each addition until mixture holds together. Press over bottom and side of 9-inch pie plate. Bake for 10 minutes. Cool.

Yield: 1 pie shell. Approx Per Pie Shell: Cal 755; Prot 13.6 gr; Carbo 67.4 gr; T Fat 48.8 gr; Chol 124.0 mg; Calc 39.3 mg; Potas 243.0 mg; Sod 389.0 mg.

Green Beans and Artichokes

2	**(16-ounce) cans French-style green beans**
2	**(8-ounce) cans artichoke hearts**
1	**cup herb-flavored bread crumbs**
½	**cup chopped parsley**
½	**cup Parmesan cheese**
½	**teaspoon garlic powder**
½	**teaspoon onion powder**
½	**olive oil**

Preheat oven to 350 degrees. Drain and rinse green beans. Drain and chop artichokes, reserving ¼ cup liquid. Combine bread crumbs, parsley, cheese, garlic powder and onion powder in bowl. Layer green beans, artichokes and crumb mixture ¼ at a time in 2-quart baking dish. Mix olive oil and reserved artichoke liquid in small bowl. Pour over layers. Bake for 45 minutes.

Yield: 8 servings. Approx Per Serving: Cal 119; Prot 6.2 gr; Carbo 19.7 gr; T Fat 2.7 gr; Chol 4.6 mg; Calc 144.0 mg; Potas 325.0 mg; Sod 644.0 mg.

Creamed Onions with Mushrooms and Carrots

Cook onions in salted boiling water to cover in saucepan for 8 to 10 minutes or just until tender. Remove onions with slotted spoon. Add carrots to cooking liquid. Cook for 3 minutes or just until tender. Drain, reserving ½ cup liquid. Blend butter and flour in saucepan. Cook over medium heat for 2 minutes, stirring constantly. Stir in cooking liquid, milk, salt, thyme and pepper. Bring to a boil, stirring constantly. Simmer for 3 minutes. Add mushrooms. Cook over low heat for 5 minutes. Add onions and carrots. Cook, covered, for 3 minutes. Spoon into serving bowl.

Yield: 8 servings. Approx Per Serving: Cal 90;
          Prot 2.4 gr; Carbo 8.7 gr; T Fat 5.6 gr;
          Chol 15.8 mg; Calc 50.7 mg;
          Potas 247.0 mg; Sod 270.0 mg.

24	*small white onions*
1½	*cups diagonally sliced carrots*
3	*tablespoons melted butter or margarine*
2	*tablespoons all-purpose flour*
1	*cup milk*
¾	*teaspoon salt*
¼	*teaspoon thyme*
⅛	*teaspoon pepper*
8	*ounces mushrooms, thinly sliced*

Maple Sweet Potatoes

Preheat oven to 400 degrees. Place sweet potatoes on baking sheet. Bake for 50 minutes or until tender. Cool slightly; peel. Press through sieve into bowl. Add syrup, butter, cloves and salt; mix well. Spoon into buttered baking dish. Chill in refrigerator if desired. Sprinkle with walnuts. Bake for 20 minutes or until bubbly.

Yield: 8 servings. Approx Per Serving: Cal 242;
          Prot 3.1 gr; Carbo 35.5 gr; T Fat 10.5 gr;
          Chol 15.5 mg; Calc 58.1 mg;
          Potas 449.0 mg; Sod 196.0 mg.

8	*medium sweet potatoes*
¼	*cup maple syrup*
¼	*cup melted butter or margarine*
	Pinch of cloves
½	*teaspoon salt*
½	*cup chopped walnuts*

Brown Rice and Walnut Casserole

Melva Rouse, Florida

Preheat oven to 350 degrees. Combine rice, walnuts, onion, green pepper, mushrooms, celery, parsley, garlic, eggs, coriander and salt in bowl; mix well. Mix in 1½ cups cheese. Spoon into greased 3-quart baking dish. Top with remaining ½ cup cheese. Bake for 30 minutes.

Yield: 10 servings. Approx Per Serving: Cal 284;
          Prot 10.8 gr; Carbo 24.1 gr; T Fat 16.6 gr;
          Chol 78.6 mg; Calc 198.0 mg;
          Potas 225.0 mg; Sod 273.0 mg.

4	*cups cooked brown rice*
1	*cup ground English walnuts*
½	*cup chopped onion*
½	*cup chopped green pepper*
10	*medium mushrooms, sliced*
1	*cup chopped celery*
2	*tablespoons chopped parsley*
1	*clove of garlic, minced*
2	*eggs, beaten*
1	*teaspoon coriander*
½	*teaspoon salt*
2	*cups shredded Cheddar cheese*

Giblet and Mushroom Stuffing

Giblets of 1 turkey
4 cups chopped celery
8 ounces mushrooms, sliced
1 cup chopped onion
1 cup butter or margarine
16 cups soft bread cubes
1 tablespoon salt
1½ teaspoons poultry seasoning
½ teaspoon sage
½ teaspoon pepper
Hot chicken broth

Preheat oven to 350 degrees. Cook giblets in water to cover in saucepan until tender; drain, cool and chop. Sauté celery, mushrooms and onion in butter in skillet. Combine with bread cubes, seasonings, giblets and enough broth to moisten; mix well. Stuff turkey or spoon into greased casserole. Bake casserole, covered, for 45 minutes. Bake, uncovered, for 15 minutes longer.

Yield: 15 servings. Approx Per Serving: Cal 266; Prot 7.1 gr; Carbo 26.3 gr; T Fat 14.8 gr; Chol 77.1 mg; Calc 83.7 mg; Potas 242.0 mg; Sod 811.0 mg.

Dirty Rice Dressing

Maria Hart, Illinois

1 cup long grain rice
Giblets of 1 turkey
¾ cup chopped onion
1 cup chopped celery
Salt and pepper to taste
1 cup chopped onion
1 cup chopped celery
1 cup chopped green pepper
3 tablespoons butter or margarine
½ envelope brown gravy mix
1 cup chopped green onions

Cook rice according to package directions. Cook giblets with ¾ cup onion, 1 cup celery and salt and pepper to taste in water to cover in saucepan until tender; drain. Process in food processor until chopped. Sauté 1 cup onion, 1 cup celery and green pepper in butter in skillet until tender. Add gravy mix according to package directions. Cook until thickened, stirring constantly. Add green onions. Cook for several minutes. Add rice; mix well.

Yield: 10 servings. Approx Per Serving: Cal 151; Prot 6.9 gr; Carbo 20.1 gr; T Fat 4.5 gr; Chol 75.4 mg; Calc 28.9 mg; Potas 195.0 mg; Sod 440.0 mg.

Triple Grain Peanut Butter Bread

Lois Ferguson, California

1 cup all-purpose flour
½ cup quick-cooking oats
½ cup yellow cornmeal
½ cup nonfat dry milk powder
½ cup sugar
1 tablespoon baking powder
½ teaspoon salt
⅔ cup peanut butter
1 egg
1½ cups milk

Preheat oven to 325 degrees. Mix first 7 dry ingredients in bowl. Cut in peanut butter until crumbly. Beat egg and milk in small bowl. Pour into crumb mixture; mix well. Pour into greased loaf pan. Bake for 1 hour and 10 minutes or until bread tests done. Cool in pan for 10 minutes. Remove to wire rack to cool completely.

Yield: 12 servings. Approx Per Serving: Cal 219; Prot 8.6 gr; Carbo 27.0 gr; T Fat 9.3 gr; Chol 27.5 mg; Calc 93.7 mg; Potas 229.0 mg; Sod 263.0 mg.

Golden Onion Loaves

Essie Frost, Oregon

Dissolve yeast in warm water in bowl. Add 2 table-spoons butter, cheese, 2 cups flour, sugar and salt. Beat at medium speed for 2 minutes. Add enough remaining flour gradually to make easily handled dough. Knead on floured surface until smooth and elastic. Place in greased bowl, turn-ing to grease surface. Let rise, covered, in warm place for 30 minutes or until doubled in bulk. Divide into 2 portions. Roll into 11 x 16-inch rectangles on floured surface. Spread with mixture of onion soup mix and ½ cup butter. Roll as for jelly roll from long side; seal edge. Place seam side down on greased baking sheets. Make lengthwise cut halfway through each loaf. Let rise until doubled in bulk. Preheat oven to 350 degrees. Bake for 35 minutes or until loaves test done. Cool on wire rack.

Yield: 24 servings. Approx Per Serving: Cal 145;
Prot 3.6 gr; Carbo 17.9 gr; T Fat 6.5 gr;
Chol 17.4 mg; Calc 35.2 mg;
Potas 43.3 mg; Sod 224.0 mg.

2   **packages (2 tablespoons) dry yeast**
1   **cup warm (115-degree) water**
2   **tablespoons butter or margarine, softened**
1   **cup shredded Velveeta cheese**
2   **cups all-purpose flour**
2   **tablespoons sugar**
1   **teaspoon salt**
2   **to 2½ cups all-purpose flour**
1   **envelope dry onion soup mix**
½   **cup butter or margarine, softened**

Sweet Potato Muffins

Preheat oven to 400 degrees. Cream margarine and brown sugar in mixer bowl until light and fluffy. Blend in eggs. Add sweet potatoes and buttermilk. Beat until smooth. Add mixture of dry ingredients; mix just until moistened. Stir in pecans and raisins. Spoon into greased muffin cups. Bake for 20 to 25 minutes or until brown.

Yield: 18 servings. Approx Per Serving: Cal 166;
Prot 3.0 gr; Carbo 26.6 gr; T Fat 5.6 gr;
Chol 30.7 mg; Calc 36.0 mg;
Potas 140.0 mg; Sod 96.5 mg.

¼   **cup margarine, softened**
¾   **cup packed light brown sugar**
2   **eggs**
1   **cup leftover mashed sweet potatoes**
½   **cup buttermilk**
2   **cups all-purpose flour**
2   **teaspoons baking powder**
1   **teaspoon cinnamon**
1   **teaspoon allspice**
¼   **teaspoon cloves**
½   **cup chopped pecans**
½   **cup raisins**

Applesauce Doughnuts

Jean Cadoret, Vermont

4	**eggs**
1	**cup sugar**
1	**cup packed light brown sugar**
3	**tablespoons oil**
1	**teaspoon vanilla extract**
4½	**cups all-purpose flour**
1	**tablespoon baking powder**
1	**teaspoon cinnamon**
½	**teaspoon cloves**
½	**teaspoon salt**
1	**teaspoon soda**
2	**cups applesauce**
	Oil for deep frying
	Sugar

Beat eggs, 1 cup sugar, brown sugar, oil and vanilla in mixer bowl until thick. Add mixture of flour, baking powder, spices and salt; mix well. Mix soda with applesauce. Stir into batter. Drop by spoonfuls into hot oil. Fry until golden brown. Drain on paper towel. Shake warm doughnuts in bag with additional sugar, coating well.

Yield: 60 servings. Nutritional information not available.

Cranapple Squares

1½	**cups sifted all-purpose flour**
¼	**cup packed light brown sugar**
½	**cup melted butter or margarine**
½	**cup chopped pecans**
6	**cups sliced peeled apples**
2	**cups cranberries**
3	**cups water**
⅓	**cup sugar**
1	**(6-ounce) package peach gelatin**
2	**(3-ounce) packages vanilla pudding and pie filling mix**
8	**ounces whipped topping**
¼	**cup chopped pecans**

Preheat oven to 375 degrees. Mix flour, brown sugar, butter and ½ cup pecans in bowl. Press over bottom of 9 x 13-inch baking dish. Bake for 20 minutes. Cool. Combine apples, cranberries and water in saucepan. Bring to a boil; reduce heat. Simmer for 5 minutes or until apples are tender, stirring frequently. Stir in sugar, gelatin and pie filling mix. Bring to a full rolling boil over high heat, stirring constantly; remove from heat. Let stand for 5 minutes. Pour over cooled crust. Chill in refrigerator. Top with whipped topping; sprinkle with ¼ cup pecans. Chill until serving time.

Yield: 15 servings. Approx Per Serving: Cal 331; Prot 3.1 gr; Carbo 49.9 gr; T Fat 14.3 gr; Chol 16.6 mg; Calc 12.9 mg; Potas 111.0 mg; Sod 170.0 mg.

Midnight Nibbles

Preheat oven to 325 degrees. Combine sugar, butter and water in saucepan. Bring to a boil over medium heat, stirring occasionally. Add chocolate chips; stir until melted. Cool. Add eggs; mix well. Mix flour, soda and salt in bowl. Add chocolate mixture; mix well. Fold in vanilla and nuts. Pour into greased 9-inch square baking pan. Bake for 25 to 30 minutes or until brownies pull from side of pan. Cool. Sprinkle with confectioners' sugar. Cut into squares.

Yield: 24 servings. Approx Per Serving: Cal 115; Prot 1.5 gr; Carbo 12.7 gr; T Fat 7.4 gr; Chol 25.4 mg; Calc 7.5 mg; Potas 56.3 mg; Sod 46.1 mg.

½	**cup sugar**
2	**tablespoons butter or margarine**
2	**tablespoons water**
1⅓	**cups Hershey's miniature chocolate chips**
2	**eggs**
⅔	**cup all-purpose flour**
¼	**teaspoon soda**
¼	**teaspoon salt**
1	**teaspoon vanilla extract**
¾	**cup chopped nuts**
	Confectioners' sugar

Sliced Pumpkin Pie

Edith Woodward, Maine

Prepare pastry. Roll into 2 circles. Line 9-inch pie plate with 1 circle. Peel pumpkin; remove seeds. Slice thinly. Measure 5 cups. Preheat oven to 400 degrees. Combine sugar, flour, lemon juice and spices in bowl; mix well. Add pumpkin slices. Spoon into pastry-lined pie plate. Dot with butter. Top with remaining pastry. Trim and flute edge; cut vents. Bake for 1 hour or until golden brown. Cool.

Yield: 6 servings. Approx Per Serving: Cal 552; Prot 4.9 gr; Carbo 65.7 gr; T Fat 23.7 gr; Chol 15.5 mg; Calc 35.4 mg; Potas 418.0 mg; Sod 418.0 mg.

1	**recipe 2-crust pie pastry**
1	**small pumpkin**
1	**cup sugar**
1	**tablespoon all-purpose flour**
1	**tablespoon lemon juice**
1	**teaspoon cinnamon**
½	**teaspoon nutmeg**
3	**tablespoons butter or margarine**

Hot Spiced Cranberry Tea

Patricia Ann McComas, Missouri

Combine cranberries and 1 cup water in saucepan. Cook until cranberry skins burst. Strain and reserve juice. Tie cloves in cheesecloth bag. Combine with 1 cup water, sugar and candies in saucepan. Bring to a boil, stirring until candies dissolve. Simmer for 5 minutes; remove cloves. Add cranberry juice, lemon juice, orange juice concentrate and 2 cups hot water. Bring just to the simmering point. Pour into cups.

Yield: 4 servings. Approx Per Serving: Cal 240; Prot 0.2 gr; Carbo 62.1 gr; T Fat 0.1 gr; Chol 0.0 mg; Calc 5.9 mg; Potas 53.7 mg; Sod 3.5 mg.

4	**ounces fresh cranberries**
1	**cup water**
3	**whole cloves**
1	**cup water**
1	**cup sugar**
¼	**cup red hot cinnamon candies**
2	**tablespoons lemon juice**
3	**tablespoons frozen orange juice concentrate**
2	**cups hot water**

December

Frozen Fruit Cups

Marcia Nestler, Iowa

1   *(6-ounce) can frozen
    lemonade concentrate*
1   *(6-ounce) can frozen orange
    juice concentrate*
1   *(10-ounce) package frozen
    sliced strawberries*
1   *(8-ounce) can crushed
    pineapple*
2   *medium bananas, sliced*
½   *cup chopped maraschino
    cherries*
½   *cup sugar*
1½ *cups water*

Thaw lemonade, orange juice and strawberries. Combine with pineapple, bananas, cherries, sugar and water in bowl; mix well. Spoon into plastic glasses. Freeze until firm. Let stand at room temperature for 10 minutes before serving.

Yield: 6 servings. Nutritional information not available.

Holiday Pâté

Wash chicken livers and pat dry. Sauté chicken livers and onion in butter in skillet for 10 minutes. Add ¾ cup chicken broth, Sherry, Bourbon, garlic, Tabasco sauce, paprika and salt. Cook for 5 minutes. Place in blender or food processor container. Process until smooth. Soften gelatin in ¾ cup broth in double broiler pan. Heat over boiling water until gelatin is dissolved. Combine with liver mixture and walnuts in bowl; mix well. Pour into 6-cup mold. Chill until firm. Unmold onto serving plate.

Yield: 20 servings. Approx Per Serving: Cal 155;
Prot 7.2 gr; Carbo 1.8 gr; T Fat 12.0 gr;
Chol 162.0 mg; Calc 13.0 mg;
Potas 88.2 mg; Sod 130.0 mg.

1	*pound chicken livers*
1	*small onion, chopped*
¾	*cup butter or margarine*
¾	*cup chicken broth*
2	*tablespoons Sherry*
½	*cup Bourbon*
1	*clove of garlic, minced*
⅛	*teaspoon Tabasco sauce*
½	*teaspoon paprika*
	Salt to taste
1	*envelope unflavored gelatin*
¾	*cup chicken broth*
1	*cup chopped walnuts*

Pear Honey

Combine pears, sugar and pineapple in 5-quart saucepan. Cook for 30 to 45 minutes or until thickened to desired consistency. Pour into hot sterilized jars, leaving ½-inch headspace; seal with 2-piece lids. Process in boiling water bath for 10 minutes.

Yield: 224 tablespoons. Approx Per Tablespoon:
Cal 39; Prot 0.0 gr; Carbo 10.0 gr;
T Fat 0.0 gr; Chol 0.0 mg; Calc 1.0 mg;
Potas 8.7 mg; Sod 0.3 mg.

5	*cups ground firm Kieffer pears*
10	*cups sugar*
2	*cups crushed pineapple*

Velvety Pumpkin Bisque

Contessa Mueller, California

Sauté green onion in butter in 2-quart saucepan over medium heat. Stir in pumpkin, water, brown sugar, bouillon, cinnamon, salt and white pepper. Simmer for 5 minutes or until bubbly. Stir in half and half. Cook just until heated through; do not boil. Ladle into soup bowls. Garnish each with lemon slice and parsley.

Yield: 6 servings. Approx Per Serving: Cal 179;
Prot 3.6 gr; Carbo 12.7 gr; T Fat 13.5 gr;
Chol 40.2 mg; Calc 115.0 mg;
Potas 301.0 mg; Sod 433.0 mg.

2	*tablespoons minced green onion*
2	*tablespoons butter or margarine*
2	*cups pumpkin purée*
1	*cup water*
2	*teaspoons light brown sugar*
1	*chicken bouillon cube*
⅛	*teaspoon cinnamon*
½	*teaspoon salt*
⅛	*teaspoon white pepper*
2	*cups half and half*
1	*lemon, thinly sliced*
	Chopped parsley

Hot Turkey Sandwiches

Jackie Gibson, California

1 **(4-pound) turkey breast**
1 **cup dry white wine**
¼ **cup water**
⅛ **teaspoon sage**
⅛ **teaspoon thyme**
½ **teaspoon salt**
⅛ **teaspoon pepper**
12 **slices pumpernickel bread**
2 **tablespoons all-purpose flour**
12 **(1-ounce) slices Cheddar cheese**
¼ **cup chopped parsley**
¼ **cup chopped almonds**

Preheat oven to 325 degrees. Wash turkey breast and pat dry. Place meaty side down in roasting pan. Bake for 40 minutes. Combine wine, water, sage, thyme, salt and pepper in bowl. Turn turkey breast meaty side up; drizzle with wine sauce. Bake for 45 minutes longer or until tender and golden brown, basting frequently. Remove turkey breast to serving platter; reserve drippings. Let stand for 30 minutes or chill if desired. Slice turkey thinly. Mound slices on pumpernickel bread. Blend flour into reserved drippings. Cook until thickened, stirring constantly. Place open-face sandwiches on baking sheet. Spoon gravy over turkey. Top with cheese. Broil until bubbly. Sprinkle with parsley and almonds.

Yield: 12 servings. Approx Per Serving: Cal 464;
Prot 55.9 gr; Carbo 17.3 gr; T Fat 16.8 gr;
Chol 135.0 mg; Calc 266.0 mg;
Potas 662.0 mg; Sod 539.0 mg.

Frozen Cherry Salad

Joyce McClain, Tennessee

8 **ounces cream cheese, softened**
8 **ounces sour cream**
¼ **cup sugar**
¼ **teaspoon salt**
2 **cups canned dark sweet cherry halves**
1½ **cups chopped peeled red plums**
1 **cup drained crushed pineapple**
2 **cups miniature marshmallows**

Beat cream cheese in mixer bowl until fluffy. Blend in sour cream, sugar and salt. Fold in fruit and marshmallows. Tint with red food coloring if desired. Spoon into 9x13-inch dish. Freeze, covered, for 6 hours. Cut into squares.

Yield: 12 servings. Approx Per Serving: Cal 302;
Prot 3.3 gr; Carbo 51.1 gr; T Fat 6.6 gr;
Chol 29.0 mg; Calc 46.5 mg;
Potas 176.0 mg; Sod 145.0 mg.

Tahitian Steak Strips

Syd Burnett, Texas

Cut steak into ⅛ x 2-inch strips. Brown in shortening in skillet. Add onions and water. Simmer, covered, for 30 minutes. Combine pineapple juice, brown sugar, cornstarch, vinegar, soy sauce and ginger in saucepan; mix well. Cook until thickened, stirring constantly. Stir into steak mixture. Add pineapple and mushrooms. Simmer, covered, for 5 minutes. Slice tomatoes and avocado into wedges. Add to skillet. Cook until heated through. Serve over rice.

Yield: 8 servings. Approx Per Serving: Cal 551; Prot 37.3 gr; Carbo 65.8 gr; T Fat 15.0 gr; Chol 93.4 mg; Calc 51.3 mg; Potas 926.0 mg; Sod 764.0 mg.

2	**pounds (½-inch thick) round steak**
1	**tablespoon shortening**
2	**medium onions, sliced**
½	**cup water**
⅔	**cup pineapple juice**
½	**cup packed light brown sugar**
2	**tablespoons cornstarch**
2	**tablespoons vinegar**
⅓	**cup soy sauce**
1	**teaspoon ginger**
2	**cups fresh pineapple chunks**
1	**cup sliced mushrooms**
2	**medium tomatoes**
1	**medium avocado**
6	**cups hot cooked rice**

Pork Crown Roast with Cranberries

Preheat oven to 325 degrees. Place crown roast in roasting pan. Cover ends of bones with foil. Sauté bread cubes, onion and garlic in butter in skillet for 10 minutes. Add cranberries, sugar, wine and seasonings; mix well. Spoon into center of roast. Roast for 3½ hours or to 185 degrees on meat thermometer. Remove roast with stuffing carefully to serving platter. Replace foil with white paper frills.

Yield: 10 servings. Approx Per Serving: Cal 1014; Prot 106.0 gr; Carbo 13.0 gr; T Fat 56.1 gr; Chol 360.0 mg; Calc 51.4 mg; Potas 1366.0 mg; Sod 590.0 mg.

1	**(7-pound) pork crown roast**
4	**cups bread cubes**
2	**tablespoons grated onion**
1	**clove of garlic, minced**
½	**cup butter or margarine**
1½	**cups chopped fresh cranberries**
¼	**cup sugar**
½	**cup dry white wine**
½	**teaspoon marjoram**
¼	**teaspoon thyme**
1	**teaspoon salt**
	Freshly ground pepper to taste

Meatball Shepherd's Pie

Scheree Krueger, Wisconsin

1½	cups green peas
1½	cups sliced carrots
1½	pounds ground beef
½	cup dry bread crumbs
¼	cup chopped onion
1	egg
½	cup milk
1	teaspoon marjoram
2	teaspoons salt
	Pepper to taste
⅓	cup oil
1	cup sliced mushrooms
¼	cup chopped onion
1	(10-ounce) can cream of mushroom soup
½	cup milk
1	teaspoon Worcestershire sauce
¼	cup beef bouillon
3	cups mashed potatoes
	Paprika to taste

Preheat oven to 350 degrees. Cook peas and carrots separately in a small amount of water in saucepan until tender. Drain. Combine ground beef, bread crumbs, ¼ cup onion, egg, ½ cup milk, marjoram, salt and pepper in bowl; mix well. Shape into 36 meatballs. Brown on all sides in oil in skillet; remove with slotted spoon. Drain skillet, reserving 2 tablespoons drippings. Sauté mushrooms and ¼ cup onion in pan drippings. Stir in soup, ½ cup milk, Worcestershire sauce and beef bouillon. Bring to a boil. Place meatballs, peas and carrots in 3-quart baking dish. Pour soup mixture over top. Spoon mashed potatoes around edge. Sprinkle potatoes with paprika. Bake for 30 minutes or until bubbly.

Yield: 8 servings. Approx Per Serving: Cal 501; Prot 27.9 gr; Carbo 30.8 gr; T Fat 30.4 gr; Chol 115.0 mg; Calc 105.0 mg; Potas 764.0 mg; Sod 1243.0 mg.

Baked Chicken Curry

3	pounds chicken pieces
¼	cup all-purpose flour
1	teaspoon salt
¼	teaspoon pepper
2	tablespoons butter or margarine
1	cup beef consommé
8	ounces bacon, chopped
½	cup chopped onion
1	tablespoon curry powder
1	tablespoon applesauce
1	tablespoon tomato sauce
1	teaspoon sugar
¼	cup lemon juice
1	tablespoon all-purpose flour
1	tablespoon cream
	Garlic powder to taste
1	cup flaked coconut
2	cups hot cooked rice

Preheat oven to 450 degrees. Coat chicken with mixture of ¼ cup flour, salt and pepper. Place skin side up in baking pan. Dot with butter. Bake for 20 minutes. Combine consommé, bacon, onion, curry powder, applesauce, tomato sauce, sugar, lemon juice, 1 tablespoon flour, cream and garlic powder in saucepan; mix well. Cook for 10 to 15 minutes, stirring occasionally. Spoon over chicken; sprinkle with coconut. Reduce oven temperature to 350 degrees. Bake for 30 minutes longer or until chicken is tender. Serve over rice.

Yield: 4 servings. Approx Per Serving: Cal 941; Prot 71.4 gr; Carbo 39.7 gr; T Fat 53.9 gr; Chol 217.0 mg; Calc 65.9 mg; Potas 902.0 mg; Sod 1856.0 mg.

Broccoli Elegant
Dot Ogden, Maryland

Preheat oven to 350 degrees. Cut broccoli into spears. Cook in a small amount of water in saucepan until tender-crisp; drain. Bring ¼ cup margarine and 1½ cups water to a boil in saucepan; remove from heat. Stir in stuffing mix. Let stand, covered, for 5 minutes. Spoon around edge of buttered 9 x 13-inch baking dish. Arrange broccoli spears in center. Blend flour into 2 tablespoons melted butter in heavy saucepan. Cook over low heat for 1 minute, stirring constantly. Add bouillon and milk gradually. Cook until thickened, stirring constantly. Add cream cheese and salt. Stir until smooth. Stir in green onions. Spoon over broccoli. Sprinkle with cheese and paprika. Bake, covered, for 35 minutes. Bake, uncovered, for 10 minutes longer.

Yield: 6 servings. Approx Per Serving: Cal 338;
Prot 10.9 gr; Carbo 19.6 gr; T Fat 24.5 gr;
Chol 39.6 mg; Calc 228.0 mg;
Potas 345.0 mg; Sod 874.0 mg.

2	**bunches broccoli**
¼	**cup margarine**
1½	**cups water**
1	**(6-ounce) package corn bread stuffing mix**
2	**tablespoons all-purpose flour**
2	**tablespoons margarine**
1	**chicken bouillon cube**
¾	**cup milk**
3	**ounces cream cheese, softened**
¼	**teaspoon salt**
4	**medium green onions, sliced**
1	**cup shredded Cheddar cheese Paprika to taste**

Christmas Cabbage
Mary Muller, Arkansas

Slice cabbages into separate bowls. Combine red cabbage, vinegar, sugar, ½ teaspoon salt and 3 tablespoons oil in saucepan. Cook for 25 minutes or until cabbage is tender, stirring occasionally. Stir in peas. Cook until heated through. Combine green cabbage with remaining ingredients in saucepan. Cook for 20 minutes or until cabbage and onion are tender, stirring occasionally. Arrange as desired on serving platter.

Yield: 10 servings. Approx Per Serving: Cal 115;
Prot 2.3 gr; Carbo 8.7 gr; T Fat 8.4 gr;
Chol 0.0 mg; Calc 38.5 mg;
Potas 196.0 mg; Sod 246.0 mg.

1	**medium head red cabbage**
1	**medium head green cabbage**
2	**tablespoons red wine vinegar**
1	**teaspoon sugar**
½	**teaspoon salt**
3	**tablespoons oil**
1	**(10-ounce) package frozen peas**
1	**medium onion, chopped**
½	**teaspoon caraway seed**
½	**teaspoon salt**
3	**tablespoons oil**

Spinach and Mushroom Casserole

4 (10-ounce) packages frozen
   chopped spinach
1 pound mushrooms, sliced
¼ cup butter or margarine
⅓ cup mayonnaise
⅔ cup sour cream
⅔ cup Parmesan cheese
2 medium tomatoes, sliced
⅔ cup bread crumbs
½ cup melted butter or
   margarine
⅓ cup Swiss cheese

Preheat oven to 350 degrees. Cook spinach according to package directions; drain well. Sauté mushrooms in ¼ cup butter in skillet. Combine mayonnaise, sour cream and Parmesan cheese in bowl; mix well. Stir in spinach and mushrooms. Spoon into buttered 9x13-inch baking pan. Arrange tomato slices over top. Mix bread crumbs, melted butter and Swiss cheese in small bowl. Sprinkle over casserole. Bake for 20 minutes or until bubbly and brown.

Yield: 8 servings. Approx Per Serving: Cal 351; Prot 11.4 gr; Carbo 17.0 gr; T Fat 28.7 gr; Chol 67.5 mg; Calc 388.0 mg; Potas 747.0 mg; Sod 508.0 mg.

Applesauce Bread

Lyn Bell Agellyrs, Maryland

1   cup raisins
5   tablespoons Brandy
½   cup butter or margarine,
     softened
1   cup sugar
1   egg, beaten
1⅔   cups all-purpose flour
1   teaspoon soda
½   teaspoon salt
1   teaspoon cinnamon
½   teaspoon nutmeg
¼   teaspoon allspice
¼   teaspoon cloves
1   cup applesauce
1   cup chopped pecans
⅓   cup all-purpose flour

Combine raisins and Brandy in bowl. Chill, covered, overnight. Preheat oven to 350 degrees. Cream butter and sugar in mixer bowl until light and fluffy. Beat in egg. Combine 1⅔ cups flour, soda, salt and spices in bowl. Add to creamed mixture alternately with applesauce, beginning and ending with flour. Drain raisins, reserving Brandy. Stir Brandy into batter. Toss raisins and pecans with ⅓ cup flour to coat. Fold into batter. Pour into greased and floured loaf pan. Bake for 1 hour and 15 minutes or until loaf tests done. Cool in pan for 10 minutes. Remove to wire rack to cool completely. Store, tightly wrapped in foil, in refrigerator.

Yield: 12 servings. Approx Per Serving: Cal 346; Prot 3.8 gr; Carbo 50.3 gr; T Fat 15.1 gr; Chol 43.5 mg; Calc 20.2 mg; Potas 182.0 mg; Sod 231.0 mg.

Brown Rice Muffins

Michelle Mahoney, Indiana

Preheat oven to 375 degrees. Combine walnuts, pineapple, honey, dates, eggs, oil, rice and buttermilk in bowl; mix well. Add mixture of flour, brown sugar, soda and cinnamon. Spoon into greased muffin cups. Bake for 25 minutes.

Yield: 12 servings. Approx Per Serving: Cal 246; Prot 5.7 gr; Carbo 43.2 gr; T Fat 7.0 gr; Chol 46.4 mg; Calc 53.5 mg; Potas 253.0 mg; Sod 140.0 mg.

½	**cup chopped walnuts**
⅓	**cup crushed pineapple**
⅓	**cup honey**
⅔	**cup chopped dates**
2	**eggs**
2	**tablespoons corn oil**
1	**cup cooked brown rice**
1	**cup buttermilk**
2	**cups whole wheat flour**
⅓	**cup packed light brown sugar**
1½	**teaspoons soda**
1½	**teaspoons cinnamon**

Christmas Muffins

Kathy Smith, Maryland

Preheat oven to 375 degrees. Sprinkle cranberries with ¼ cup sugar in bowl. Let stand for several minutes. Combine flour, ¼ cup sugar, baking powder, cinnamon, allspice and salt in bowl. Make well in center. Mix orange juice, egg, orange rind and butter in bowl. Pour into well; stir just until moistened. Fold in cranberries and walnuts. Spoon into greased muffin cups. Bake for 15 to 20 minutes or until golden.

Yield: 12 servings. Approx Per Serving: Cal 163; Prot 2.6 gr; Carbo 22.6 gr; T Fat 7.2 gr; Chol 36.5 mg; Calc 21.4 mg; Potas 69.6 mg; Sod 282.0 mg.

1	**cup fresh cranberries, coarsely chopped**
¼	**cup sugar**
1½	**cups all-purpose flour**
¼	**cup sugar**
2	**teaspoons baking powder**
½	**teaspoon cinnamon**
¼	**teaspoon allspice**
1	**teaspoon salt**
¾	**cup orange juice**
1	**egg, beaten**
¼	**teaspoon grated orange rind**
⅓	**cup melted butter**
¼	**cup chopped walnuts**

Peppery Cheese Bread

Bernadette Harrison, New York

Dissolve yeast in warm water in mixer bowl. Add 1⅓ cups flour, sugar, salt, soda, sour cream and egg. Beat for 2 minutes. Stir in 1 cup flour, cheese and pepper. Spoon into 2 greased 1-pound coffee cans. Let rise in warm place for 1 hour. Batter will rise but not double. Preheat oven to 350 degrees. Bake for 40 minutes or until brown. Remove from cans. Cool on wire rack.

Yield: 24 servings. Approx Per Serving: Cal 88; Prot 3.0 gr; Carbo 10.1 gr; T Fat 3.9 gr; Chol 20.6 mg; Calc 48.8 mg; Potas 37.6 mg; Sod 135.0 mg.

1	**package (1 tablespoon) dry yeast**
¼	**cup warm (115-degree) water**
1⅓	**cups all-purpose flour**
2	**tablespoons sugar**
1	**teaspoon salt**
¼	**teaspoon soda**
1	**cup sour cream**
1	**egg**
1	**cup all-purpose flour**
1	**cup shredded Cheddar cheese**
¼	**teaspoon pepper**

Whole Wheat Zucchini Bread

Wanda Doud, Oregon

3	**eggs**
1	**cup sugar**
1½	**cups packed light brown sugar**
2	**teaspoons black walnut flavoring**
1	**teaspoon vanilla extract**
1	**cup oil**
2	**cups shredded zucchini**
2	**cups whole wheat flour**
1	**cup all-purpose flour**
2	**teaspoons baking powder**
1	**teaspoon soda**
1	**teaspoon salt**
1	**tablespoon cinnamon**
1	**cup chopped walnuts**

Preheat oven to 350 degrees. Beat eggs in mixer bowl until thick and lemon-colored. Add sugars, flavorings and oil; mix well. Stir in zucchini. Add sifted dry ingredients. Stir in walnuts. Pour into 2 greased 5 x 9-inch loaf pans. Bake for 1 hour or until loaves test done. Cool on wire rack.

Yield: 24 servings. Approx Per Serving: Cal 259;
Prot 3.4 gr; Carbo 34.0 gr; T Fat 13.1 gr;
Chol 34.2 mg; Calc 32.2 mg;
Potas 161.0 mg; Sod 167.0 mg.

Frozen Plum Pudding

Sally Brunson, Indiana

½	**cup sugar**
5	**egg yolks**
½	**cup sugar**
¼	**teaspoon salt**
2	**cups milk**
2½	**cups light cream**
8	**ounces macaroons, crushed**
¾	**cup finely chopped candied fruit**
⅓	**cup golden raisins**
½	**cup chopped almonds**

Sprinkle ½ cup sugar in heavy skillet. Cook over low heat until melted and light brown, stirring constantly. Cool. Beat egg yolks, ½ cup sugar and salt in mixer bowl. Bring milk to the boiling point in double boiler pan. Stir a small amount of hot milk into egg mixture; stir eggs into hot milk. Cook over hot water until thickened, stirring constantly. Stir in caramelized sugar. Cool. Stir in cream gradually. Fold in crushed macaroons, candied fruit, raisins and almonds. Pour into shallow dish. Freeze until firm.

Nutritional information not available.

Christmas Spice Cake

Preheat oven to 350 degrees. Grease four 8-inch round cake pans; line bottoms with greased waxed paper. Cream butter and sugar in mixer bowl until light and fluffy. Beat eggs with milk in small bowl. Sift flour and baking powder together. Add flour mixture to creamed mixture alternately with egg mixture, beginning and ending with flour mixture and mixing well after each addition. Add vanilla. Spoon half the batter into 2 prepared pans. Stir spices and raisins into remaining batter. Spoon into 2 remaining pans. Bake for 30 to 35 minutes or until layers test done. Cool in pans for several minutes. Invert onto wire racks to cool completely; remove waxed paper. Mix cranberry sauce and 1 can coconut in bowl. Spread evenly on cake layers. Stack plain and raisin layers alternately on cake plate. Sprinkle with remaining coconut.

Yield: 16 servings. Approx Per Serving: Cal 557;
          Prot 6.7 gr; Carbo 97.5 gr; T Fat 18.1 gr;
          Chol 108.0 mg; Calc 60.9 mg;
          Potas 440.0 mg; Sod 167.0 mg.

1	*cup butter or margarine, softened*
2	*cups sugar*
4	*eggs*
1	*cup milk*
3¼	*cups sifted all-purpose flour*
1	*teaspoon baking powder*
1	*teaspoon vanilla extract*
1	*teaspoon cinnamon*
1	*teaspoon allspice*
¼	*teaspoon cloves*
4	*cups raisins*
1	*(16-ounce) can whole cranberry sauce*
1½	*(3½-ounce) cans flaked coconut*

Frosted Black Walnut Cake

Thelma Borger, Iowa

Preheat oven to 350 degrees. Beat sugar with cream in bowl until well mixed. Add flour gradually, mixing well after each addition. Stir in black walnuts, baking powder and salt. Add eggs; mix well. Pour into 3 greased and floured 9-inch cake pans. Bake for 25 minutes or until cake tests done. Remove to wire rack to cool. Spread Black Walnut Frosting between layers and over top and side of cake.

Yield: 16 servings. Approx Per Serving: Cal 358;
          Prot 8.0 gr; Carbo 58.6 gr; T Fat 10.9 gr;
          Chol 101.0 mg; Calc 92.4 mg;
          Potas 164.0 mg; Sod 133.0 mg.

2	*cups sugar*
2	*cups cream*
3	*cups all-purpose flour*
½	*cup chopped black walnuts*
1	*tablespoon baking powder*
	Pinch of salt
3	*eggs*

Black Walnut Frosting

Combine sugar, cornstarch and eggs in saucepan; mix well. Stir in milk gradually. Cook over low heat until thickened, stirring constantly. Stir in black walnuts. Cool until of desired spreading consistency.

1	*cup sugar*
2	*tablespoons cornstarch*
2	*eggs*
2	*cups milk*
½	*cup chopped black walnuts*

Pecan Candy Logs

1 *(7-ounce) jar marshmallow creme*
1 *(16-ounce) package confectioners' sugar*
1 *tablespoon vanilla extract*
1 *(14-ounce) package light caramels*
3 *tablespoons evaporated milk*
3 *cups finely chopped pecans*

Combine marshmallow creme and confectioners' sugar in bowl or plastic bag; mix well. Mixture will be stiff and dry. Add vanilla. Knead until mixture holds together. Shape into four 1½-inch diameter logs. Place in waxed paper-lined dish. Freeze for 1 hour. Combine caramels and evaporated milk in double boiler pan. Cook over hot water until caramels melt. Dip marshmallow rolls in caramel mixture to coat or spoon caramel over rolls. Coat with pecans. Let stand until caramel is cool. Chill until firm. Store, wrapped in plastic wrap, in refrigerator. Cut into slices.

Yield: 48 servings. Approx Per Serving: Cal 134; Prot 1.0 gr; Carbo 20.5 gr; T Fat 6.0 gr; Chol 0.6 mg; Calc 18.8 mg; Potas 49.5 mg; Sod 22.4 mg.

Holiday Toffee

½ *cup boiling water*
1 *cup packed light brown sugar*
1 *cup sugar*
⅓ *cup light corn syrup*
⅛ *teaspoon salt*
⅓ *cup butter or margarine*
1 *cup semisweet chocolate chips, melted*
¾ *cup chopped toasted almonds*

Combine boiling water, brown sugar, sugar, corn syrup and salt in saucepan. Stir until sugars are completely dissolved. Cook, covered, over high heat for 2 minutes or until steam washes sugar crystals from side of pan. Cook, uncovered, to 240 degrees on candy thermometer, firm-ball stage; do not stir. Add butter. Cook to 300 degrees on candy thermometer, hard-crack stage; do not stir. Pour into lightly buttered 9 x 13-inch dish. Let stand until firm. Blot with paper towel. Spread half the melted chocolate over top; sprinkle with half the almonds. Let stand until chocolate is set. Invert onto waxed paper-lined surface; blot with paper towel. Spread with remaining chocolate; sprinkle with remaining almonds. Let stand until chocolate is set. Break into pieces.

Yield: 32 ounces. Approx Per Ounce: Cal 134; Prot 1.3 gr; Carbo 19.6 gr; T Fat 6.5 gr; Chol 5.1 mg; Calc 24.7 mg; Potas 84.8 mg; Sod 33.6 mg.

Almond Crisps

Bobby Easton, California

Preheat oven to 350 degrees. Beat eggs with oil and sugar in bowl until thick and lemon-colored. Add flour, baking powder, almonds, lemon juice, lemon rind and vanilla; mix well. Shape into six 1 x 12-inch rolls. Sprinkle with cinnamon-sugar. Bake for 30 minutes. Cool. Slice rolls diagonally ½ inch thick. Place on baking sheet. Bake for 15 minutes on each side or until brown.

Yield: 144 cookies. Approx Per Cookie: Cal 38; Prot 0.7 gr; Carbo 4.1 gr; T Fat 2.2 gr; Chol 7.6 mg; Calc 5.5 mg; Potas 12.4 mg; Sod 11.3 mg.

4	**eggs**
1	**cup oil**
1	**cup sugar**
4	**cups all-purpose flour**
4	**teaspoons baking powder**
1	**cup slivered almonds**
	Juice and grated rind of 1 lemon
1	**tablespoon vanilla extract Cinnamon-sugar**

Mini-Chip Brownies

Preheat oven to 350 degrees. Combine butter, brown sugar, egg and vanilla in mixer bowl. Beat until light and fluffy. Add mixture of flour and salt; mix just until blended. Stir in chocolate chips. Pour into greased 9-inch square baking pan. Bake for 25 minutes or until brownies pull from side of pan. Cool. Cut into squares.

Yield: 24 servings. Approx Per Serving: Cal 125; Prot 1.1 gr; Carbo 16.5 gr; T Fat 6.7 gr; Chol 21.8 mg; Calc 13.3 mg; Potas 64.7 mg; Sod 84.7 mg.

½	**cup melted butter or margarine**
1	**cup packed light brown sugar**
1	**egg**
1	**teaspoon vanilla extract**
1	**cup all-purpose flour**
½	**teaspoon salt**
1	**cup Hershey's miniature chocolate chips**

Orange Florentines

Preheat oven to 350 degrees. Combine orange peel, almonds, sugar, milk and flour in bowl; mix well. Batter will be thin. Drop by spoonfuls onto heavily greased cookie sheet. Flatten with back of spoon. Bake for 15 minutes. Remove immediately with spatula to wire rack, reshaping gently with fingers. Cool. Place cookies upside down on serving plate. Spread with chocolate. Chill until firm.

Yield: 12 servings. Nutritional information not available.

¾	**cup finely chopped candied orange peel**
1	**cup slivered blanched almonds**
½	**cup sugar**
⅓	**cup milk**
2	**tablespoons all-purpose flour**
2	**ounces semisweet dipping chocolate, melted**

Minty Chocolate Pies

Dollee Meredith, Washington

2 cups crushed chocolate wafers
¼ cup melted margarine
½ cup margarine, softened
1½ cups confectioners' sugar
3 eggs, beaten
2½ (1-ounce) squares unsweetened chocolate, melted
¼ teaspoon peppermint extract
¼ teaspoon vanilla extract
2 cups whipping cream
1 (10-ounce) package miniature marshmallows
½ cup crushed peppermint candy
Chocolate curls

Mix cookie crumbs and melted margarine in bowl. Press over bottom of 2 greased 9-inch pie plates. Cream ½ cup margarine and confectioners' sugar in mixer bowl until light and fluffy. Add eggs, melted chocolate and flavorings; beat until smooth. Spread in prepared pie plates. Freeze for several minutes or until firm. Whip cream in mixer bowl until soft peaks form. Fold in marshmallows. Spread over chocolate layers. Sprinkle with crushed candy and chocolate curls. Chill until serving time.

Yield: 12 servings. Approx Per Serving: Cal 527; Prot 3.2 gr; Carbo 58.9 gr; T Fat 32.9 gr; Chol 67.7 mg; Calc 45.9 mg; Potas 114.0 mg; Sod 252.0 mg.

Custard Crunch Pie

Barbie Lamie, Oklahoma

3 eggs, well beaten
1 cup sugar
¼ cup melted margarine
1 cup milk
3 tablespoons all-purpose flour
¼ cup maple syrup
1 teaspoon vanilla extract
¼ cup quick-cooking oats
½ cup coconut
¼ cup chopped pecans
1 unbaked 9-inch pie shell

Preheat oven to 350 degrees. Combine eggs, sugar, margarine, milk, flour, maple syrup and vanilla in bowl. Beat until smooth. Stir in oats, coconut and pecans. Pour into pie shell. Bake for 30 minutes or until set.

Yield: 6 servings. Approx Per Serving: Cal 527; Prot 7.8 gr; Carbo 64.1 gr; T Fat 27.6 gr; Chol 142.0 mg; Calc 91.8 mg; Potas 183.0 mg; Sod 328.0 mg.

Coffee Grogg

Pam Simmons, Indiana

Place 1 teaspoon Grogg Mix in each of six 6-ounce mugs. Add 1 strip lemon rind, 1 strip orange rind and 2 tablespoons cream to each mug. Fill mugs with hot coffee.

Yield: 6 servings. Approx Per Serving: Cal 134; Prot 0.9 gr; Carbo 8.1 gr; T Fat 11.4 gr; Chol 41.7 mg; Calc 43.4 mg; Potas 153.9 mg; Sod 26.6 mg.

2	**tablespoons Coffee Grogg Mix**
6	**strips lemon rind**
6	**strips orange rind**
¾	**cup heavy cream**
4¼	**cups hot coffee**

Coffee Grogg Mix

Cream butter in mixer bowl until light and fluffy. Add brown sugar gradually, mixing until smooth. Add salt, flavoring and spices; mix well. Store in covered containers in refrigerator.

Yield: 60 teaspoons. Approx Per Teaspoon: Cal 22; Prot 0.0 gr; Carbo 4.7 gr; T Fat 0.4 gr; Chol 1.0 mg; Calc 4.3 mg; Potas 16.9 mg; Sod 11.6 mg.

2	**tablespoons butter or margarine, softened**
1⅓	**cups packed light brown sugar Dash of salt**
1	**teaspoon rum flavoring**
⅛	**teaspoon cinnamon**
⅛	**teaspoon nutmeg**
⅛	**teaspoon allspice**
⅛	**teaspoon cloves**

Hot Strawberry Tea

Crush 1 cup strawberries. Combine with tea, cloves, cinnamon and mint in large teapot. Add boiling water. Steep for 5 minutes. Stir in sugar. Strain. Add remaining strawberries and serve at once.

Yield: 8 servings. Approx Per Serving: Cal 68; Prot 0.2 gr; Carbo 17.5 gr; T Fat 0.1 gr; Chol 0.0 mg; Calc 8.8 mg; Potas 82.9 mg; Sod 0.5 mg.

3	**cups individually frozen whole strawberries**
8	**teaspoons tea leaves**
1	**teaspoon whole cloves**
1	**cinnamon stick**
1	**teaspoon dried mint leaves**
6	**cups boiling water**
½	**cup sugar**

Hot Spiced Wassail

Combine tea, juices, sugar and spices in saucepan. Cook until sugar is dissolved, stirring constantly. Simmer for 15 minutes. Strain into punch bowl. Serve hot.

Yield: 14 servings. Approx Per Serving: Cal 148; Prot 0.4 gr; Carbo 37.5 gr; T Fat 0.2 gr; Chol 0.0 mg; Calc 10.6 mg; Potas 209.0 mg; Sod 9.0 mg.

1	**quart tea**
1	**quart cranberry juice**
1	**quart apple juice**
2	**cups orange juice**
¾	**cup lemon juice**
1	**cup (or less) sugar**
12	**whole cloves**
3	**cinnamon sticks**

Index

FOR ORDERING INFORMATION

Favorite Recipes Press
a division of Great American Opportunities, Inc.
P.O. Box 305142, Nashville, TN 37230
or
Call Toll-free
1-800-251-1542